From Dirt
to
Dreams

A 30–40 Month
Guideline for Success

Dedication

This book is dedicated to Larry Justice, who spent years researching and writing this book, but transitioned to heaven prior to publishing. This book is also dedicated to his mom Barbara, dad Larry Sr., dad George and brother Michael along with his children, Malcolm, Vinnie, Roman, Sophia, Kieara and grandson Jasper, his extended family and family of Word of Life Christian Center who were all close to his heart. Thank you for your unconditional love.

DISCLAIMER

The advice and recommendations contained in this book are derived from Larry Justice's extensive research. Always consult local authorities on specific rules related to putting the advice and recommendations made in this book into practice in a particular locality.

From Dirt to Dreams

A 30–40 Month Guideline for Success

By Larry Justice

From Dirt to Dreams: 30-40 Month Guideline for Success

Written by Larry Justice
Copyright © 2022 Larry Justice/Keri Wilkins
Illustrations by Larry Justice
Cover and Interior DelSheree Gladden
Published by Larry Justice/Keri Wilkins

TABLE OF CONTENTS

XII

From Dirt to Dreams
30–40 Month Guideline for Success

PHASE I TIMELINE
Zero to Six Months

PREPARATION

- Clear and prepare fields
- Build greenhouses
- Build barns, corrals, and storage
- Purchase feed, etc.
- Set up aquaponics

PLANTING

- First planting
- First harvest
- Second planting
- Second harvest
- First crop rotation
- First batch of compost
- Soil testing daily to weekly

LIVESTOCK: FIRST WAVE

- Chickens
- Goats
- Dogs
- Rabbits
- Cattle

PRODUCTS READY FOR SALE

- Livestock
- Eggs
- Dairy
- Candies
- Jams
- Jellies
- Compost Pots

BUSINESS PLANNING

- Submit a Doing Business As (DBA) if needed
- Register business license
- File 501c3/LLC paperwork
- Obtain insurance
- Write a business plan
- Set up business bank accounts
- Business office set-up
- Begin organizing community sales and networking
- Develop Co-op/CSA and membership sales structures

Notes

- There is no particular order to Phase 1 processes
- Steps may be completed concurrently

From Dirt to Dreams

PHASE 2 TIMELINE
Six to Twelve Months

PREPARATION

- Complete farm set-up
- Install root cellar
- Plan cover crops
- Develop handmade product lines

PLANTING

- Third planting
- Second crop rotation
- Plant cover crops
- Third harvest

LIVESTOCK

- Complete additional livestock areas
- Add therapy livestock

PRODUCTS READY FOR SALE

- Homemade product lines
- Dairy, candies, cheese, milk, yogurt, candles, soaps, pelts, hides,

coats/jackets, feathers, canned items, ciders, etc.
- Self-sustainable kits for homesteading and camping

BUSINESS PLANNING (CONTINUED)

- Business development
- Community outreach and engagement
- Develop networks
- Sales avenues
- Hire a bookkeeper
- Hire out online marketing (websites, online sales)

WORKSHOPS/THERAPY

- Begin self-sustaining lifestyle workshops
- Begin therapy sessions

Phase 3 Timeline
Twelve to Eighteen Months

Preparation/Operations

- Continue normal operations
- Continue developing professional skills

Planting

- Continue crops

Livestock

- Final livestock additions
- Develop permanent breed strains

Product Sales

- Permanent sales established
- Set up sales stands
- Set up sales trailers

Business Planning

- Maintain community and business relationships
- Add new networks and relationships daily

WORKSHOPS/THERAPY

- Add therapy classes
- Conduct on-going self-sustaining education

PHASE 4 TIMELINE
Eighteen to Twenty-Four Months

PREPARATION/OPERATIONS

- Continue normal operations

PLANTING

- Continue crops

LIVESTOCK

- Continue livestock
- Build as needed

PRODUCT SALES

- Continue sales

BUSINESS PLANNING

- Begin research of café and market
- Develop business plan for café and market
- Build cobb and straw bale housing for select women's, men's,

and teen's, graduates, and for rental retreats

Workshops/Therapy

- Continue therapy and workshops
- Add new sessions as needed
- Develop annual self-sustaining lifestyle workshop

PHASE 5 TIMELINE
Twenty-Four to Forty Months

PREPARATION/OPERATIONS

- Continue normal operations
- Continue developing professional skills
- Break ground on market/café
- Launch "From Dirt to Dreams" program

PLANTING

- Continue crops

LIVESTOCK

- Final livestock additions
- Finalize permanent breed strains

PRODUCT SALES

- Continue permanent sales
- Operate sales stands
- Operate sales trailers

Business Planning

- Open café and market
- Maintain community and business relationships
- Add new networks and relationships

Workshops/Therapy

- Additional therapy classes
- On-going self-sustaining education

HOMESTEADING BASICS

Human Needs

When establishing a homestead, basic human needs must be considered as well as the physical elements, such as designing and developing a homestead.

Critical human needs to take into account include water, food, medicine and first aid, communication, shelter, electrical power and light, financial security, heating and cooling, transportation, air, protection, sleep, and hygiene and sanitation.

Consider Maslow's Hierarchy of Needs when establishing which needs should be met in which order.

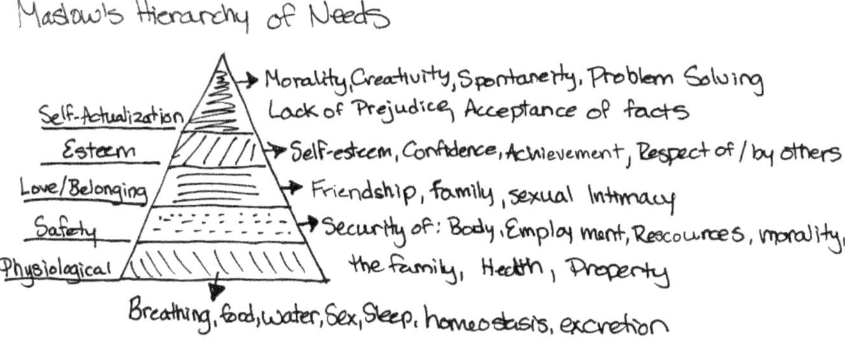

Designing an Efficient Homestead

Designing an efficient homestead takes careful consideration of multiple elements, such as indoor needs, yard and farm areas and uses, garden functions, energy sources, potable water sources, food and cooking supplies and storage, medical care and knowledge, and more. This section will cover topics necessary for establishing an efficient and successful homestead.

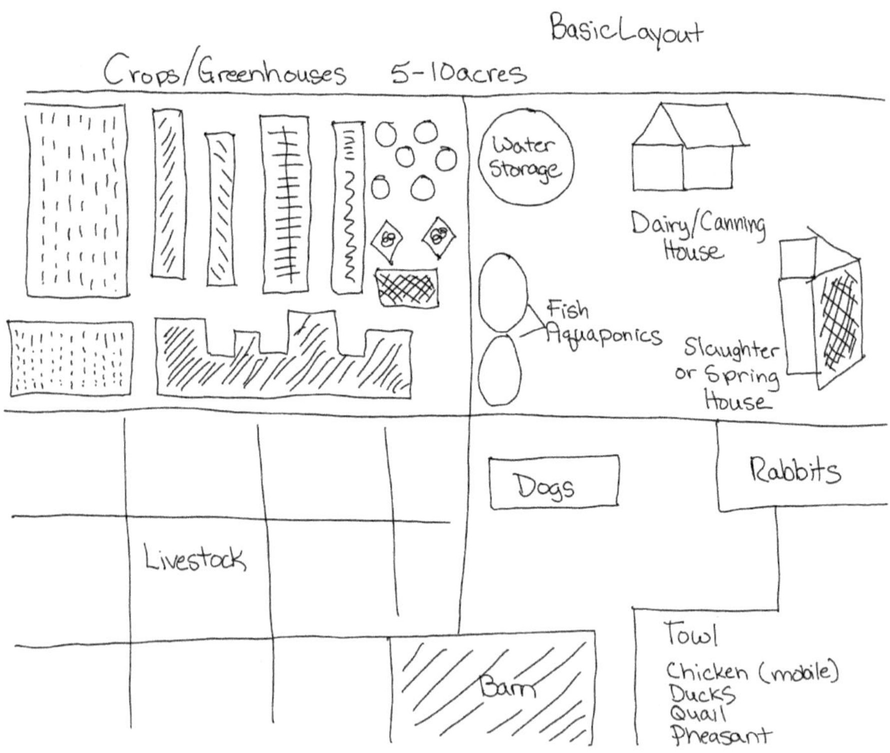

INDOOR HOMESTEAD ELEMENTS

Container garden for year-round food production
Light source for indoor garden
Rainwater collection for gardening and drinking
Living space for occupants
Solar, wood, or electric heat and light
Waste disposal systems for food, water, and human waste
Food preservation methods and supplies
Knowledge and supplies for manufacturing living necessities

ADDITIONAL LARGE HOMESTEAD ELEMENTS

Intensive and/or row garden
Large grain production
Large orchard
Greenhouse
Storage and preparation facility
Rainwater for gardening and drinking
Stream, fishpond, or river
Cow and horse shelter and grazing areas

BACKYARD HOMESTEAD ELEMENTS

Intensive garden for consumption and/or market
Small grain production
Small orchard
Greenhouse

Rainwater collection for gardening and drinking
Solar, wood, or electric heat
Solar, fire, or electric light for outbuildings and yards
Human and animal waste disposal systems
Duck, chicken, and goose areas
Goat shelter and grazing areas
Beehives
Food preservation structure, such as a root cellar

Types of Gardens to Consider

Human food garden
Cooking herb garden
Medicinal herb garden
Animal food garden/forage
Soil fertilizing/green manures
Windbreak/erosion control
Building materials
Cloth production
Fuel production
Insect control

Energy Conservation

KEEPING COOL IN THE SUMMER

Having an outdoor kitchen can reduce heat buildup in the living space, as will eating mostly raw or grilled food. Open the windows at night to let in cooler air and close them in the morning. Use blackout or heavily insulated curtains in the sunniest windows. Take cool showers, go swimming, or take naps during hot afternoons. Work at night when possible and drink higher amounts of water and fruit juice.

KEEPING WARM IN WINTER

Seal windows and doors with heavy plastic, cloth, or blankets during the winter months. Use only one door to reduce losing heat in multiple areas. If possible, have a separate entryway.

Alternatives to Electric Appliances

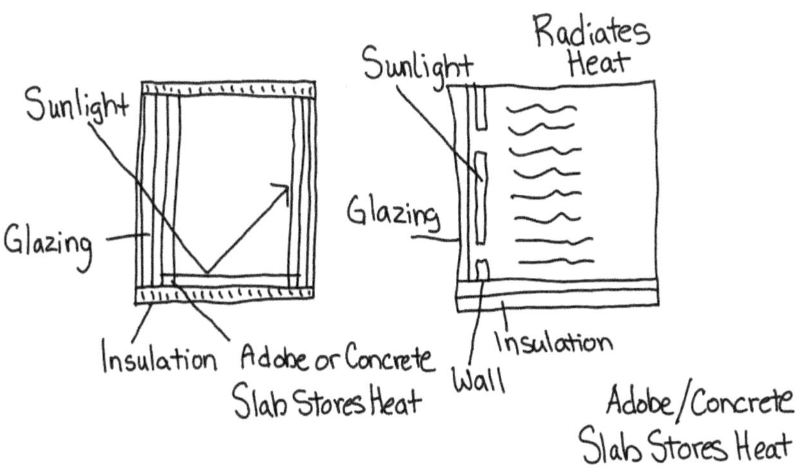

Passive solar designs can replace electric baseboard heating and other types of electric heating.

Woodstoves can replace space heaters.

Wood cookstoves can replace electric stoves.

A solar or compost water heater can replace electric or gas water heaters. Compost water heaters use biomass, a mass of decaying organic matter found in plant materials, heaped into a pile large enough that it produces enough heat to make hot water and kill fungi and bacteria living in organic matter.

Clotheslines can replace electric or gas dryers.

Handwashing dishes replaces electric dishwashers.

Hand tools or DC powered tools can replace electric shop equipment.

Replacing electric refrigerators is more challenging, but possible. If the homestead is located in an area with spring temperatures lower than 40 degrees Fahrenheit, food can be put in waterproof containers and stored outside of a refrigerator. A large-scale version is to build an insulated stone or block springhouse with a cement trough flowing with spring water through it.

A heat exchanger is a container or material which absorbs the heat from hot compost and transfers it to the desired element, such as water to air, thus making hot water or warming a room. Simple heat exchangers could be flexible plastic pipe attached to a cold-water source. In this setup, water sits in a pipe, warming until the tap is turned on. It then flows out of the pipe to the tap. As with a traditional water heater, the user must then wait for water to heat again. A 1.5 in diameter pipe that is 100 ft long holds 9 gallons, which is enough hot water for several hot showers or a load of laundry.

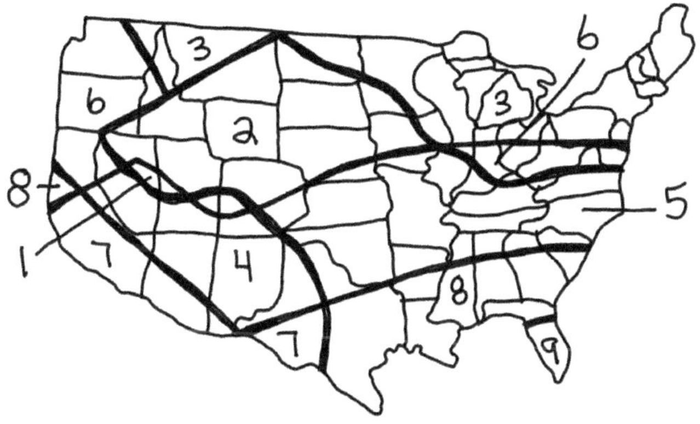

1. High heat demand, lots of sun.
2. High heat demand, good sun.
3. High heat demand, fair sun.
4. Medium heat demand, lots of sun.
5. Medium heat demand, good sun.
6. Medium heat demand, fair sun.
7. Low heat demand, lots of sun.
8. Low heat demand, fair sun.
9. Low heat demand, lots of sun.

Electric Wattage Reference Chart

Tool/Appliance	Rated Watts	Surge Watts	Required Voltage
Essentials			
Light bulbs	40-100	-	120
Deep freezer	500-600	1,200	120

Sump pump	800	2,000	120 or 240
Refrigerator	500-800	2,000	120
Water well pump	1,000-2,500	5,600-7,500	120-240
Electric water heater	4,000		120-240
Heating			
Heat pump	4,000-15,000	2x rated	120-240
Electric furnace	8.000-26,000	2x rated	120-240
Furnace fan (gas heater)	875	2,300	120-240
Space heater	600-1.800	-	120
Electric blanket	200-400	-	120
Cooling			
Central A/C (2.5 tons)	1,500-6,000	4x rated	120-240
Window A/C	1,200	3,000-4,800	120
Window fan	300-800	600-1200	120
Kitchen			
Microwave oven	800-1,000	-	120
Coffee maker	1,500	-	120
Electric range (1 element on)	1,500	-	120-240
Toaster	800-1,000	-	120
Dishwasher	1,500	3,000	120
Oven	3.400		120-240
Family Room			
Color TV	300	-	120
DVD/CD player	100	-	120
Stereo receiver	450	-	120
Computer system	300-800	-	120
Laptop	100	-	120
Other			

Security system	180-500	-	120
AM/FM clock radio	300	-	120
Garage door opener	480-750	-	120
Washer	1,150	3,400	120-240
Dryer, electric	4,000-5,400	6,750	120-240
Dryer, gas	700	2,500	120-240

Single-Use Battery Comparison

Type	Energy Density	Shelf Life	Cost	Risk of Leakage	Comments
Heavy duty	Poor	2+ years	Low	Higher	N/R
Alkaline	Good	5+ years	Low	Higher	Acceptable
Nickel Oxyhy-droxide (NiOOH)	Very good	6+ years	Moderate	Lower	Better than alkaline
Lithium (Li)	Excel-lent	10+ years	High	Lower	Best

Rechargeable Battery Comparison

Type	Energy Density	Self-Dis-charge	Shelf Life	Cost	Comments
Nickle metal hydride (NiMH)	Good	30% more	1-2 months	High	Acceptable

NiMH low self-dis-charge	Good	1.5-3% per month	1-2 years	High	Best
Nickle Cadmium (Ni Cd)	Low	10-15% per month	3 months	Moderate	
Lithium ion (Li Ion)	Very good	5-10% per month	6 months	High	

Heater and Heating Systems

When setting up a heating system, plan for proper ventilation. All unvented, fuel-burning heaters require ventilation of 1 sq ft per 1,000 BTUs.

THREE METHODS FOR SELECTING A PROPER HEATER

Method one is the simplest method. Multiply the square footage of the area which needs to be heated by 25. This will give you the number of BTUs per hour needed. For example: x = sq ft and y = BTUs per hour. If 200 sq ft needs to be heated, the calculation is: 200 * 25 = 5,000 BTUs/hr.

Method two is slightly more accurate. It requires measuring the volume of air to be heated and specifying the minimum temperature difference desired between the interior of the home and outside. The equation is: volume * 4T * 0.133 = the number of BTUs/hr. For example, if the room which needs to be heated is 200 sq ft with 8 ft ceilings, 1,600 sq ft of air needs to be heated. If the outside air temperature can fall as low as 10 degrees Fahrenheit, and the inside temperature should be maintained at 60 degrees Fahrenheit, the temperature difference is 50 degrees Fahrenheit. The minimum heater size is then determined by the calculation: 1,600 x 50 x 0.133 = 10,640 BTUs/hr.

Method three is an even more accurate method because it takes into account a home's level of insulation, but no longer considers specific temperature differences. Instead, this method multiplies the area to be heated by the insulation factor. The equation is: Area * RF factor. For example, if a house has an average RF factor of 50-70 and the area to be heated is 200 sq ft, the range is calculated using the minimum and maximum RF factors. The best option is 200 * 50 = 10,000 BTUs/hr. The worst option is 200 * 70 = BTUs/hr.

Insulation Factor (RF) Chart

Poor insulation, RF 90-110: No insulation in the walls, ceiling, or floors. No storm windows. Windows and doors are not sealed well.

Average insulation, RF 50-70: R-11 insulation in the walls and ceilings. No insulation in the floors. No storm windows. Doors and windows are fairly tight.

Good insulation, RF 29-35: R-19 insulation in the walls. R-30 insulation in the ceilings. R-11 insulation in the floors. Tight-fitting storm windows or double-paned windows.

Superior insulation, RF 21-25: R-24 insulation in the walls. R-40 insulation in the ceilings. R-19 insulation in the floors. Tight-fitting storm windows or double-paned windows. Vapor barrier is sealed carefully during construction.

Earth sheltered, RF 10-13: An earth sheltered house with little exposure that is well insulated.

Types of Heating Systems

Fireplaces
Masonry heaters
Wood/coal/pellet stoves
Electric space/baseboard heaters
Kerosene space heaters
Oil-filled radiators
Propane or natural gas heaters/furnaces

Heating with Wood and Other Fuels

Even with a small morning fire, masonry heaters radiate heat throughout the day.

Wood can burn in a coal stove, but not vice versa.

Fireplaces are terribly inefficient, but using a Texas Fire Frame can help.

A cord of wood measures 4 ft x 4 ft x 8 ft.

Fuel Equivalency

Fuels listed below are roughly equivalent to each other:

1 cord of wood
150 gallons of No. 2 fuel oil
230 gallons of liquid propane
21,000 cu ft of natural gas
6,158 kilowatt hours of electricity

To calculate the amount of wood needed, use the equation: Cords = PF * EPF/W * EW

PF = Primary fuel
W = Wood

EPF= Energy efficiency of primary fuel
EW= Energy efficiency of wood

Example: Assume a 2,000 sq ft home normally uses 60,000 cu ft of natural gas per year. The efficiency of natural gas is about 65% and the efficiency of wood is about 55%. The number of cords of wood needed to supply the homestead's heating needs for a full year would be calculated as:

Cords = 60,000 x 0.65/21,000 x 0.55 = 3.4

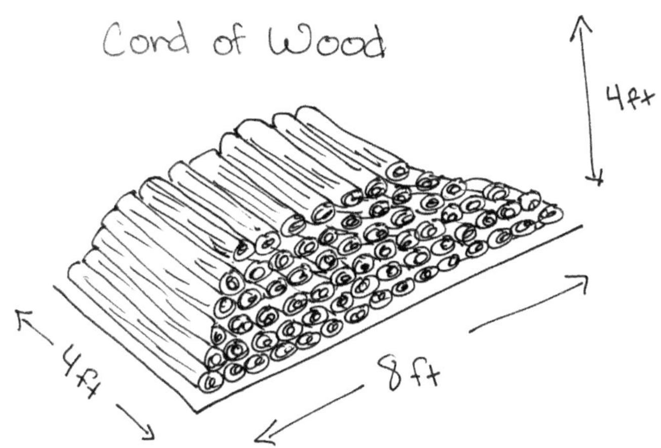

Heating Comparisons for Vented Room Heaters

Fuel Type	Fuel Unit	Fuel Heat Content per Unit (BTUs)	Cost per Million	Efficiency	Cost with Efficiency
Coal (anthracite)	Ton	25,000,000	$8.00	75%	$10.67
Solid wood	Cord	22,000,000	$9.09	55%	$16.53

Corn (kernels)	Ton	16,500,000	$12.12	68%	$17.83
Natural gas	Therm	100,000	$12.27	65%	$18.88
No. 2 fuel oil	Gallon	138,690	$17.01	78%	$21.81
Pellets	Ton	16,500,000	$15.15	68%	$22.28
Propane	Gallon	91,333	$21.27	65%	$32.73
Electric	Kilo-watt-hour	3,412	#33.85	100%	$33.85

Water

PROCURING WATER AT HOME

The average American uses about 100 gallons of water per day. A single person on the homestead should have at least a 1000-gallon tank. Families need a tank twice that size.

PROCURING WATER IN THE WILDERNESS

A main concern with using water found in the wilderness is contamination. Mountain streams can be contaminated with the parasite giardia and underground water can be contaminated with agricultural chemicals. Both sources can be purified, however, via a home distiller or purifier. Rain water is typically purer, but may contain higher levels of acid.

In order to find natural sources of water, there are landmarks and formations which may indicate water, such as limestone caves, dry canyons which cut through sandstone, and granite-loaded areas.

Water may not be immediately visible and may require digging or other methods of extraction. The following are possible methods of procuring water. Dig a hole on the greenest, grassiest hillside. Dig a hole in valley floors with loose soil to locate ground water. Dig a hole in low forests, seashores, and river plains. On clear nights, collect dew with cloth or a sponge. Dig in dry streambeds in the mountains. Melt snow in the sun. In the desert, watch where animals, ants, and bugs drink. In arid climates, dig where cattails, greasewood, willow, elderberry, or salt grass grow, or where it looks damp. Collect rainwater. At the beach, dig behind windblown sandhills at back of the beach. Ocean fish contain fresh water and can be diced up and laid on a cloth then wrung out. Condense ocean water, or use condensation to collect moisture.

Certain plants also contain water. Look for plants with fleshy leaves or stems which have water inside. Do not drink any milky or colored juices. Cut off the top of the barrel of a cactus, mash the pulp inside, and then drink. Desert oak and bloodwood roots can be pried out, chopped into 2 ft lengths with the bark stripped, and then suck out the water. Some vines have edible sap. To harvest it, cut deep notches as high as can be reached. Cut it off the at the base and let the water drip into a cup or the mouth.

Springs, places where water comes from the ground without mechanical pumping, are great natural sources of water. A spring which produces 100 to 150 gallons per day is typically adequate in any season and should not dry up easily. Springs located uphill from a homestead will provide 1 lb of pressure per 2 ft of elevation.

Dams are another way of creating a sustainable water source for a homestead. There are several types of dams, but barrier dams are most common on homesteads. A barrier dam is built across flowing water, blocking it completely or partially. It can create a useful pond and water storage. Contour dams are also used. They are built on very small slopes and are used for irrigation.

WATER CONTAMINATES

There are several important water contaminants to be aware of when establishing or using a water source on a homestead. Below is a list of common water contaminants.

Iron and magnesium: To remove, utilize chlorination, a greensand filter, or water aeration.

Nitrates: Levels of 10-20 milligrams per liter can be harmful, mainly for infants. Higher levels can be removed via reverse osmosis, distillation, and anion exchange.

Chloride and sulfates: These may be removed with an acid base-exchange unit.

Fluoride: Small amounts are harmless, but excess amounts can be harmful and should be removed via distillation, reverse osmosis, or iron exchange using bone char or activated alumina.

Metals: If water has pH levels lower than 7.0, treat it via reverse osmosis, distillation, or running water through soda ash or limestone chips.

Radium and radon: Both are harmful to health and should be removed. Ion exchange and reverse osmosis remove radium. Granular activated carbon and aeration remove radon.

DISTILLATION

Distillation is a common method of treating water.

To distill water, heat it to its boiling point, 212 degrees Fahrenheit (100 degrees Celsius), and allow the steam to collect into a cooler such as spiral copper tubing, etc. The water then returns to liquid as it cools and collects into a container.

WATER STORAGE AND CONSUMPTION

When storing water, be sure to follow FDA guidelines by using Department of Transportation (DOT) approved No. 34 opaque containers. Store water away from light, pesticides, gasoline, paint, and other chemicals. Store water containers where they will not freeze. Cycle stored water every six months, unless the water is treated with a water preserver. Always pretreat water that comes from untreated sources, such as wells.

To calculate how much water is needed on a homestead, first determine whether the stored water is to be used for potable or non-potable purposes.

For potable, or drinkable, water, the USDA recommendation is 1 gallon per person per day for drinking, and for hygiene activities, the recommendation is 1 gallon per person per day as well.

For non-potable water, the USDA recommendation is 2-7 gallons per person per day to be used for sanitation purposes.

To calculate water needs for potable water, use the equation: $A * B * C = D$, with A=people, B=gallons per day, C=number of days, and D=the total number of gallons per day.

A minimum recommended amount of water to store is a supply large enough for fourteen days, or to have access to that amount of water. Non-potable water storage will always be greater than potable water storage due to sanitation needs. The average ratio is 3:1.

WATER PURIFICATION

Water can be purified in a variety of ways. The most common methods are boiling, filtering or purifying, chemical disinfection, reverse osmosis, and ultraviolet light. Distillation and reverse osmosis are considered the best methods by the USDA.

Using bleach and iodine are common methods of disinfection, but it is very important to use correct ratios. Below is a chart providing safe and effective ratios for each substance.

Water Quantity	Clear Water	Cloudy Water
1 qt/liter	2 drops bleach 2 drops iodine	4 drops bleach 10 drops iodine
1 gallon	8 drops bleach 20 drops iodine	16 drops or ¼ tsp bleach ½ tsp iodine
5 gallons	½ tsp bleach 1 tsp iodine	1 tsp bleach 2 tsp iodine
10 gallons	1 tsp bleach 2 tsp iodine	2 tsp bleach 4 tsp iodine
55 gallons	5 ½ tsp bleach 11 tsp iodine	11 tsp bleach 22 tsp iodine

* 1 drop = 0.05 MH
* Water disinfected with iodine is not recommended for pregnant women, people with thyroid problems, people hypersensitive to iodine, or for continuous use for more than a few weeks at a time.
* The cloudy-to-clear ratio is 2:1.

Disposing of Waste

There are several options for human waste disposal. The most basic would be establishing an outhouse. Outhouses are suitable when there is no existing plumbing or waste disposal options, and when the homestead is not within city limits or an area that disallows their use.

Septic tank absorption fields are more commonly used than outhouses. This system can only be used in areas where the groundwater water table is low enough, such as when bedrock is far from the soil surface. The soil when a septic tank is installed must also have a reasonable percolation speed, meaning it must be steady. There may be other regional factors to consider as well.

A mound system may be used to install a septic tank where groundwater table is too high for a conventional

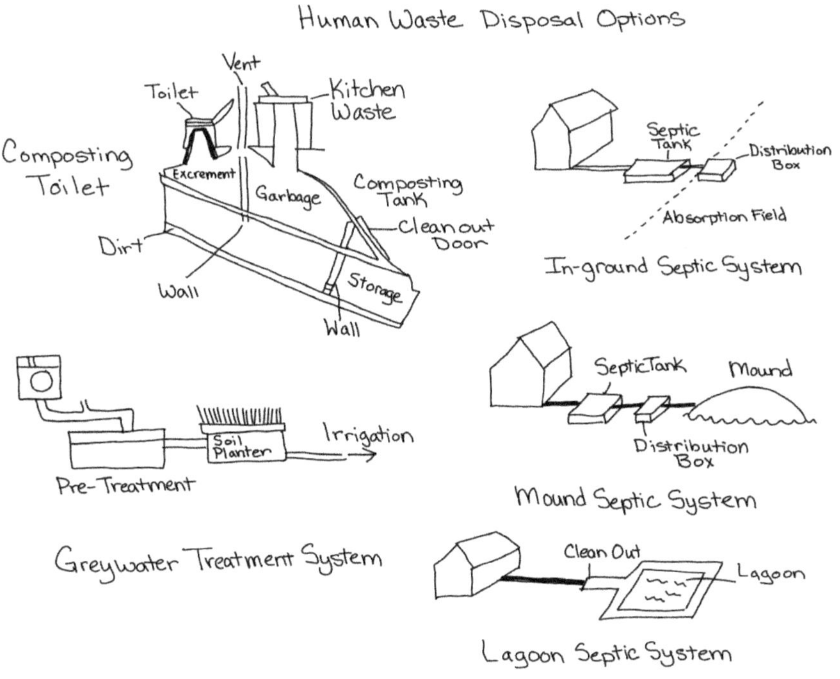

septic tank. The tank is placed in a mounded area to remain higher than the water table.

A lagoon is a suitable option for areas where the percolation rate is too slow for a regular septic tank. It uses aerobic treatment instead of anaerobic treatment and requires energy to run a compressor or a stirrer.

A composting toilet is a toilet that puts waste into a tank where it composts waste material naturally.

Primitive Heat and Light

Fire

When preparing to start a fire outdoors, make a ring with rocks. Clear all burnable material within a 10 ft diameter around the ring. Have water nearby or build the fire near a water source for safety. Gather tinder, small pieces of dry wood or brush, along with larger pieces of wood. Build a fire in the center of the ring. If using a fireplace, regularly clean out the old ashes.

Methods of Starting a Fire

Flint

Starting a fire with flint involves striking flint with a stone, both of which are held over spongy, dry wood. Continue striking the flint until sparks ignite the tinder.

Pocketknife

1. Take a rectangular piece of bark, big enough to put

one knee on with plenty of space left to work, and notch a triangle in the edge.

2. Find a 1-2 in. diameter stick about 1 ft long and sharpen its end to a point.

3. Tie a cord of twisted grass, rope, yarn, or similar material to each end, making a bow with a loose string.

4. Obtain a flat stone, preferably with a hollow middle.

5. Find a square, smaller piece of bark.

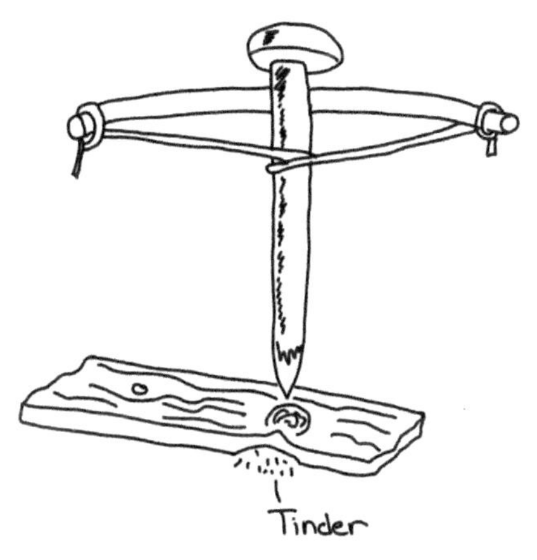

6. Place a larger piece of bark on the smaller piece that has the notch in the middle.

7. Kneel down with the knee on the larger piece of bark.

8. Stand the stick straight up on the larger piece of bark right next to the tip of the notch.

9. Twist the bow cord halfway around, making a loop on the stick. Put the stone on top, making a primitive drill.

10. Place one hand on the stone, pressing down firmly, while the other hand holds the bow.

11. The drill should work by making a sawing motion horizontally with the bow. Hold the stick steady with the stone so the stick twists back and forth, drilling into the bark.

12. Keep working the drill quickly and smoothly until a black powder forms in the notch and it starts to smoke.

13. When red coals are observed in the black powder, quickly add tinder and stop drilling.

14. Keep adding bigger and bigger sticks until the

fire gets as big as needed. A large fire is not needed to cook and keep warm.

Cooking

Cooking with Fire

In order to cook well using fire, it is important to be able to estimate the temperature of a fire. This can be done using a person's hand. To estimate the temperature of a fire, hold the hand 3 in. above the fire and count how many seconds pass until the hand must be removed because it is too hot. If the hand is removed before 1 second (a count of "one thousand one"), the temperature is roughly 450-500 degrees Fahrenheit. If the hand is removed between 2 and 3 seconds, it is 400-450 degrees Fahrenheit. If the hand is removed at 6 or more seconds, the fire is not hot enough.

Dutch Oven Cooking

Dutch ovens can be used for cooking a variety of foods. It is important to know the size and capacity of the Dutch oven being used. Below is a list of size and capacity equivalencies for easy reference.

5 in = 1 pt
8 in. = 2 qt
10 in. = 4 qt/1 gal
12 in. = 6 qt/1 ½ gal
12 in. deep = 8 qt/2 gal
14 in. = 8 qt/2 gal
16 in. = 12 qt/3 gal

Seasoning a Dutch Oven

Wash with hot water and dry to remove the factory coating. Spread olive, vegetable oil, vegetable shortening, or lard over the inside and outside of the pan, including the legs. Do not use aerosolized oil spray because it will leave a sticky film. Put the lid on the pan and turn it upside down in the oven with foil on the rack below it to catch drips. Bake the pan at 350 degrees Fahrenheit for 1 hour. This will cause the pan to smoke and it will create a strong odor. Open windows to vent the room or season the pan using an outdoor brick oven.

Using a Dutch Oven

After a fire forms hot coals, which usually takes about 30-45 min of burning, place coals evenly atop and below the Dutch oven. After using a Dutch oven, scrape out excess foods and place the pan under hot water, but never submerge the pan completely. Scrub the pan with steel wool or a tool like a Brillo pad. Dry the pan with a towel. Apply thin coat of olive or vegetable oil over the Dutch oven. Never keep the lid on tightly when storing because the oil coating can become rancid. Place a spacer between the lid and the oven so air can circulate.

When making soup in a Dutch oven for twenty or more people, dig a hole twice as big as the oven. Make a fire in the hole and burn it down to red hot coals. Make a hole in the coals to place the oven in. Cover the oven with dirt. The soup should be done in four to eight hours.

To make bread in a Dutch oven, grease and preheat the oven. Set a loaf in it that has already risen and is ready to bake. For cornbread or cake, do not preheat. Pour the batter directly into the oven. Prepare the fire and a hole the same way as for soup, then place the oven into the hole, making sure it is level. Cover it with coals and dirt. Cook for three hours.

To make biscuits, grease and preheat the oven. Place chunks of firm dough in the bottom of the oven while it is sitting on the coals. Turn them over when brown and place the lid on the oven. Place coals on the lid and cook for ten minutes.

To cook a pie, prepare the pie in a regular pie tin and place the entire tin into the oven, then cook similar to bread.

Types of Cheeses

Soft: non-ripe, fresh cheese such as cottage, cream, pot, ricotta, gjetost, Neufchatel, brie, and camembert. Double and triple cream cheeses ripen naturally in a few days.

Semi-soft: Basic Swiss, brick, muenster, Liederkranz, limburger, port salut, Roquefort, and gorgonzola. These cheeses are ripened using specially developed molds and bacteria.

Firm: Cheddar, Chesire, Lancashire, Caciocavallo, Swiss Emmental gruyere, and Jarlsberg.

Hard: Asiago, parmesan, Romano, and sapsago. Firm cheeses are matured longer to make them grainier.

Common Ingredients for Jam

Apple
Apricot
Cherry
Citrus
Grape
Peach
Pear
Quince
Strawberry
Blackberry

Raspberry
Blueberry
Cranberry

FOOD STORAGE

Establishing food storage is recommended for homesteads to supplement lean growing years, to reduce store-bought grocery costs, and to create a reserve for times of financial instability.

Food Storage Amounts

Listed amounts are for two adults and three children for one year.

25 lbs wheat
50 -12 oz cans of evaporated milk
60 lbs flour (self-rising and regular)
160 lbs granulated sugar
109 lbs cornmeal
50 lbs brown sugar
150 lbs rolled oats
4-10 lbs molasses
260 lbs rice
20 lbs honey
13 lbs pearled barley
12 lbs corn syrup (karo: light, dark)
150 lbs pasta
25 lbs jams, jellies, and marmalades
180 lbs dried beans
24 lbs powdered fruit drink (Kool-Aid)
8 lbs each of dry lima, soybean, split pea, lentils
10 lbs Jell-O

28 lbs dry soup mix
25 lbs salt (kosher, sea, etc.)
19 qts cooking oil
2 lbs dry yeast
10 qts shortening
10 lbs baking soda
4 qts (1 gal) mayonnaise
10 lbs baking powder
4 qts (1 gal) salad dressing
10 gal water
15 qts peanut butter
Supply of canned fruit and veggies
56 lbs nonfat dry milk

General Guide for Food Storage Items

Adjust selected items based on family preferences and eating habits.

Food Type	Amount per Adult per Year	Amount per Child per Year (Ages 1-5 years old)
Baking powder	1 lb	1 lb
Baking soda	1 lb	1 lb
Brown sugar	3 lbs	3 lbs
Canned fruit	5 #10 cans (more if possible)	3 #10 cans (more if possible)
Cooking oil	2 gal	1 gal
Cornmeal	30 lbs	12 lbs
Dry beans	45 lbs	15 lbs
Dry lentils	5 lbs	2 lbs
Dry lima beans	5 lbs	2 lbs
Dry pasta	40 lbs	22 lbs

Dry potatoes	5 #10 cans 65 cups	3 #10 cans 39 cups
Dry soup mix	7 lbs	5 lbs
Dry soybean	40 lbs	20 lbs
Dry split peas	5 lbs	2 lbs
Dry yeast	½ lb	½ lb
Flour (self-rising /regular)	25 lbs	12 lbs
Rice	80 lbs	30 lbs
Evaporated milk	12 12 oz cans (2 lbs)	6 12 oz cans (1 lb)
Honey	3 lbs	1 lb
Jam/jellies	5 lbs	2 lbs
Jell-O	1 lb	1 lb
Mayonnaise/salad dressing	2 qt/1 qt	1 qt/ 1 qt
Molasses	1 lb	1 lb
Peanut butter	4 lbs	2 lbs
Pearled barley	80 lbs	5 lbs
Powdered eggs	3 #10 cans (39 cups)	2 #10 cans (26 cups)
Powdered fruit drink	6 lbs	3 lbs
Powdered milk	60 lbs	30 lbs
Rolled oats	50 lbs	12 lbs
Salt (sea, kosher, etc.)	10 lbs	5 lbs
Shortening/lard	4 lbs	2 lbs
Sugar	40 lbs	20 lbs
Tomato	5 #10 cans (sauces or slices)	3 #10 cans (sauces or slices)
Tuna or canned meat	10 cans or more	5 cans or more
Vinegar/wheat	½ gal/200 lbs	½ gal/75 lbs

Other Miscellaneous Food Storage Items

Spices (garlic powder, onion powder, basil, oregano, pepper (white and black), chili powder, cinnamon, etc.)
Packaged dried fruit and raisins
Beef and chicken bouillon
Baking cocoa
Ketchup and mustard
Salsa and picante
Vanilla
Seeds for sprouts (alfalfa, radish, peas, mung, and lintels)
Pancake mix
Pickles
Boxed cereals
Crackers (graham, baby, saltines, etc.)
Cans of nuts
Ground, vacuum-sealed coffee
Tea
Vitamins (children and adults)
Baby cereal and formula
Boxed meals (macaroni and cheese, etc.)

Proper Care of Food Storage

Moisture and rodents are top concerns for maintaining food storage. Food storage items should be stored at a temperature of 70 degrees Fahrenheit or less, in a cool, dry, dark space. All food should be stored in air-tight, rodent-proof containers, such as those made of metal or glass.

Food storage items should be rotated on a regular basis. Below is a list of common food storage items and when they should be rotated out.

Food	Storage Time
Baking powder	18 months
Baking soda	2 years
Beans/peas (dried)	1 year (airtight container)
Biscuit, brownie, muffin mixes	9 months (airtight container)
Bouillon cubes, granules	1-2 years
Breadcrumbs (dry)	6 months
Bread	3-5 days
Cakes mixes	1 year
Canned foods, unopened	2 or more years
Catsup, chili sauce	1 year unopened/1 month opened, sealed well and refrigerated
Cereal, ready to eat	6-12 months unopened/2-3 months opened, sealed well
Cheese, grated parmesan	10 months unopened/2 months opened, sealed well and refrigerated
Chocolate: unsweetened/semi-sweet/syrup	18-24 months unopened/6 months opened syrups, sealed well and refrigerated
Cocoa	Indefinitely
Cocoa mixes	8 months
Coconut, shredded/canned	1 year unopened/6 months opened, sealed well and refrigerated
Coffee	2 years unopened cans and bags/2 weeks opened, stored in an airtight container/1-2 years unopened instant coffee/1-2 months opened, stored in an airtight container
Coffee creamer	9 months unopened/6 months opened, sealed well

Cookies	2-3 weeks homemade, sealed in an airtight container/2 months packaged
Corn syrup	Up to 3 years (refrigerate to extend life)
Cornmeal	1 year in an airtight container
Cornstarch	18 months in an airtight container
Crackers	3 months in an airtight container
Fish, canned/packaged	3-5 years
Flour: white	6-8 months in an airtight container
Flour: wholewheat	6-8 months in an airtight container
Frosting: canned/mix	3 months canned, unopened/8 months mix, unopened
Fruit: dried/fresh	6 months dried, stored in an airtight container/3-5 days fresh (longer if refrigerate)
Fruit juice: canned/drink boxes	9 months
Gelatin	18 months
Grits	1 year in an airtight container
Honey	1 year. If crystallized, warm the open jar in hot water
Hot roll mix	18 months
Hot sauce	2 years
Jellies/jams	1 year (refrigerate after opened)
Marshmallows	2-3 months in an airtight container
Mayonnaise	4-6 months unopened/2 months opened and refrigerated
Milk	1 year condensed, unopened/1 year evaporated, unopened/6 months powdered, non-fat dry in an airtight container/2-3 months shelf-stable, unopened
Molasses	2 years unopened/6 months opened and refrigerated

Mustard, prepared yellow	2 years unopened/6-8 months opened and refrigerated
Nuts	4-6 months in shell, unopened/1-3 years vacuum can, unopened/3 months opened
Pancake syrup	18 months unopened/3-4 months opened and refrigerated
Pasta: spaghetti, macaroni, etc.	2 years in an airtight container/6 months egg noodles in an airtight container
Peanut butter	6-9 months unopened/2-3 months opened. Natural peanut butter must be refrigerated after opening
Pie crust mix	8 months
Pies and pastries	2-3 days. Refrigerate whipped cream or custard fillings
Popcorn, unpopped	2 years in an airtight container
Potatoes: instant mix, fresh	6-12 months instant mix in an airtight container/2-4 weeks fresh, kept in a dry place
Powdered drink mix	18-24 months
Pudding mix	1 year
Rice	2 years white, brown/6-12 months wild/6 months flavored or herb
Salad dressing	10-12 months bottled, unopened/3 months bottled, opened, refrigerated/2 weeks made form a mix, refrigerated
Shortening (solid)	8 months
Sauces and gravy mixes	6-12 months
Soft drinks	6 months
Soup mixes, dry	1 year
Soy sauce	3 years unopened/9 months opened, sealed well
Spices and herbs	6 months-2 years depending on type, sealed in an airtight container

Syrup	18 months unopened/1 year opened and refrigerated
Sugar	4 months brown sugar in an airtight container/18 months confectioners' sugar in an airtight container/2 years granulated sugar and artificial sweetener
Tea	18 months bags in an airtight container/3 years instant/2 years loose in an airtight container
Toaster pastries (aka Pop-Tarts)	2-3 months in an airtight container
Vanilla (and other extracts)	2 years unopened/1 year opened, sealed well
Vegetables	2 weeks fresh/2-4 weeks onions and potatoes/1-2 weeks sweet potatoes
Vegetable oils	6 months unopened/1-3 months opened
Vinegar	2 years unopened/1 year opened

Refrigerator and Freezer Food Storage

Food may also be stored in a refrigerator and stored long-term in a freezer. Foods still need to be rotated to maintain freshness. Below is a list of common foods stored in refrigerators and freezers and how long they remain fresh.

Food	Refrigerator	Freezer
Eggs: fresh (in the shell)	4-5 weeks	Do not freeze
Eggs: hard boiled	1 week	Do not freeze
Raw yolks or whites	4-5 days	1 year
Egg substitute	10 days unopened, 3 days opened	1 year unopened/ do not freeze if opened

Mayonnaise	2 months	Do not freeze
Tv dinners/frozen casseroles	Keep frozen until eaten	3-4 months
Deli and vacuum-packed products:		
Egg, chicken, and macaroni salad	3-5 days	Do not freeze
Stuffed pork, lamb, or chicken	1 day	Do not freeze
Stored, cook convenience meals	3-4 days	Do not freeze
Vacuum packed dinners	2 weeks	Do not freeze
Raw meats and poultry		
Ground beef, turkey, pork, veal	1-2 days	3-4 months
Steaks	3-5 days	6-12 months
Pork chops	3-5 days	4-6 months
Roasts	3-5 days	4-12 months
Tongue, kidney, liver, heart	1-2 days	3-4 months
Chicken, turkey: whole	1-2 days	6-12 months
Chicken, turkey: parts	1-2 days	6-9 months
Giblets	1-2 days	3-4 months
Bacon: store packed	7 days	1 month
Bacon: vacuum sealed	1-2 months	6-12 months
Sausage: raw, stored packed	1-2 days	3 months
Sausage: factory packed	1-2 days opened/1-3 months unopened	3 months opened/6-12 months unopened
Cooked meats and poultry		
Fried chicken	3-4 days	4 months
Chicken nuggets	1-2 days	1-3 months
Cooked poultry dishes	3-4 days	4-6 months

Cooked beef, pork, veal or cooked meat dishes	3-4 days	2-3 months
Gravy and meat broth	1-2 days	2-3 months
Soups and stews	1-2 days	2-3 months
Ham, full cooked	7 days whole/3-5 days half or sliced/6-9 months canned	1-2 months whole, half, or sliced. Do not freeze canned
Fish and shellfish		
Lean fish	1-2 days	6 months
Fatty fish	1-2 days	2-3 months
Canned fish	3-4 days opened	2 months
Shellfish	1-2 days	3-6 months
Cooked fish	3-4 days	4-6 months
Smoked fish	14 days	2 months
Hot dogs and lunchmeat		
Hot dogs	1 week opened/2 weeks unopened	1-2 months
Lunchmeat	3-5 days opened/2 weeks unopened	1-2 months
Breads, pastries, and cakes		
Bread or rolls: unbaked	2-3 weeks	1 month
Bread or rolls: baked	Do not refrigerate	2-3 months
Cookie dough: unbaked	3 days	3 months
Cookies: bakes	Do not refrigerate	6-12 months
Cake batter	Do not refrigerate	1 month
Cake: baked, unfrosted	3 days	2-4 months
Cake: baked, frosted	3 days	1 month
Fruit pie	2-3 days baked/1-2 days unbaked	6-8 months baked/2-4 months unbaked
Cheeses		
Cottage, ricotta	1-2 weeks	4 weeks

Soft cream, opened	5 days	Do not freeze
Hard and wax-coated	1-2 months	6-8 months
Sliced	2 weeks	Do not freeze
Parmesan, Romano: grated	2 months	Do not freeze
Processed	3-4 weeks	6-8 months
Fruits and vegetables		
Fruits and vegetables	Varies, based on type and freshness	6 months (blanching required)

Food Storage Containers

#10 aluminum cans
Foil pouches
Canning jars
PETE (Polyethylene Terephthalate) plastic bottles
Plastic buckets with food liners

Water Storage Amounts

The general rule for storing water is to have 14 gallons per person per two weeks. If water is plentiful in the area, a simple purifier is a great investment.

Food Storage Tips

Store a minimum of 30 days of non-perishable food.
Store what will be eaten, eat what is stored.
Rotate food by putting the newest food to the back and the oldest to the front: First In, First Out (FIFO).
Always keep pantry food in a cool, dry place and in tightly sealed containers.
Sweeteners, oils, and seasonings are not critical to survival, but can ease the hardship by making food more

enjoyable.

Consult product labels and shelf-life tables to determine how long food will store safely.

Consult the USDA food pyramid when deciding what to store: www.mypyramind.com.

Do not forget to stock up on non-food and special needs items.

Food poisoning can turn a bad situation into a deadly one. Practice these four steps to avoid food poisoning: clean, separate, cook, and chill.

Stockpile food, preferably a minimum of 30 days of food that generally satisfies the guidelines of the USDA new food pyramid and does not rely heavily on refrigeration.

Use refrigerator and freezer thermometers to properly set the temperatures.

Store non-food items, such as aluminum foil, paper products, plastic utensils, plastic storage bags, napkins, and cooking utensils as well.

Have a general, all-purpose cookbook(s) on hand.

Homesteading Supplies

Personal and Household Items

Toilet paper
Personal hygiene items
First aid kits
Board games
Waterproof matches
Flashlights and batteries
Wind-up and solar radios
Candles and holders
Wool blankets
Pocket knives
Epson salts

Ropes
14 cu ft freezer
Weather thermometer/humidity gauge
Refrigerator
Assorted storage bins and buckets
4x4 crew cab truck
Kerosene/oil lamps and fuel
Sleeping bags and pillows
Thermal underclothes
Socks
Steel-toe boots
Tents and tarps
Vaseline
Sewing kits
1 year saving plus emergency cash
1 year dried and canned food storage
Smoke and CO_2 alarms (battery powered)
Dust pans
Batteries (all sizes)
Brooms
Woodstove
Flat iron
Wood cookstove
Baskets
Wash tub (galvanized)
Sewing machine
Clothesline and clothespins

Cooking Equipment

Thermometers
Cooking stones
Ceramic crocks and crockpots
Steel brushes and wool
Hand grain mill
Scouring pads

Bucher knives
Cutting boards
Steel bowls
Rolling pins
Cast iron cookware
Dish pan and wash pan
Unbleached muslin
Drain rack
Enamel canner
Large bowls (glass, plastic, steel, etc.)
Pressure canner and gauge
Stainless steel teakettle
Jar rack and wire racks
Tea pot
Canning jars and lids
Cooling rack and colanders (strainers)
Hydrometer (for water content)
Bread board
Metal ice chest
Whisks and utensils
Roasting pans
Wooden cooking spoons
Bread pans
Pie and cookie tins/pans
Muffin pans
Potholders and dish towels
Pizza pans
Butter churn and paddle

Tools and Equipment

A heavy-duty truck, either a ¾-1 ton diesel or extended crew cab, is essential for work on a homestead. A used truck may be acquired for $10, 000-$20,000 in many areas. When buying a used truck, look for one with

100,000 miles or less. A flatbed truck is preferable in many situations.

A livestock trailer and a utility trailer will also be useful for homestead work. A reasonable price range is $5,000-$15,000 depending on the condition.

A shipping or storage container can serve many purposes on a homestead. Typically, one may be purchased for $1,500-$4,000.

A tractor, with attachments suitable to specific work to be done, is also essential to working on a homestead. A price range of $15,000-$20,000 is common.

Depending on the size of the homestead, a four-wheeler or OHV may also be useful. Basic models may be purchased at a price of $3,000-$5,000.

Other necessary and desirable equipment and tools are listed below:

85 cc 24 in. chainsaw
35 cc 14 in. chainsaw
Chainsaw sharpening kit
9 ft chainsaw mill
Gasoline
Circular saw
16 in. saw and blades
Hacksaw
Hard hats and safety glasses
12 ½ in portable planer
De-barker
Drills and bits
Hammers and sledgehammers
45 lb anvil
Ax and hatch
Blacksmithing kit
Splitting maul
Saws

Saw sharpening kit
2 in. x 8 in. clamp
4 in. x 16 in. clamp
Chisels
Chainsaw
5 lb wood splitting wedge
Sandpapers and sanding blocks
Low angle hand plane
Linseed oil
2 ft x 4 ft levels
Torpedo level
Screwdrivers
Brass plumb bob
Ratchet sets
Chalk line and blue chalk
Sawhorses
Pickax
Maddox
T-square and square
Tape measures (50 ft and 100 ft)
Pipe wrenches
Nails and spikes
Rope (hemp, etc.)

EMERGENCY KIT ITEMS

Cold climates

Blankets
Matches and candles
Warm coat
Caps and gloves
Walking shoes/hiking boots and overshoes

Desert Climate

Sun protection clothes (long sleeves)
Sun hats and block
Water for drinking and usage

All climates

Compass and maps
Knives and hatchets
High-calorie nonperishable foods
2 tow ropes/chains
Transistor radio
Flashlight and first aid kit
Extra batteries
Jumper cables

Farm Equipment

Seeds for planting
Pots for planting
Gloves (leather, cotton, Mechanix, etc.)
Pulleys (different sizes)
Pitchforks
Chains and locks
Post hole digger
Fence stretcher (come along)
Garden hoses
Scythe and sharpening stone
Plow and tiller
Machete
Mowers
Rakes (lawn, steel, potato, etc.)
Hoes (spade, Dutch Flat, etc.
Wheelbarrow and baskets

Shovels: snow, spade, square, dung, etc.
Hand water pump and pipes

Animals and Animal Care Equipment

Draft animals
Dogs (working, herding)
Livestock
Chickens and rooster
Vapor rub
Deworming medicine
Stainless steel milk container
Chicken feeders and water dishes
Harnesses and carts
Feed, hay, and dog food
Farrier tools and grooming tools
Chicken wire
Horse blankets
Fencing and barbed wire
Lead ropes, halters, and bridles
Iodine
Chisel, file, and hoof pick
Bottles and nipples
Dust pans and brooms
Old blankets

Modern Conveniences and Electricity

Appliance	Average Wattage	Average hrs. per yr.	Kilowatt hour per year
Dehumidifier	257	1467	377
Attic fan	370	786	291
Infrared heat lamp	250	52	13
Humidifier	177	921	163

Portable space heater	1322	133	176
Blender	386	39	15
Coffee maker	894	119	106
Dishwasher	1201	302	363
Garbage disposal	445	67	30
Microwave	1450	131	190
Mixer	127	102	13
Range and oven	12,200	96	1171
Rang/self-cleaning oven	12,200	99	1208
Toaster	1146	34	39
Waffle iron	1116	20	22
15 cu ft upright freezer	341	3504	1195
15 cu ft upright/FL freezer	440	4002	1761
12 cu ft refrigerator	241	3021	728
12 cu ft FL refrigerator	321	3791	1217
14 cu ft fridge/freezer	326	3488	1137
14 cu ft FL fridge/freezer	615	2774	1829
Curling iron	40	50	2
Hair dryer	750	51	38
Shaver	14	129	2
Radio	71	1211	86
Television	300	2200	660
Sewing machine	75	147	11
Vacuum	630	73	46

Dryer, clothes	4856	205	995
Hand iron	1008	143	144
Auto washing machine (2500 kwh)	512	208	107
Water heater	4474	1075	4811
Desktop PC	150		

Additional Convenience Appliances

Juicer
Dehydrator
Air fryer
Bread maker
Stand mixer

FIRST AID AND HOMEOPATHIC CARE

Herbal Vinegar

Herbal vinegars are best made with apple cider vinegar and the following herbs:

Apple mint (*Menta sp.*) leaves, stalks
Bee balm (*Monarda didyma*) flowers, leaves, stalks
Bergamot (*Monarda sp.*) flowers, leaves, stalks
Burdock (*Arctium lappa*) roots
Catnip (*Nepeta cataria*) leaves, stalks
Chicory (*Cichorium intybus*) leaves, roots
Chives, especially chive blossoms
Dandelion (*Taraxacum officinalis*) flower buds, leaves, roots

Dill (*Anethum graveolens*) herb, seeds
Fennel (*Foeniculum vulgare*) herb, seeds
Garlic (*Allium sativum*) bulbs, greens, flowers
Garlic mustard (*Alliaria officinalis*) leave and roots
Goldenrod (*Solidago sp.*) flowers
Ginger (*Zingiber off.*), wild ginger (*Asarum canadense*) roots
Lavender (*Lavandula sp.*) flowers, leaves
Mugwort (*Artemisia vulgaris*) new growth leaves and roots
Orange mint (*Mentha sp.*) leaves, stalks
Orange peel, organic only
Peppermint (*Mentha piperita* and etc.) leaves, stalks
Perilla (Shiso)(*Agastache*) leaves, stalks
Rosemary (*Rosmarinus off.*) leaves, stalks
Spearmint (*Mentha spicata*) leaves, stalks
Thyme (*Thymus sp.*) leaves, stalks
White pine (*Pinus strobus*) needles
Yarrow (*Achillea millefolium*) flowers, leaves

Herbs as a Calcium Supplement

Take 2-4 tsp vinegar daily.

Amaranth (*Amaranthus retroflexus*): leaves
Cabbage leaves
Chickweed (*Stellaria media*): whole herb
Comfrey (*Symphytum officinalis*): leaves
Cronewort/mugwort (*Artemisia vulgaris*): young leaves
Dandelion (*Tarazacum off.*): leaves, roots
Kale leaves
Lambsquarter (*Chenopodium album*): leaves
Mallow (*Malva neglecta*): leaves
Mint leaves of all sorts, especially sage, motherwort, lemon balm, et.

Nettle (*Urtica dioica*): leaves
Parsley (*Petroselinum sativum*): leaves
Plantain (*Plantago majus*): leaves
Raspberry (*Rubus species*): leaves
Red clover (*Trifolium pratense*): blossoms
Violet (*Viola odorata*): leaves
Yellow dock (*Rumex crispus* and other species): roots

First Aid Kit for a Modern House

Adhesive medical tape
Splints (metal and popsicle sticks/tongue depressors)
Antiseptic ointment (triple antibiotic ointment, Polysporin)
Eyewash and distilled water
Band aids (fabric and waterproof), butterfly band aids
Standard first aid book (American Red Cross book preferred)
Flashlight and batteries
Ipecac syrup
Blankets
Tweezers (several sizes)
Cold packs
Hydrogen peroxide
Disposable gloves
Betadine (diluted)
Sterile gauge pads and rolls
Tylenol/acetaminophen, ibuprofen and Motrin
Hand sanitizer
Dental floss
Plastic bags
Soft dental/orthodontic wax
Scissors and bandage scissors
Cotton balls and swabs (Q-tips)
Knife

Tamanol/Cavit filling
Steri-strip wound closure strips
Toothache meds (Red Cross, Dentis, Orajel)
Spenco second skin (moleskin)
Clove oil
Liquid skin (liquid band aid)
Catgut sutures
Prescription medicine
Personal sanitation supplies
Disposable dishes and utensils
Plant identification book for food foraging
½ gallon of water per person per day in glass jar or jugs
Disposable diapers (if necessary)
2 rolls of toilet paper per person per week
Candles, 3 or more per day
Matches, woodstove, and 2-4 cords wood
Battery fire detector
Oil lamps and fuel
Flashlights and batteries

First Aid Kit for a Primitive House

Clean cloths (sanitation)
Pocket knife
½ gallon water per person per day in glass jar or jug
Cloth diapers (if necessary)
Paper and cloth scraps for toilet paper
Candles, lamps, matches, and fuel
Flint
Canned and dried food

Medication and Uses

Pain: Tylenol/acetaminophen, aspirin, Naproxen, ibuprofen/Advil/Motrin, etc.

Fever: Tylenol/acetaminophen
Inflammation: Ibuprofen/Advil/Motrin, NSAIDs
Anti-diarrheal: Imodium, Pepto-Bismol, Kao pectate, etc.
Anti-nausea: Dramamine
Poisoning: Ipecac
Rash, itching: hydrocortisone cream
Cough medicine: dextromethorphan
Earache: Tylenol/acetaminophen, ibuprofen/Advil/Motrin
Eye drops: saline-based solutions

Aspirin should only be used after injury or pain for adults, never for children, because it has been linked to Reye's Syndrome. It should also never be given for viral pain or other illness. Aspirin is also used to prevent heart attacks.

Natural Wound Cleaners

Garlic
Honey
Iodine
Saltwater
Sphagnum moss (contains natural iodine)

Homemade Disinfectants

Solution of 1 part bleach to 1 part water
Hydrogen peroxide and vinegar, applied separately

Comprehensive First Aid Kit

1 large first aid bag with individual compartments to contain first aid supplies

1 bottle of alcohol or alcohol wipes for disinfection

1 bottle of betadine and/or hydrogen peroxide for cleaning wounds

1 bottle of hand sanitizer and/or sanitizer wipes for sanitizing hands

1 bottle of mineral and/or baby oil to float insects out of ears

1 bottle of saline solution and/or eye wash to flush contaminants from eyes

1 bottle of decongestant spray to clean blood clots from the nose

1 tube antiseptic with benzocaine to treat mouth pain

10 individual doses of burn gel (e.g., water gel) to treat burns and sunburns

1 bottle of aloe vera lotion or gel to treat sunburns

1 bottle of calamine lotion to treat poison ivy or sunburn

1 tube of hydrocortisone cream to treat insect bites and rashes

1 tube of triple antibiotic cream or ointment to apply to wounds to prevent infection

2 pair of rubber/latex gloves to protect against infection

1 pair of tweezers to remove foreign objects

1 needle in a protective case to remove splinters

1 penlight to examine the eyes, ears, and throat

1 pair of bandage scissors to cut gauze and tape

1 pair of rescue shears to cut away clothing

1 magnifying glass for examining wounds

6 safety pins or bandage clips to secure bandages

1 digital/mercury thermometer for measuring temperature

10 small plastic bags for disposal

1 plastic measuring spoon for giving correct medicine dosage

2-5 rolls of medical tape (1 in. x 10 yds) to secure bandages and splints

1 3 oz bulb syringe to irrigate wounds and unblock noses

1 pack of cotton swabs (Q-tips) for cleaning wounds, ears, etc.

3 instant, disposable cold packs to reduce swelling and relieve pain

1 structural aluminum malleable (SAM) splint: 1 finger, 1 large (36 in.) to immobilize a limb

2 rolls duct tape to immobilize a limb

1 rescue blanket to treat for shock

1 epinephrine auto-injector to treat anaphylactic shock

1 save-a-tooth storage system for taking tooth to a dentist or the ER

2 or more pocket masks for protection when giving CPR

2 bottles of pain relievers, such as Tylenol or Ibuprofen to relieve pain and reduce swelling

2 bottles of liquid pain relievers for treating children

2 bottles/boxes of Benadryl to treat allergic reaction

2 bottles/packages of pink bismuth tab/liquid to treat upset stomach, diarrhea, etc.

50 fabric adhesive bandages of assorted sizes for covering scrapes, cuts and punctures

20 gauze pads of assorted sizes for covering wounds, cuts, cleaning etc.

20 non-stick gauze pads of assorted sizes to cover burns, blisters, and wounds

2 conforming gauze rolls about 4 in. wide to secure bandages and compress joints

2 eye pads to protect an injured eye

10 trauma pads, sizes 5 in. x 9 in. and 8 in. x10 in., to stop bleeding in deep wounds

2 multi-trauma dressings, size 10 in. x 30 in. to

protect and pad major wounds

2 blood stopper compress dressings to stop bleeding in deep wounds

2 water-gel burn dressing, sizes 4 in x 4 in. and 4 in. x 16 in., to treat burns

20 fingertip and knuckle bandages to protect wounds on fingers/toes

2 triangle bandages, size 40 in., to cover large wounds and secure limbs

25 butterfly wound closure strips of assorted sizes to hold wound edges together

2 note pads, pens, and markers for writing down patient info/vital signs

1 first aide manual to guide first aid efforts

Keep the first aid kit well stocked. Adjust its contents according to the regional area, due to each region having its own specific injury risks. For example, northern regions will have more cases of frost bite than southern regions.

ARTS AND CLOTHING

Soap Making

Making homemade soap not only provides for the homestead's needs, but it can also create a product to be sold for additional income. Two important aspects of soap making are fat and lye temperatures and additives.

Fat and Lye Temperatures

Sweet rancid fat should be in a temperature range of 97-100 degrees Fahrenheit with the lye temperature in the range of 75-80 degrees Fahrenheit.

Sweet lards and soft fats should be in a temperature range of 80-85 degrees Fahrenheit with the lye temperature in the range of 70-75 degrees Fahrenheit.

A half-lard and half- tallow mixture should be in a temperature range of 100-110 degrees Fahrenheit with the lye temperature in the range of 80-85 degrees Fahrenheit.

Tallow should be in a temperature range of 120-130 degrees Fahrenheit with the lye temperature in the range of 90-95 degrees Fahrenheit.

Vegetable fats should be in a temperature range of 100-120 degrees Fahrenheit with the lye temperature in the range of 90-95 degrees Fahrenheit.

Soap Additives

Additives are an important aspect of making homemade soap. Below is a list of common additives, how to use them, and the additive's useful properties.

Almond can be used as an additive when blanched and ground into a fine meal. It helps to unclogs pores and absorb oil.

Aloe vera gel can be used as an additive. It also heals abrasions and tones skin.

Apricot can be used as an additive either fresh or dried. It softens skin and adds vitamins.

Bran, the ground up outer husk of any grain, can be used as an additive as well. It acts as a mild abrasive to clean out pores and remove dried skin.

Calendula can be used as an additive, using fresh or dried petals. The seeds should be removed. It softens and soothes sensitive and dry skin.

Carrots can be used as an additive to add vitamins.

Powdered clay   can be used as an additive to absorb oils and help with drying.

Fresh, unbrewed coffee grounds can be used as an

additive to absorb odors.

Cornmeal can be used as an additive to absorb oil and unclog pores.

Grated cucumber can be used as an additive as a mild cleaner and to clean pores.

Elderberry can be used as an additive after distilling the flowers and using the liquid. It softens and tones skin.

Goat milk should be used as an additive when fresh. It cleanses skin.

Raw honey can be used at an additive. It softens and smooths skin.

Kelp, a large, leafy algae, can be used as an additive. It cleans and adds vitamin C.

Oil from lemon peels can be used as an additive to add antibacterial properties.

Lettuce has antibacterial properties. Fresh, clean leaves can be used as an additive.

Marshmallow, *Althea officinalis*, can be used as an additive. It softens skin.

Oatmeal, ground up rolled oats, can be used as an additive. It soothes sensitive and irritated skin.

Rosemary, *Rosmarinus officinalis*, can be used as an additive as a mild cleanser.

Sage, *Salvia officinalis*, can be used as an additive. It is antibacterial and acts as a cleanser.

Fresh strawberry can be used as an additive. It tightens and whitens skin, and adds vitamin C.

Leather Dyes

Natural dyes can be made on the homestead using a variety of herbs and plants.

Indigo is a natural dye that comes from the indigo plant. Colors very similar to indigo can be made from a variety of plants, but most commonly elderberry. Indigo creates a dark blue color and it can dye all-natural fibers. Leather can be dyed by soaking the skin in an indigo solution. To prepare the solution, boil indigo, or alum and elderberries, in water. Wash the skins in the liquid. Another method is to boil elderberries with alum and dip the skin in the liquid once or twice and allow the skin to dry. To create a lighter, sky blue dye, steep indigo in boiling water. Allow it to cool to a lukewarm temp then spread it over the skin.

Green leather dye can be made by mashing buckthorn berries into a thick paste and spreading it over the skin. Then boil the skin in alum water.

To dye leather yellow, smear the skin with aloe and linseed oil then rinse off.

To die leather light orange, smear the skin with fustic berry paste and boil in alum water.

To dye leather dark orange, smear the skin with turmeric past and boil in alum water.

For most natural leather dyes, the ratio of fiber to solution is 4 gallons solution to 1 lb fiber, but final colors may vary depending on the quality of the ingredients and fiber.

Dyeing Other Fibers

Fibers should be scoured and mordanted before being dyed. Below is a chart of common natural dye sources and instructions on dyeing natural fibers. Only natural fibers can be dyed with natural dyes.

Dye Source	Color	Gathering	Preparing	Dying
Acorn	Brown	7 lbs off the ground	Soak overnight	Boil 2.5 hours then simmer with fiber 1 hour

Beet	Red	2 lbs		Boil 1 hour then simmer with fiber 30 minutes
Blue-berry	Blue	16 qts fully ripe berries		Boil 30 mins with 1 cup vinegar then simmer 30 minutes with fiber
But-terfly weed	Yellow	1 bushel of blossoms in full bloom	Soak 1 hour	Boil 1 hour then simmer 30 minutes with fiber
Celery leaves	Yellow	2 lbs fresh green leaves		Boil 1 hour then simmer 30 minutes with fiber
Cherry, fruit	Pink	16 qts ripe berries		Boil 1 hour then simmer 30 minutes with fiber
Cherry root	Blue	2 lbs		Boil 30 minutes with 1 cup vinegar then simmer 30 minutes with fiber
Core-opsis	Yellow	2 bushels of blossoms	Soak 40 minutes to 1hour	Simmer with fiber for 30 minutes
Dan-delion root	Red	2 lbs		Boil 1 hour then simmer 30 minutes with fiber
Elder-berry	Laven-der	16 qts ber-ries		Boil 30 minutes with 1 cup vinegar then simmer 30 minutes with fiber
Gold-enrod	Yellow	2 lbs blos-som and stems		Simmer 30 minutes then again with fiber
Grapes	Blue	16 qts ripe grapes		Boil 1 hour then simmer 30 minutes with fiber
Grass	Green	2 lbs. fresh green grass		Boil 1 hour then simmer 30 minutes with fiber

Juniper berries	Brown	16 qts ripe berries		Boil 30 minutes with 1 cup vinegar then simmer 30 minutes with fiber
Lily of the Valley	Light green	2 lbs fresh green leaves		Simmer 1 hour then simmer with fiber 20 minutes
Madder	Red	2 lbs madder root		Boil 1 hour then simmer 30 minutes with fiber
Marigold	Brown	2 bushels of blossoms		Simmer 1 hour then simmer with fiber 1 hour
Onion skin	Yellow	2 lbs of dry outer skin		Simmer 20 minutes. Do not overcook. Simmer with fiber 20 minutes.
Red onion skin	Red	2 lbs of dry outer skin		Simmer 20 minutes. Do not overcook. Simmer with fiber 20 minutes.
Pokeberry	Yellow	16 qts ripe berries		Boil 30 minutes with 1 cup vinegar then simmer 30 min with fiber
Privet	Gray	1 lb fresh green leaves		Simmer 30 minutes-1 hour then simmer 20 minutes with fiber
Queen Anne's Lace	Green	1-bushel of blossoms and stems		Simmer 30 minutes then simmer with fiber 30 minutes
Red raspberries	Pink	16 qts ripe berries		Boil 30 min with 1 cup vinegar then simmer 30 min with fiber
Red cabbage	Blue	2 lbs leave		Boil 1 hour then simmer 30 minutes with fiber
Red cedar root	Purple	2 lbs red cedar root		Boil 1 hour then simmer 30 minutes with fiber

Rho- doden- dron	Green	3 lbs fresh green leaves	Soak leaves overnight	Boil 1 hour then simmer 30 minutes with fiber
Rose hips	Red	2 lbs rose hips		Boil 1 hour then simmer 30 minutes with fiber
Sassa- fras	Or- ange	2 lbs fresh green leaves		Boil 1 hour then simmer 30 minutes with fiber
Spin- ach	Green	2 lbs fresh leaves		Boil 1 hour then simmer 30 minutes with fiber
Straw- berries	Pink	16 qts ripe berries		Boil 30 min with 1 cup vinegar then simmer 30 minutes with fiber
Sumac	Black	2 lbs fresh leave		Boil 1 hour then simmer 30 minutes with fiber
Tea (no Mor- daunt)	Light brown	½ lb dried leaves		Cover with boiling water and steep 15 min then simmer 20 minutes with fiber
Vir- ginia creeper	Peach	2 lbs all parts of Virginia creeper		Boil 1 hour then simmer 30 minutes with fiber
Walnut	Brown	7 lbs of hulls off the ground	Soak overnight	Boil 2.5 hours then sim- mer 1hour with fiber

OTHER SOURCES OF INCOME

Homesteads often need additional sources of income, especially when first starting up. Below is a list of possible products which can be sold for additional income, as well as a small sample of stay-at-home jobs.

Homestead Products

Aquatic plants
Berries and fruits
Craft supplies
Fishing supplies
Firewood
Flowers
Furniture and handmade items
Gourmet food products
Herbal preparation
Herbs and seeds
Useful animals
Organic fresh food
Organic processed food
Organic insecticide for plant nurseries

Stay at Home Jobs

Writer
Artist
Newsletter writer
Publisher
Illustrator
Photographer
Designer
Musician
Artist
Mail-order products
Internet-sold products
Bed and breakfast operator
Carpenter
Crafter
Freelance consultant
Daycare provider

Pet sitter

Family tree researcher

CYCLES OF WORK

Homesteading has cycles of work which remain fairly steady and predictable throughout the year. This section provides a sample of homestead work cycles, though dates and months listed below may need to be adjusted depending on climate and growing zones.

January

Fun: New Year's Day.

Personal: Mend tools. Make clothes for the year. In cold climates, put cod liver oil in the bird feeder.

Fowl: Watch for broody geese and collect eggs.

Rabbit: Check water twice daily for freezing.

Goats: Trim hooves.

Sheep: Deworm ewes if they were last treated in November. Examine sheep for ticks, trim hooves, vaccinate all sheep, and tag ewes before lambing. Give ewes a pregnancy check at the end of the month.

Horses: Shoe and deworm horses. Clean tack once a week.

Cattle: Finish drying up pregnant milk cows.

February

Fun: Valentine's Day.

Trees: Chop down maple trees in preparation for making syrup. Cut fruit tree scions for grafting.

Bees: Order new bees.

Rabbits: Check water twice daily for freezing.

Goats: Trim goat's hooves. Young goats should be on solid food and eating well. Begin separating the young from their mothers.

Sheep: Watch pregnant ewes for lambing. Dock newborn lambs and castrate non-breeding males at two weeks old.

Horses: Shoe and deworm horses. Clean tack weekly.

March

Fun: St. Patrick's Day. Hold a "sugaring off" party. March 21st is first day of spring.

Trees: Tap maple trees. When the time is right, plant new trees (depending on the variety). Prune older trees. Start grafting trees when buds start to swell.

Personal: Take down storm windows and winter sealing.

Garden: Start transplants for an early garden, around March 1st. Plant a bee garden.

Field: Plow fields when the soil is dry enough. Plant grain amaranth and wheat, usually after the last frost. Plant sweet sorghum two weeks after the last frost.

Bees: Watch for swarming bees. If more hives are desired, do not make any changes. If more hives are not desired, pinch out the queen cells.

Fowl: Prepare the goose pasture. Rooster mating season starts.

Rabbits: Continue to check water.

Goats: Check goat's hooves. Buy young bucks or use bucks from the herd. Deworm goats and vaccinate before turning them out to pasture.

Sheep: Buy weaned lambs. Sheer and clean wool. Treat ewes and lambs for ticks and lice. Vaccinate lambs.

Horses: Shoe and deworm horses. Check pastures for weeds. Clean tack weekly. Clip horses for plowing.

Cattle: Watch for bred dairy cows calving from the 1st

to around the 15th.

April

Fun: April Fool's Day. Easter. Arbor Day. Passover.

Personal: Store winter quilts and clothes. Weave clothes during spare time. Beginning of danger of Lyme disease.

Farm: Clean barn of manures.

Field: Turn over the virgin soil that was turned the previous fall. Disc old pastures and broadcast grass seeds. Check sheep pastures for weeds with burrs.

Garden: Plant early garden transplants or plant seeds in the garden from the 1st through the 15th. Start spring garden transplants on the 1st.

Fowl: Rooster fertility ends.

Goats: Check goat's hooves. Goats bred in November should be due around the 1st.

Sheep: Feed hay, vaccinate, and cull out old ewes, and then turn them out. Treat ewes for lice. Wean lambs one week prior to turning out.

Horses: Shoe and deworm horses. Turn horses out to pasture. Clean tack weekly.

May

Fun: May Day. Mother's Day. Memorial Day. Victoria Day (Canada).

Garden: Harvest the earliest garden vegetables. Plant spring garden transplants around the 15th, or sow seeds from the 1st through the 15th. Start the latest spring garden transplants around the 1st.

Field: Harvest wheat, plant sorghum, and plant alfalfa hay for the goats and sheep.

Pond: Blanket weed will cover ponds and can be

removed.

Bees: Catalog bees should be arriving if ordered.

Goats: Check goat's hooves.

Sheep: Watch for foot rot and isolate infected animals. Weigh lambs and choose replacements.

Horses: Shoe and deworm horses. Clean tack weekly.

Cattle: Breed cows who are in heat from the 15th through the end of the month.

June

Fun: Father's Day. Midsummer. Summer begins on the 21st.

Personal: Gather flowers for dyes and materials for baskets.

Garden: Harvest early and spring gardens. Plant the latest spring garden transplants around the 15th, or sow seeds in the garden from the 1st through the 15th. Start summer garden transplants around the 1st.

Field: Harvest sweet sorghum on a clear, chilly day. Harrow the pasture and irrigate.

Goats: Check hooves and deworm.

Sheep: Check lambs for diseases and deworm lambs.

Horses: Shoe and deworm horses. Clean tack weekly.

July

Fun: Independence Day (US). Canada Day.

Personal: Gather flowers and berries for dyes.

Garden: Harvest the spring garden and the latest spring garden. Plant the summer garden transplants around the 15th, or sow seeds in the garden around the 15th. Start the latest summer garden transplants around the 1st. Harvest fruit.

Field: Harvest grain amaranth and alfalfa hay. Plant broomcorn 10-14 days after the amaranth harvest.

Goat: Check goat's hooves.

Sheep: Rotate pastures. Purchase a ram, if necessary. Shear all rams and replacement ewe lambs early in the month.

Horses: Shoe and deworm horses. Clean tack weekly.

August

Fun: County fair.

Personal: Gather berries for dyes. Gather cornhusks for baskets and beds.

Garden: Harvest spring gardens. Sow late summer garden seeds, if transplants were not used, from the 1st to the 15th. Start fall garden transplants.

Trees: Harvest nuts and apples. Cut trees for firewood.

Goats: Check goat's hooves. Deworm goats. Butcher meat goats.

Bees: Collect honey.

Sheep: Put overweight ewes on diets.

Horses: Shoe and deworm horses. Clean tack weekly.

September

Fun: Labor Day. School starts. Grandparent's Day. Fall starts on the 23rd.

Personal: Gather cattail stalks, husks, and basket materials. Gather bayberry for candles. Clean out barns.

Field: Test the soil of all pastures and fields. Turn virgin soil and plow fields. Plant winter grain.

Garden: Add materials to compost the garden. Harvest the latest spring garden, the summer garden, and the late summer garden. Plant fall garden transplants around the 15th or sow seeds from the 1st through the 15th.

Trees: Harvest nuts.

Bees: Start feeding bees.

Fowl: Chickens may start molting.

Goats: Check goat's hooves. Dry up goats who are kidding in November.

Sheep: Flush, tag, and check hooves on ewes on the 1st. Check rams for injury or illness. Shear sheep on the 1st.

October

Fun: Halloween. Thanksgiving (Canada).

Personal: Lyme Disease season ends. Prepare to butcher large animals when daily temperatures reach 40 degrees Fahrenheit. Change feathers in beds. Store up quilts, clothes, and candles. Make soup. Collect berry vines for baskets.

Garden: Harvest summer gardens and the fall garden. Plant the winter garden.

Fowl: Goose molting season starts. Collect feathers.

Goats: Check hooves and deworm only the does 6-8 weeks before kidding. Start giving grain to does who will kid.

Sheep: Finish breeding season by the 20th. Breed ewe lambs by mid-October.

Horses: Shoe and deworm horses. Clean tack weekly.

Cattle: Butcher male calves over 15 months old.

November

Fun: Thanksgiving Day (US). Remembrance Day (Canada).

Personal: Chop wood, put up storm windows, and seal cracks.

Garden: Harvest late summer and fall gardens.

Trees: Plant new trees (check variety) and prune old trees.

Goats: Check goat's hooves. Stop milking by the 1st and breed ewes by the 14th. Cull older ewes.

Fowl: Cull old, non-laying geese.

Sheep: Flush, eye, tag, and check hooves of ewes on the 1st.

Horses: Keep up maintenance.

Rabbits: Check water twice daily for freezing.

December

Fun: Advent. St. Nicholas day. St. Lucia day. Christmas. Chanukah. New Year's Eve. Boxing Day (Canada). Winter begins on the 22nd.

Personal: Put cod liver oil in bird feed in cold climates. Plan next year's farming.

Goats: Check and trim hooves. Taper off the doe's grain around the 15th.

Sheep: Plan for lambing and watch for health issues.

Horses: Keep up maintenance.

Rabbits: Keep up maintenance.

Cattle: Start drying up pregnant milk cows.

Everyday, year-round work on a homestead also includes weeding and watering gardens and rinsing out sprout jars. The list of work tasks above will vary for individual homesteads.

WEATHER

Becoming familiar with the seasons, weather indicators, and wind can help homesteaders better plan growing seasons and prepare for adverse conditions.

Beginning Dates of Seasons in the Northern Hemisphere

Summers solstice: June 21st. The north pole leans

most toward the sun. This is longest day of the year.

Winter solstice: Dec. 22nd. The south pole leans most toward sun. This is the shortest day of year.

Vernal (ring) equinox: Mar. 21st. Earth is almost sideways to the sun. Day and night are the same length.

Autumnal equinox: Sept. 23rd. Earth is most sideways to the sun. Day and night the same length.

Season Lengths in the Northern Hemisphere

Spring: 92 days and 20 hours
Summer: 93 days and 14 hours
Fall: 89 days and 19 hours
Winter: 89 days and 1 hour

Natural Weather Indicators

Good indicators include a red sunset, flying beetles, busy spiders, high flying birds, heavy dew, grey mornings, soft-edged clouds, and pinecones with their scales open.

Bad indicators include a pale yellow sky at sunset, a red sunrise, a red eastern sky, dogs sniffing the air frequently, birds ruffling their feathers and huddling, hard-edged clouds, pinecones with their scales closed.

During lightning storms, count the seconds between the flash and the thunder. Lightning is about 1 mile away per every 5 seconds' count.

Wind Speed Measurements

1-3 mph: Smoke rises straight up.
4-7 mph: Leaves rustle slightly.
8-12 mph: Loose paper scraps will lift. Wind is felt on the face.

13-18 mph: Loose dust is blown, and small branches move.

19-24 mph: Small trees sway.

25-31 mph: Large branches move constantly.

32-38 mph: Entire trees in are in motion. Walking is affected.

39-46 mph: Walking becomes difficult.

47-54 mph: Gale winds with slight building damage.

55-63 mph: Trees are uprooted. There is heavy building damage.

64-75 mph: Very violent storms.

Wind Chill Chart

Wind Speed	30°	25°	20°	15°	10°	5°	0°	-5°	-10°	-15°
5 mph	25	19	13	7	1	-5	-11	-16	-22	-28
10 mph	21	15	9	3	-4	-10	-16	-22	-28	-35
15 mph	19	13	6	0	-7	-13	-19	-26	-32	-39
20 mph	17	11	4	-2	-9	-15	-22	-29	-35	-42
25 mph	16	9	3	-4	-11	-17	-24	-31	-37	-44
30 mph	15	8	1	-5	-12	-19	-26	-33	-39	-46
40 mph	13	6	-1	-8	-15	-22	-29	-36	-43	-50
50 mph	12	4	-3	-10	-17	-24	-31	-38	-45	-52

ANIMAL BASICS AND HEALTH

No matter what livestock is raised, medical care is a high priority. Having a basic understanding of animal care and emergency treatment is important for any homesteader. Having the right supplies on hand will make caring for livestock more manageable.

Animal Care First Aid Kit

Toolbox
Restraint equipment (for individual animals)
Digital rectal thermometer with a string and alligator clip
Stainless steel bucket
16-,18-, 20-gauge hypodermic needles (1-1.5 in. long)
5 cc, 12 cc, 60 cc syringes
IV complex hose
Obstetric chains and handles
Neonatal resuscitator
Neonatal esophageal feeder
Stomach tube (sized for individual animals)
Small fridge for medicine
Flashlights and batteries
Funnel and soft tubing (rubber)
Cotton balls
Cotton rags
Cotton swabs

Animal Wound Kit

Rubber gloves.
Antiseptic cream
Betadine
Hydrogen peroxide
Nonstick gauze pads
4 in. x 4 in. standard gauze pads
Roll cotton
Veterinary wrap
Medical tape

LARRY JUSTICE

Deworming

Species specific deworming medication – injections
are the easiest, but oral paste is the cheapest method
Administration supplies (needles and syringes)

Bees

Types of bees

There are three main breeds of bees common to beekeeping: Italian, Caucasian, and Carniolan. Italian bees work hard. Caucasian bees sting less. Carniolan bees are the gentlest.

African bees escaped from a lab in San Paulo, Brazil. They attack in a swarm and can be lethal. They can be out run at 15 mph for 5-7 minutes or 8-10 city blocks. They are immune to bug spray. Use soapy water and high pressure to kill them.

Wasps, yellow jackets, and hornets don't pollinate or consume flower nectar. Instead, they eat bugs, fruit, and other foods. They are helpful in gardens for pest control, but can sting for any reason. They can sting multiple times, while honeybees only sting once. They leave the stinger then die.

BEEKEEPING EQUIPMENT

Tools for hive work include:

Hive tool
Bee smoker
Bee brush (optional)
Equipment for one hive
Hive stand (optional)
Standard bottom board

Brood chambers (standard hive bodies with frames)
Honey supers (shallow with frames)
Hive cover (an inner cover with telescope style)
Queen excluder
Wax comb foundation
Sugar syrup feeder

Equipment for honey extraction includes:

Electric uncapping knife
Honey extractor
Honey storage tank (optional)

Beekeeping clothing includes:

PROTECTIVE CLOTHING:

Bee veil
White coveralls
Work boots (optional)
Bee gloves (optional)

It is preferred to purchase beekeeping clothing to ensure it adheres to safety guidelines, but it can be made or assembled. Gloves should be very thick leather. Gauntlets should cover from the gloves to the elbows and need to fasten tightly around the arm. They should be baggy and made of canvas. Work boots should be tightly sealed with the pants tied tightly around the outside so the bees cannot get in and crawl up the leg. It is preferable to have an additional cover over the pants and boots.

White, one-piece baggy coveralls made of ripstop nylon are preferred because bees cannot walk on them. Jungle-style construction hard hats or bee-proof straw hats with a firm wide brim are preferred for head coverings.

Bee veils can be difficult to make, but should go over the top of the hat and sit on the brim. It is then tied firmly with a drawstring. If using a hard hat or other hats without a back-of-the-neck protector, attach cardboard to the back of the hat with duct tape.

Specific tools, such as a bee smoker or a stick with a burning rag attached to it, are useful to have available close to the hive. Other items such as hive tools for standard hives, bee brushes, and syrup feeders should also be readily available.

Bee skeps are dome-shaped structures made of coiled or braided straw. Straw is gathered into long bundles, wrapped around with a thick strip of wood then coiled. There should be a hole that is the height of one coil cut out for a door. Bee skeps are easily made, but are not favored because they have a higher risk for disease because they are not easy to clean out or regularly examine.

BEEHIVES

Standard Hive

COMPONENTS: BOTTOM TO TOP

Stand: The stand keeps hive level

Cotton/Bottom board: The bottom board holds up the brood chamber

Brood chamber: The bees live in the brood chamber. The queen lays eggs here and the cells house the bee larvae, or brood.

Supers/Honey supers: Supers are shallow boxes that sit on the brood chamber and hold honey. Although the bottom supers sometimes hold additional brood, it is preferable to have shallow boxes rather than deep ones so the supers do not get too full and too heavy. Each super holds 10 removable vertical frames, on which bees build wax cells. Each frame, or "foundation" or "flat sheet," of beeswax will typically have hexagons imprinted on it as a template for bees to build cells. These can be made or purchased.

Components of a Hive

Brood cells have dark colored caps. These cells contain bee larvae.

Queen cells are one inch long, and hang away from the rest of the comb. They are similar in shape to a peanut shell. These cells contain the larvae and the queen.

Drone cells protrude from the comb like queen cells, but do not protrude as far and have bullet-shaped tops. These cells contain baby drones.

The queen bee has a one-inch long, tapered body. Her only job is to lay eggs. Other bees will not crowd her. It takes 16 days for a queen bee to hatch and she can live seven to eight years.

Drones are heavier and larger, but do not have a stinger. Drones have big eyes and their only job is to mate with queen. Drones take 24 days to hatch.

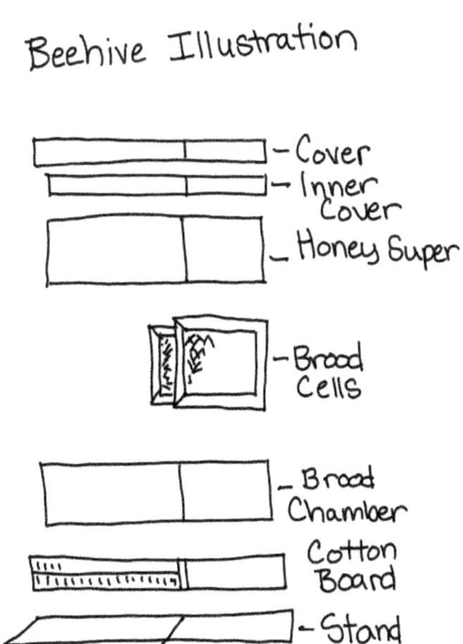

Worker bees have stingers and are the main workforce which keeps the hive going. Workers take 21 days to hatch.

The Ideal Bee Environment

Bees tend to have better survival rates in milder climates. During the first and second years, a new colony will produce about 1 to 2 gallons of honey per hive per summer and up to 4-5 gallons over time. It can take three years for bees to reach the full, expected amount of honey.

When setting up the hive, orient the door in the direction of the expected or desired bee flight path. This should typically be toward the morning sun and away from people and animals. Place hives away from any vibrating equipment.

Bees thrive best in heat zones 7 and 8, with zone 7 being more ideal. The best hardiness zones for bees are zones 6A and 6B.

Plants and Honey Production

Bees should also have plenty of nearby plants from which they can harvest nectar. Below is a list of plants which are favorites of bees.

Alfalfa produces a light-colored honey with a mild, delicate flavor. It is a major source of commercial honey production.

Aster produces a white, minty honey that granulates readily. It is a major source of fall honey and pollen.

Basswood produces a light, aromatic honey. Because of its abundance, it is one of the leading sources of honey.

Clover produces a light, delicate honey. Because of its abundance, it is also a leading source of honey

Dandelion produces a yellow to amber colored honey with a strong flavor. It is an important early spring source of nectar and pollen.

Goldenrod produces a thick, golden honey. It is mostly used for winter food for bees and is an excellent fall source of pollen and nectar.

Orange and other citrus produce a fragrant and mild honey that is often used for blending with other honeys. It is one of the most popular honeys.

Sage produces a light-colored honey that is mild in flavor. It is important in west. Most sage honey does not granulate.

Tupelo produces a mild, greenish–amber honey. It is known for not granulating and is a favorite in health food stores.

Hive and Colony Maintenance

To perform regular maintenance, open the hive and remove every frame. Locate the queen. During the spring, look for queen cells as well. Determine the total number of bees in the colony, the total number of brood cells, and what types and how much honey is being produced. Determine whether more supers are needed. Having adequate supers prevents over crowding, which in turn prevents swarming.

Ensure there is clean, fresh, non-stagnant water in the area. If a source of fresh water is not available, let an outside faucet drip onto a slanted board.

Check the heat level of the hive. A hive that is too hot may need remediation. If bees are observed frequently standing around outside the door of the hive, it is likely they cannot cool the hive. Move the hive into the shade, make the entrance larger or stagger supers for improved ventilation. During winter, the door should be only one quarter inch wide to keep heat in and to also prevent mice.

Having a food source is critical for bees' survival.

Bees need to be near herb gardens, orchards, honeysuckle plants, clover, and alfalfa. Even cabbage and mustard flowers make good honey. Do not use pesticides, because bees eat their own honey during the winter. Find out if your neighbors use pesticides, as well. One hive needs 50 to 100lbs of honey for the winter. If they get low on honey, give them artificial pollen or just pour white sugar between the frames. Never give them brown sugar. The molasses in brown sugar can be toxic to bees.

Artificial pollen should be one part brewer's yeast, three parts soy flour, and one part nonfat dry milk. Use as much natural pollen as possible.

BEEKEEPING CALENDAR

In the early spring make sure bees have enough food. Begin distributing artificial pollen and check the cleanliness of the hive. Workers should keep it clean. If there are dead bees, that usually means there is a failed queen, except in cold climates where bee deaths may be related to cold temperatures.

In the late spring or early summer, add another section once the hive has grown to the desired size. This will hold increased comb production. This is time to split the hive if desired. Bees may swarm if the hive becomes over-full. Leave the bees in a group if they swarm. They should not sting, but they may be tracked down and coaxed back.

In the fall, on a sunny day in the afternoon, remove honey from the hive. Be sure to leave 50 to 100lbs for the bees to eat over the winter.

During the winter, keep the hive ventilated and protected from wind. Check the food supply and add sugar, or sugar water, as needed.

Preventing Diseases

Preventing disease requires being aware of the quality of anything introduced into the hive or colony. Do not buy honey from unfamiliar suppliers. Only buy bees from a dealer with a good reputation. Do not buy used equipment unless has been inspected by a state-approved inspector. The governing agency is different depending on the state. Put in new hive foundations every two to four years and check for signs of disease every time the hive is opened.

Types of Diseases and Pests

Acarine are small mites which bore holes in the air passages of bees one to eight days old and feed on their blood. Keep bees producing larvae to prevent the population from diminishing, but acarine will continue to feed on them unless treated. In order to re-populate colonies affected by acarine, treat with terramycin.

American Foulbrood (AFB) is the worst type of brood disease. It is caused by the spore-forming bacterium *Paenibacillus* larvae. These bacteria cause larvae to rot. Cell caps appear sunken and become perforated. Punctured cells will contain larvae which are dark brown and slimy. Affected hives will smell of rotten eggs (sulfur). To prevent AFB, treat with terramycin powder in the fall and the spring. AFB infections are spread by infected nurse bees passing spores to larvae during feeding. There is no cure for AFB. Infected colonies and hives should be destroyed and equipment should be irradiated. By law, AFB must be reported to the state.

The presence of ants in a hive typically means there are other problems. It is possible that the queen has fled or the colony has become weakened with disease. This provides room for ants to plunder, which may cause bees to leave.

Chalkbrood is a fungus, *Ascosphaera apis*, which

causes larvae to die once they are sealed in cells as pupae. Pupae turn white to grey to black then hard and chalky. Chalkbrood is most common in the spring when temperatures are cooler and the colony is expanding. To prevent the fungus from spreading, take out infected combs and burn them. The foundation should also be replaced.

Chilled brood is not a disease. The brood is too big for outer edge to keep warm in cold temperatures. Larvae will lose color and turn black. Bees will be found dead at all stages.

European foulbrood (EFB) looks like the American strain, but is caused by the bacterium *Melissococcus plutonius*. The brood will have a brown-yellow mottled appearance and brood cells will be uncapped. It often takes an experienced keeper examining the larvae to tell the difference between American and European strains. EFB is more common when a colony is under stress. There is no treatment for EFB. Affected combs should be replaced.

Nosema is caused by the spore-forming microsporidian *Nosema apis*. It is a naturally carried parasite in the intestines of bees. An affected bee will be swollen and crawling outside the hive with its wings shaking. Nosema can be prevented with Fumidil-D. If bees do not get enough pollen, Nosema will multiply and kill the bees.

Sacbrood is a rare virus making cell caps dark and sunken. Larvae which have recently died appear yellow and are highly infectious. Larvae which have been dead several months appear brown or grey-black and are not infectious. The appearance can be similar to foulbrood. The virus may be spread by feeding larvae infected pollen. Affected combs should be replaced. Antibiotic treatment is not effective against sacbrood.

Stonebrood is a very rare disease caused by the fungi *Aspergillus flavus* and *Aspergillus fumigatus*, which is present in soil. The fungus causes cells to become green and mildewy. Bees are typically able to fight this disease naturally.

Varroa destructor is a mite from India which kills European bees. They are light brown, oval and have eight legs. The six-legged varroa are harmless. *V. destructor* kills drone cells. Prevent these mites from entering a hive by using plastic pesticide strips.

Wax moths eat beeswax and larvae. Adult moths also lay eggs on the combs. When moth larvae hatch, they continue to eat as they burrow through the hive. This reduces the yield and salability of honey. Evidence of wax moth infestation includes fine gray webs around paths and tunnels chewed through the comb. A strong colony will kill the moths, but diseased, stressed, or declining colonies may not be able to fight them off.

Poultry

Poultry is an integral component of sustainable living. Choosing the right stock and ensuring proper care requires considering multiple factors, which will be discussed in this chapter. Important resources on basic and in-depth information about breeds, standards of care, and harvesting include the American Poultry Association (APA) and *Standard of Perfection,* aka "the standard," an APA publication.

Poultry Species Characteristics

Coturnix quail have good raisability and disease resistance. They produce egg and meat well in small and limited spaces.

Guinea fowl have fair to good raisability and excellent disease resistance. They are gamy in flavor, but are good at providing insect control and raising alarm. They also thrive in hot climates.

Pigeons have good raisability and disease resistance. They are good message carriers and produce meat well in limited spaces. They are also quiet.

Chickens have fair to good raisability and disease resistance. They are good for egg and meat production, and are natural mothers. They also adapt well to cages, houses, and ranges.

Turkeys have poor to fair raisability and disease resistance. The have heavy meat production.

Geese have excellent raisbility and disease resistance. They produce meat and feathers well, and act as natural lawn mowers and help control aquatic plants. They have "watch dog" temperaments and adapt well to cold, wet climates.

Ducks have excellent raisability and disease resistance. They produce eggs, meat, and feathers and help with control of insects, snails, slugs, and aquatic plants. The adapt well to wet climates.

CHICKENS

Types

MEAT BIRDS

Meat birds have large appetites and little interest in exercise such as scratching and exploring. They grow to a large size (about 4 lbs) in a short time (6-8 weeks). They are very efficient converters of feed to meat, about 2 lbs feed to 1 lb meat, a 2:1 ratio. Meat birds are based on the Cornish rock cross. They are considered the "standard" for meat birds.

LAYING HENS

Laying hens are bred especially for laying and are designed to put their energy into eggs and not into body mass, which makes them slightly smaller than birds bred for meat. They begin laying sooner than meat or dual-purpose birds, at about five months instead of six months. At about eighteen months old they will molt, or lose their feathers. Modern egg-laying breeds are bred for shorter molting periods, which means more eggs per year. Hens stop laying when molting. The white leghorn is considered the "standard."

DUAL-PURPOSE BREEDS

Dual-purpose breeds are known for both eggs and meat. They are thought of as "old-time" breeds. They are typically more attractive to homesteaders and backyard poultry enthusiasts due to their sturdiness, attractive appearance, and self-sufficiency. These breeds are often considered endangered species.

Chicken Illustration

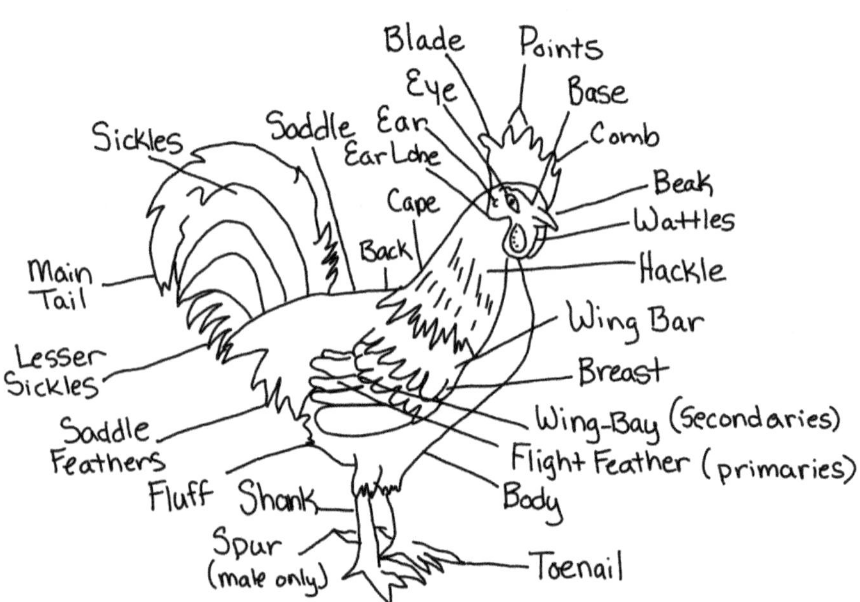

Size

Size is the greatest distinction between breeds. Sizes range from bantam to large breeds. Large breeds are known for laying and meat, and normally set the standard for production. Large breeds are typically easier to handle and work with because they are less agile as adults. Bantam breeds are best known for show, but pound-for-pound can produce as much as large breeds. Bantams are one quarter to one fifth the size of large breeds, and are considered more high-strung. They fly throughout their life. There are very few true bantam breeds. Most modern bantams are considered miniature versions of large breeds.

Appearance

Part of the "charm" of chickens are the vivid coloring and patterning of their plumage, along with their various and occasionally spectacular configurations of comb and plumage. White-feathered birds look cleaner when dressed than colored-feathered birds. Laying hens may be around for years so many homesteaders choose ones they consider attractive.

Hardiness and Temperament

Heavier and heavily-feathered breeds may produce better and longer into winter than smaller breeds in colder climates. It is a general rule to raise meat birds in the summer. Hardiness is more of a breed trait, while temperament is more of an individual trait that depends on the bird and its place in the pecking order.

Determining the Number of Birds to Raise

As a general rule, a flock should have a ratio of one rooster per ten to twenty hens. Other determining factors of flock size should take into account the type of birds being raised.

When raising meat birds, it is important to consider the available freezer space, the number of birds that are planned to be prepared and served within a given period, and how often the family prefers to eat chicken.

When raising laying birds, consider the available refrigerator space, how many egg-containing meals the family prefers to eat, and the height of egg production per season. At the height of summer, egg production typically has a one-to-one ratio, meaning one hen produces one egg per day. This tapers off as temperatures cool and stops completely during winter. At the height of production in the summer, three hens will produce about 1 ½ dozen eggs per week.

Egg Production

Egg production depends primarily on the hen's age, but can be affected by other factors as well. On average, three hens will produce two eggs per day. One hen can lay between 200-280 eggs per year for the first two years. During the first year of laying, a hen will usually lay one egg per day with decreased production over time. While egg production slows with age, eggs typically become larger.

Laying hens need 14 hours of daylight. During short winter days, hang an artificial light in the coop and use a timer to compensate for the lack of sun.

Sexual Maturity and Production

Chickens reach sexual maturity at 5-6 months and remain productive for two or more years.

The Coop

The main criterium for constructing a proper coop are light, air, protection from predators, and protection from inclement weather. It is best to have separate compartments for more versatility. Coop design should take climate into consideration, as well as land and the type of breed to be housed.

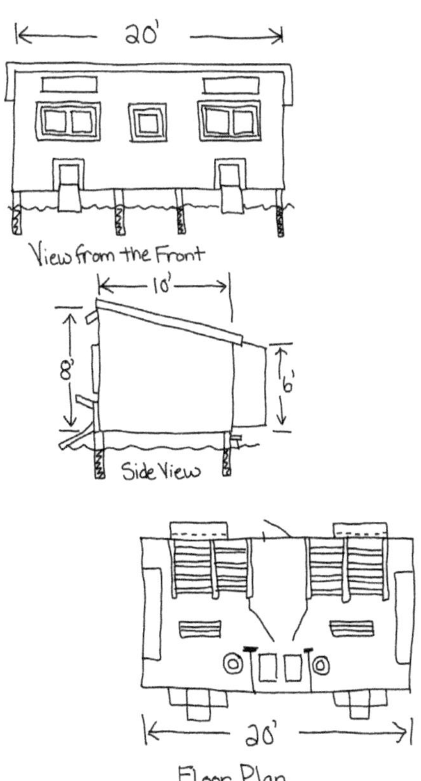

LOCATION

The coop should be oriented to face south in order to optimize the usage of sunlight. It should also be placed on the driest part of the property.

SPACE

Birds need more space if raised exclusively indoors. Birds raised indoors and outdoors require less coop space. A common rule of thumb for space needed per bird is 2-10 sq ft per bird. For example, twelve birds will require 24-

120 sq ft. This could be accommodated with a coop size of either 4 ft by 3 ft, or 10 ft by 12 ft.

Having space to separate older birds from young birds is ideal. Young birds can more easily contract diseases from older birds. Day-old chicks need 0.5 sq ft per bird until they reach 4 weeks old, at which time they need 1 sq ft per bird.

LITTER

Cover the bottom of the coop with a moisture-absorbing cover such as wood shavings. The litter should be at least 4 in. deep, and should be maintained to be loose and dry. The coop should have proper ventilation and few water spills to help maintain optimal litter conditions. Manure and debris can build up to a max of 2 ft before cleaning. Manure will resonate heat as it decomposes.

For chicks, use 1 in. of wood shavings, rice hulls, or ground cobbs. Do not use cedar chips, sawdust, or treated wood. The strong odor of these materials is overpowering for young birds and the oils and chemicals used on these products can be toxic to chicks.

LITTER MANAGEMENT

Litter should range from 5-10 in. deep. Allow as much space per bird as possible. Birds will stir their manure through scratching, especially if grain is thrown into the litter occasionally. Add more litter as necessary. With the right ratio of chicken to litter, manure will virtually disappear and begin to compost. Slow-composting litter will produce some heat if left alone all winter. A thick, soft layer of bedding also takes the strain off the birds' feet and legs.

Cleaning and Maintenance

The coop and all equipment should be disinfected before new birds arrive. Remove wet litter, moldy or wet feed, and dirty water. Clean nests with droppings in them. Once a year, the entire coop should be cleaned and painted with lime whitewash.

Temperature

Chickens do not sweat, nor can they cool themselves easy like most domestic animals. They pant like dogs and start to suffer at 95 degrees Fahrenheit or higher. Coops should be constructed with average temperatures of the geographic location in mind.

Chicks require a constant temperature of 90-95 degrees Fahrenheit for the first week of life, which often requires use of a heat lamp. As chicks age, the temperature can be reduced by 5 degrees per week until they can tolerate 70 degrees Fahrenheit. At that point, they should not need an additional heat source.

Special Considerations for Chicks

Too much heat or light, or overcrowding can result in cannibalism amongst chicks. Carefully calculate the space, light, and heat requirements for chicks when designing a coop for chicks.

Exterior Construction

Walls

Coop walls should be constructed using 2 in. by 4 in. stud walls with sheathing, such as planks or plywood, on the outside. Insulating the walls is optional. Interior sheathing is optional as well, but would create "dead-air" space insulation.

The coop should be tall enough for a person to walk into for cleaning and maintenance purposes.

ROOF

The roof should have a 1-foot slope.

FLOOR

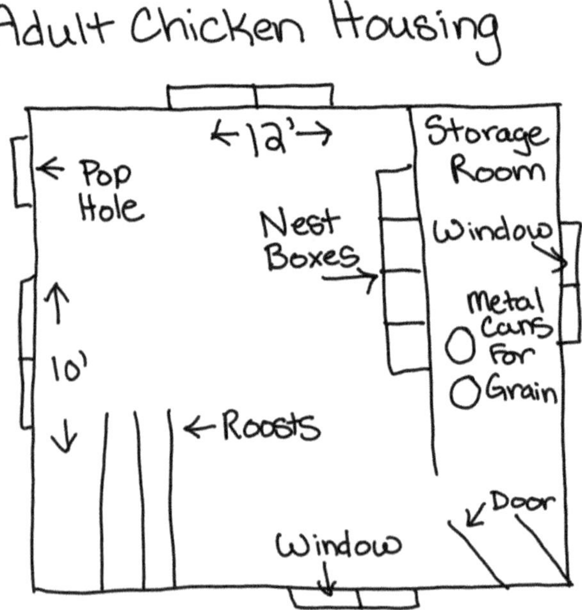

There are three basic types of coop floors: dirt, wood, or concrete. Which is used depends on budget, maintenance requirements, and preference.

Dirt flooring is the cheapest option. However, it is harder to shovel when cleaning and will turn to mud if not gravelly or sandy enough to drain well.

Wood flooring should be 1-2 in. thick. Reclaimed wood can be used if it is in good, useable condition. Wood floors require floor joists, usually of 2 in. by 6 in. beams, which rest on hangers or supports at the corners, such as cinderblocks, stones, or heavy posts sunk several feet into the ground. Wood flooring keeps birds off the ground but will rot eventually if not sealed and maintained.

Concrete flooring is the easiest to clean. It is impervious to rodents, and is more or less permanent. It is also the most expensive option.

Doors

There should be two separate doors, one for humans to enter for cleaning and egg collecting and one for birds to enter. The bird door should be a minimum of 1 ft by 1 ft. A ramp is necessary at the bird door if the entrance is more than a few inches off the ground. Attach molding or strapping every six inches on the ramp for traction.

All doors and windows should have latches so they can be closed at night for protection against predators. Child-proof latches are ideal.

Windows

Windows are necessary for air and light. There should be a minimum of 1sq ft of window space per 10 sq ft of floor space. Proper ventilation without drafts is critical for healthy birds. Chickens excrete moisture, heat, and carbon dioxide as they breathe. Moisture and ammonia rise from manure as it mixes with litter, as well. Construct a series of holes or slots 6 in. in diameter across the top of the north and south walls. This will create a natural cross ventilation without drafts. Windows should be installed vertically, not parallel to the floor, and should open to the exterior of the building. Direct sunlight helps fight bacteria and will help maintain a healthy coop environment.

Windows should be located on the south side in northern climates and on the lower side of the roof so it overhangs windows. In warm climates, a tarp may be sufficient.

Interior Construction and Design

ROOSTS

Roosts help make birds feel safer and help improve modulation of their body temperature. Roosts can be constructed of something as simple as old ladders propped up against the inside of the coop. If tree branches are used to construct roosts, they should be 1.5 in. thick for large breeds and 1 in. thick for bantam breeds.

Space roosts 18 in. away from the wall with 18 in. between parallel roosts. Allow 10 ft of linear roost per bird. Place roosts low enough that the birds can fly up to them. Roosts should be moveable or hinged to allow for cleaning. Be sure to block off the sides of the roosts so birds cannot access the area underneath the roost. Roosts should be tiered, beginning at 12 in. and then at 24 in. Four rows of 4 ft long roosts are typically adequate for 16-20 birds, a ratio of 1 roost per 4-5 birds.

Chicks should be kept separate from adult birds until six weeks of age, but the area they are kept in should still have a roost installed. At four weeks old, the roost should be installed 1 in. off the floor. The roost should be raised 1 in. per week thereafter until chicks are six weeks old, reaching a height of 3 in. By three months old, the roost can be raised to normal height, which is 24 in. high.

It is recommended to introduce chicks to hens at four weeks of age via a rabbit cage. At six weeks old, chicks can be moved to the main chicken coop area.

NESTING BOXES

Nesting boxes should be slightly bigger than the bird and open in the front to allow privacy for laying. Burlap can be placed across the opening of each box. Placing fake eggs in the boxes can encourage quicker usage. Nesting boxes are used only for laying and are not territorial areas. Nesting boxes should be removable and placed in an area that provides privacy.

The ratio of nesting boxes should be one box per 4-5 hens. For example, five boxes are needed for 25 hens. There should also be an equal number of roosts as nesting boxes in the coop. Boxes should be constructed 1 ft in height, width, and depth and should have a 45-degree pitched roof to keep other birds from nesting on top of the box. New or recycled filing cabinets work well as nesting boxes.

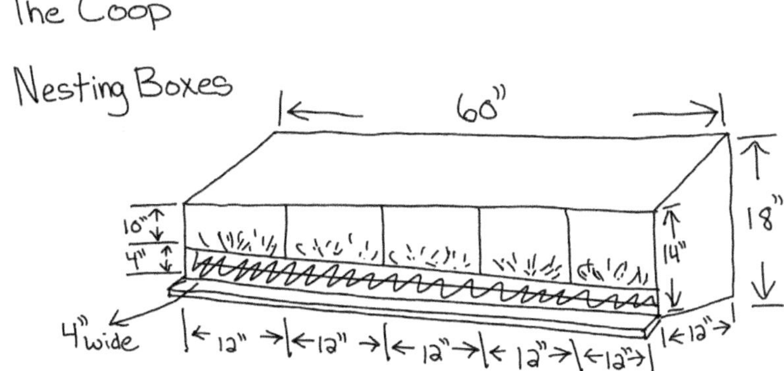

Amenities

ELECTRICITY

Having electricity run to a coop is not required, but will provide lighting and GFCI outlets. Electricity is needed to power heaters or to run heated water devices during the winter, which may be needed in colder climates. Artificial lighting can extend the laying season by continuing the lighting cycle of 14-15 hours with artificial light.

CHICKEN RUN/YARD

Chicken runs can be made using chicken wire, a 1 in. poultry netting. Galvanized chicken wire is preferred. Fencing should be a minimum of 4 ft, but 6 ft or higher is ideal. If small chicks will be kept in the run, use aviary netting, or a similar type of netting, around the bottom 12-18 in. Aviary netting or chicken wire should also be placed over the top of the run to protect from predators such as owls and hawks. Bury chicken wire 6-12 in. deep and with a 90-degree angle at the bottom to keep out burrowing predators. If possible, it is best to have at least two runs. Alternate between the two runs so one may recover as the other is used.

Litter such as straw, leaves, cornstalks, or corn cobs should be placed in the yard for the birds to scratch in. Scratching is important for foraging, social interaction, hygiene, and nesting. If birds will be raised free-range, or allowed to roam freely outside the coop during the day, they should still have a yard to protect against predators. Having a yard or chicken run can help lower feed costs and help maintain a cleaner coop.

Egg Hatching

Obtaining Fertilized Eggs

Eggs maybe purchased from a hatchery for $1-$3 each, or acquired from a personal flock or a neighbors' flocks. If hatching eggs from a personal flock, a rooster is needed to fertilize the eggs. A ratio of one rooster per ten hens is ideal for the first few years. A ratio of one rooster to five hens is ideal thereafter.

A 50% hatch rate is conservative, and a 75% hatch rate is considered a good showing.

Handling Fertilized Eggs

A typical cycle at the top of the season is one egg per 25 hours, which will provide one egg per day every 12-15 days depending upon the season. A hen will not lay in the dark. A hen's rest period is merely overnight if collecting eggs and three weeks if the hen is brooding.

If eggs are not kept warm, the embryo inside stops developing. Once the egg is warm again, development resumes quickly. When incubating eggs, or moving eggs to a different nest for another hen to brood, the caretaker's role as a chicken husband is to remove eggs as soon as possible to keep them clean and safe. Store fertile eggs at 40-60 degrees in the open air and allow them to dry for at least 12 hours. Eggs should be incubated within six days, but no later than fourteen days.

Store eggs with the large end straight up before incubating, and at a 30-degree angle once in the incubator. If eggs are soiled with manure, brush off the debris. Do not use soap and water. Eggs have built-in defenses against bacteria.

Brooding by Hen

The best reason to brood by hen is that the ideal, natural atmospheric conditions are provided beneath a setting hen. To begin brooding by hen, place about one dozen eggs in a nest and wait to see if a hen sets. If she stays setting and gets upset when someone attempts to take an egg, she is a brooder.

Active nesting boxes should be separated from other hens to avoid the risk of having the nest taken by another hen or to prevent it from being abused by coop-mates.

Because parasites can multiply and cause havoc on brooders, use cedar chips or shavings for litter in nesting boxes along with chemical parasite control sprayed or sprinkled on the chips.

Artificial Incubation

Artificial incubators are essentially boxes that attempt to replicate natural atmospheric conditions normally provided by a hen. Incubators keep eggs warm and moist, similar to having a hen setting them.

The two main types of incubators are tabletop or chest. Tabletop incubators hold two or more eggs. Chest incubators are designed to hold 300 eggs.

Still-air incubators have ventilation holes in the bottom and top. Cool, fresh air pushes through the bottom warmer and the air exits through the upper holes.

Parts of a Tabletop Incubator

See-through lid
Rack to place eggs on
Heating element and thermal switch to turn the heat

on and off

Water reservoir: located in the bottom of the incubator, maintains the humidity level

Ventilation holes: can be plugged/unplugged to adjust ventilation

Automatic egg turner: keeps embryo centered

Fan: converts still-air to forced-air

Keys to Successful Incubation

PLACEMENT

It takes twenty-one days for an embryo to develop and hatch. Place the incubator where it can remain undisturbed for the full incubation period. Pets, children, and predators should be kept away from the incubator.

Never place the incubator in direct sunlight. Maintaining a constant temperature and level of humidity is critical. Place the incubator in a room where the temperature can be maintained at 70-80 degrees Fahrenheit.

TURNING

When placing eggs in the incubator, they should lie on their side with the larger end slightly elevated. The developing chick's head will orient toward the higher end of the egg. Not only is there more room at the larger end, but there is also more air space that is needed to hatch.

Incubating eggs must always have fresh air and be turned frequently. During the first week of embryo development, it is critical that eggs be turned up to eighteen times per day. The embryo grows on top of the yolk, with the surrounding layers of egg white serving as nutrition and protection. If not turned, the embryo floats through the white to the shell membrane. This causes the embryo gets stuck and die.

After the first week, eggs should be turned a minimum of three times per day to increase hatching chances. The easiest way to keep track of the turning process is to place Xs or Os on opposite ends of the eggs. Remove the front row of eggs then roll the rest gently in one direction until all marks are on top. Place the removed row of eggs at the back. The first and last turning should be at the beginning and end of the day. Make the night resting period as short as possible.

During the last three days of incubation, eggs should not be turned.

TEMPERATURE

Different types of incubators require different temperatures, but the required temperature should remain consistent. Fluctuation more than half a degree, either way, can decrease the chances of successful hatching. Embryos can more easily tolerate lower temperatures than higher temperatures. Keep a thermometer visible in order to monitor the temperature.

As chicks develop, they begin to generate their own heat. The heat may need to be adjusted to a slightly lower temperature toward the end of the incubation period.

Turn the incubator on one day prior to loading in order to make sure the temperature is correct and holds steady.

If using a still-air incubator, be aware that the temperature can be as much as two degrees warmer at the top of the egg than at the bottom. Measure air temp at the level where embryo is developing. Because the embryo floats near the top of the egg, the thermometer bulb should be placed one quarter inch below the top of the shell when the shell is on its side.

HUMIDITY AND AIR SPACE

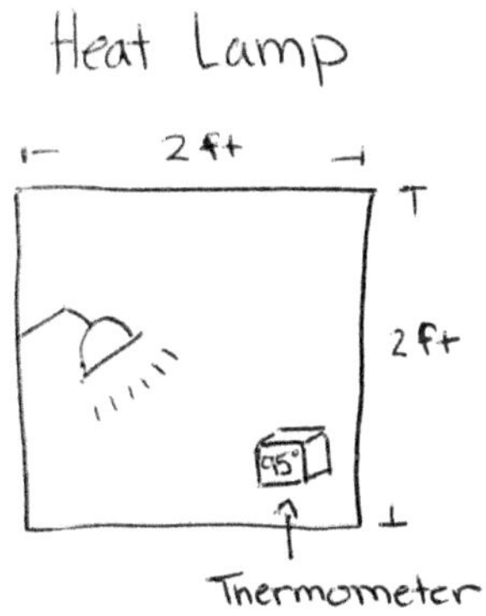

The egg shell is porous, so water constantly evaporates from it, which is why the humidity level in the incubator is so important. If it is not correct throughout incubation, the chick may not be able to hatch from the shell.

Air space forms in the large end of the egg after it is laid. It grows as fluid evaporates through the shell during incubation. When the chick hatches, it pokes its beak through the membrane that separates the development compartment from the air space, then through the shell in a circle to break off the cap of the shell over the air space.

If the chick is too dry when hatching due to evaporation, it may be dehydrated, or the shell may stick to the chick and trap it. If the humidity is too high, the air space might not be big enough. Too small of an air space will cause the chick to pip, or break through the shell in the fluids under air space. If this happens, the chick could drown.

Humidity in the incubator can be measured with a hygrometer-thermometer with a water-soaked cloth wrapped around the bulb. Forced-air incubators have hygrometers, while still-air incubators do not. Candling is the best method of measurement of air space when using a still-air incubator.

Humidity inside the incubator is measured in "degrees Fahrenheit wet-bulb." Temperature is recorded by the hygrometer as water evaporates from around the bulb. When using relative humidity measurements, the humidity level should be at 60% until the chick is hatching. During hatching, it should be raised to 70%. The wet-bulb equivalent is 84-86 degrees Fahrenheit during incubation and 90 degrees Fahrenheit during hatching.

To increase the humidity in the incubator, plug the bottom vent holes to restrict airflow. During the last few days of incubation, moisture competes with oxygen unless the humidity is increased. Do not block vents at this point because the chick needs more oxygen and needs to get rid of more carbon dioxide during development. An incubator without enough airflow can fill with carbon dioxide and suffocate the chick. One solution is to place a humidifier in the room. Another option is adding a soaked sponge to the incubator.

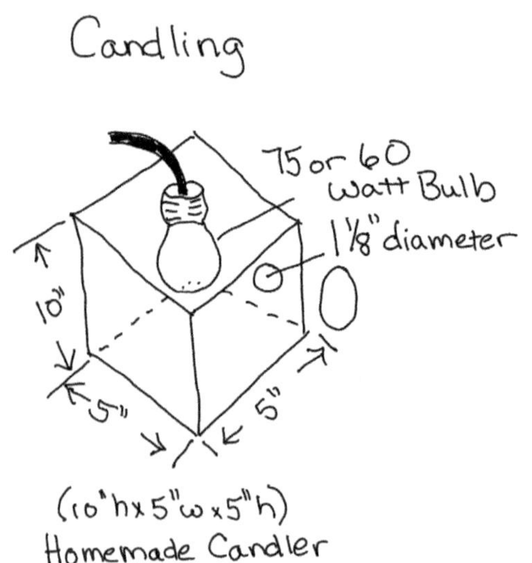

Candling can be used to check for the presence of a living embryo and to see the relative position of the airspace, which can indicate if the humidity level is high or low. Candling is accomplished by shining a light through the egg to illuminate the inside. It is best to candle eggs to check humidity and air space at the end of the second week of incubation. Remove any eggs that have died since the first candling. When approaching the third week of incubation, do not disturb the eggs, especially after day eighteen.

CHECKING FERTILITY

If an egg is not fertile or the embryo has died, it is important to determine this as soon as possible so it can be removed from the incubator. Rotten eggs produce gases that the other embryos should not breathe. Rotten eggs can also occasionally explode.

Candling eggs can help determine fertility. During candling, look for three basic configurations: 1) a small spot with spider-like legs, 2) the embryo's blood vessels-branching from the center, 3) a uniformly opaque egg with a shadow cast by a yolk that was never fertile, or an egg with a darker shadow in the middle, surrounded by a blood ring. The latter indicates an embryo that has died. The blood has moved away from the embryo, causing the blood ring.

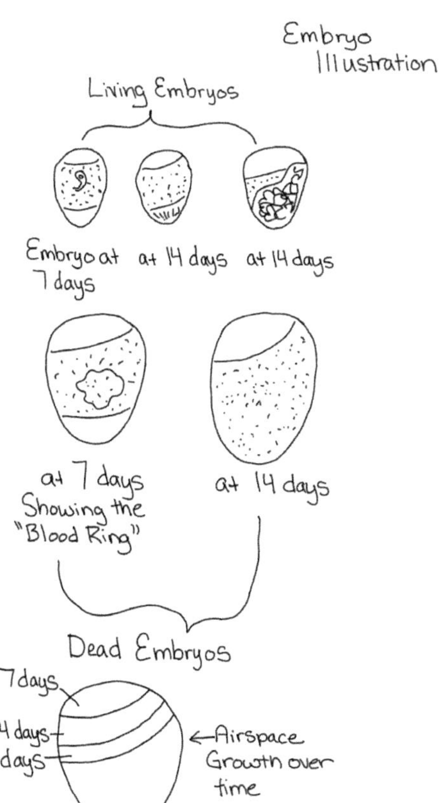

HATCHING

During days 19-21, the chick emerges from the shell, taking the yolk of the egg into the stomach through the navel and hatching fully fed. This allows the chick time to dry off and get its bearing before finding food in the outside world.

On hatching day, the temperature drops to 95 degrees Fahrenheit, but the humidity increases to 70%, or 90 degrees Fahrenheit wet bulb. A see-through incubator should be steamed up. Put double-layered cheesecloth on the top rack for the chicks once hatched.

Leave hatchlings in the incubator for 24 hours once hatched to finish drying.

Feeding

Feeding requirements for chickens depend on whether they are meat birds or laying hens, whether they are actively laying, and their age. Meat birds require feed with a higher protein content. Chicks initially need 20-24% protein for rapid growth and then can be transitioned to grower feed with lower-protein content. Laying hens require the least amount of protein but more calcium for strong shells. For example, twenty-five light-breed hens producing eggs should eat 5-7 lbs of feed per day.

Feed can be homemade, but it is important to be sure the right nutrition is provided. Homemade feed can be made from ground corn with proteins and minerals and kitchen waste. It should be offered once daily. Only put out enough to be eaten in five to ten minutes. Avoid onions and fruit peels because they can affect the flavor of the eggs. Ground eggshells or oyster shells can be sprinkled on top of feed as grit, which aids digestion.

Always change feed over the period of a week, increasing new feed from one fourth, to one half, to three fourths, and then fully to the new feed.

Chicks need special feeding processes to ensure proper growth and development. It is recommended to feed plenty of milk, as much grain as chicks want, and ample scraps, with egg or oyster shells sprinkled on top as grit.

Provide a continuous supply of forage and plenty of water. Gravel sand and pebbles can also be mixed into the feed as grit.

The feeding pan for chicks can be any size, but avoid pans that allow chicks to climb into and stand in the pan. A 3 in. by 5 in. by 2 in. rabbit dish works well for chicks. The pan should be filled twice daily. Chicks need constant nourishment and should have access to feed at all times.

Types of Feed

Commercial feed typically contains 15-16% protein. It may also contain ground-up chicken parts labeled as protein. For chicks, crumble works best, and pellets and mash work well for older birds. Commercial feed is usually packaged by age groups.

Commercial starter feed contains antibiotics. It should only be used for one week so the chicks do not become dependent on it. Do not use feed containing antibiotics within one to two weeks of when birds will be butchered.

Homemade chick feed can be made using two parts finely ground wheat, small portions of corn and oats, one part protein (fish meal, meat meal, canned cat food, hard-boiled eggs, yogurt, cottage cheese, worms, bugs, or grubs), one part greens (alfalfa meal, alfalfa greens, or fresh greens like finely chopped lettuce), and portions of wheat germ, sunflower seeds, or linseed meal. Feed should contain at least 2% protein.

Homemade adult feed is similar to chick feed but should contain 15-16% protein. Adult birds can eat peels, sour milk, pickles, meat, scraps, rancid lard, overripe or damaged fruit, vegetable pods and vines, and table scraps. Do not include onion, peppers, cabbage, or citrus fruits. Never feed birds moldy food.

WATERING

Clean, fresh water should be available at all times. If there is not a natural water source, water containers should be refilled daily. The amount of water needed depends on the number of birds and their age.

Adult chickens need to drink about a pint of water per day and it should be available at all times. Chicks should drink about 1.5 to 2 times the amount of food they eat. About 0.5 gal. of water is recommended for 25 chicks. A small poultry waterer from a feed store works well for providing water for chicks. To make a poultry waterer for chicks, use a 3 lb coffee can with a small hole cut ¾ in. from the top of each side and set it right side up inside a cake pan.

Change out fresh water as needed. Check it regularly, making sure the water has not become soiled. With new chicks, add electrolytes once a day for the first two weeks. Electrolytes may be purchased from a feed store. The added electrolytes help strengthen chicks, especially when stressed or ill.

HEALTH CARE

An important part of maintaining a healthy flock is being aware of diseases that affect chickens, vaccinations available for preventing disease, and other common maladies. If disease does affect a flock, early detection can help prevent it from spreading.

Parasites are a concern with chickens. Mites and lice are common external parasites. Roundworms, cecal worms, and capillary worms are internal parasites. Cleanliness and disease management will help to prevent them. For external parasites, dust with wood ashes or dip in 2 oz of sulfur and 1 oz of soap per gallon of water. An alternative is two parts oil with one part kerosene. Feed birds garlic and extra grit to help prevent worms.

Cannibalism occurs naturally among chickens, but is caused by stress, overcrowding, lack of food or water, malnutrition, unsuitable temperatures, or the sight of blood on a chicken. The best course of action it to address the problem causing the stress and to debeak the culprit bird. Debeaking involves removing the tip of the beak with a sharp knife or toenail clippers.

Injuries can occur at any time. A common injury is a broken leg. If the bird is otherwise healthy, the leg can be splinted with popsicle sticks and tape. If it is not healthy enough to heal, it can be used for meat.

Laying hens, or pullet, can become egg-bound. This occurs when an egg gets stuck and cannot or will not be laid. The recommended treatment is to put warm olive oil into the chicken's vent and rotate the egg out by hand.

A prolapsed vent can be caused by a pullet laying too early. The vent protrudes from the body when prolapsed. To treat this condition, wash the protruding tissue with warm water and a mild antiseptic then lubricate the area with petroleum jelly. Push the mass of tissue back into the vent gently. Dry off the bird and separate it from the flock. Feed the birds plenty of greens and fresh water. Do not feed her grain for about seven days in order to slow her laying. Watch for repeated prolapse. If it continues, the bird should be used for meat.

When chickens do not receive enough vitamin D, it can cause several problems, including thin-shelled eggs and leg deformities. During the winter, especially in far northern climates, give birds cod liver oil as a supplement to ensure proper vitamin D levels.

Vaccinations should begin before 20 weeks of age for infectious bronchitis and Newcastle disease. Starter pullets should have been vaccinated for Marek's disease as well. Consult a local veterinarian on other diseases that are common in the area.

Marek's disease is a virus that causes leg paralysis, drooping wings, and weight loss. Birds may also develop tumors on internal organs. Birds can be carriers without showing signs or symptoms and others may die. Birds can be vaccinated against the disease, but it takes three or more days for the vaccine to take effect. Infected flocks are contaminated forever.

Infectious laryngotracheitis is an acute and highly contagious viral infection. It causes birds to gasp for air and cough up blood. It is frequently fatal. Birds should be vaccinated after 4 weeks of age, then along with the rest of the flock and when additional birds are introduced. Birds may need up to five boosters yearly.

Fowlpox is a slow-spreading viral infection common to chickens and turkeys. Humans are immune to this strain. Symptoms include fever, weight loss, and scabs on unfeathered skin. Birds infected in the mouth may die of starvation and/or suffocation. The virus is spread by insect bites or open wounds. The entire flock should be vaccinated with a yearly booster

Chickens are susceptible to a variety of respiratory diseases, including Newcastle's disease, infectious bronchitis, mycoplasmosis, turkey and chicken coryza, and Avian influenza. Symptoms of these diseases are similar and include swelling of the eyes, runny noses, coughing, and poor weight gain. Diagnosis requires a blood test, bacterial culture, and virus isolation to determine which disease it is.

Molting is a natural process in most cases. Molting is the losing and re-growing of feathers yearly at the end of the laying season, and typically begins around 18 months of age and occurs during the winter months. Feathers are lost from the neck, breast, thighs, back, wings, and tail, with the wings and tail feathers being lost last. Molting is normally triggered by shortened days, but by using artificial light in the coop, molting can be delayed and egg production can be extended. Other causes of molting may include but are not limited to, temperature, food or water shortage, disease, cold temperatures, or sudden lighting changes.

Forced molting is possible and allows for longer egg production life, if molting is forced about every fourteen months. In order to force molting, turn off any artificial lighting in the coop so birds only get about eight hours of natural light per day. Keep giving water, but remove all food for ten days. Next, full-feed cracked grain for two to three weeks. Finally, for the next two to three weeks, feed birds a normal laying ration and turn artificial lighting back on. Birds will resume production in six to eight weeks. Molting lasts 12-24 weeks.

A hen may stop laying for a variety of reasons. Non-laying hens typically have a shrunken and pale comb, vent, and wattle. Their bodies are smaller and the pubic bones are closer together. They may be fatter and have a yellow coloring to the vent, eyering, earlobe, beak, and shank. The yellowing will occur first in the vent and then gradually develop in other areas. Non-laying hens can still be useful for pest control, but can also be used for meat as well.

DUCKS

Based on weight, ducks are divided into four classes: bantam, lightweight, medium, and heavy.

Bantam

This is the smallest weight class for ducks. There are six important breeds to know: Australian spotted, Call, East Indie, Mallard, Miniature Silver Appleyard, and Silkie.

Australian spotted ducks have average weights of 2.2 lbs for males and 2 lbs for females. Hens have a yearly egg production of 50-125 eggs. These birds are considered excellent at foraging and mothering. They are considered an endangered species.

Call ducks have average weights of 1.6 lbs for males and 1.4 lbs for females. Hens have a yearly egg production of 25-75 eggs. These birds are considered poor to fair at foraging and fair to excellent at mothering. They are a common species.

East Indie ducks have average weights of 1.8 lbs for males and 1.5 lbs for females. Hens have a yearly egg production of 25-75 eggs. These birds are considered excellent at foraging and mothering. They are a fairly common species.

Mallard ducks have average weights of 2.5 lbs for males and 2.2 lbs for females. Hens have a yearly egg production of 25-100 eggs. These birds are considered excellent at foraging and mothering. They are an abundant species.

Miniature Silver Appleyard ducks have average weights of 2.2 lbs for males and 2 lbs for females. Hens have a yearly egg production of 50-125 eggs. These birds are considered excellent at foraging and mothering. They are an endangered species.

Silkie ducks have average weights of 2.2 lbs for males and 2 lbs for females. Hens have a yearly egg production of 50-125 eggs. These birds are considered excellent at foraging and mothering. They are an endangered species.

LIGHTWEIGHT

Bali ducks have average weights of 5 lbs for males and 4.5 lbs for females. Hens have a yearly egg production of 120-250 eggs. These birds are considered poor to fair at mothering and excellent at foraging. They are an endangered species.

Campbell ducks have average weights of 4.5 lbs for males and 4 lbs for females. Hens have a yearly egg production of 250-340 eggs. These birds are considered poor to fair at mothering and excellent at foraging. They are a common species.

Harlequin ducks have average weights of 5.5 lbs for males and 4 lbs for females. Hens have a yearly egg production of 240-330 eggs. These birds are considered poor to good at mothering and excellent at foraging. They are a rare species.

Hook bill ducks have average weights of 4 lbs for males and 3.5 lbs for females. Hens have a yearly egg production of 100-225 eggs. These birds are considered fair to good at mothering and excellent at foraging. They are an endangered species.

Magpie ducks have average weights of 6 lbs for males and 5.5 lbs for females. Hens have a yearly egg production of 220-290 eggs. These birds are considered fair to good at mothering and excellent at foraging. They are a rare species.

Runner ducks have average weights of 4.5 lbs for males and 4 lbs for females. Hens have a yearly egg production of 150-300 eggs. These birds are considered poor to fair at mothering and excellent at foraging. They are a common species.

Medium

Ancona ducks have average weights of 6.5 lbs for males and 6 lbs for females. Hens have a yearly egg production of 210-280 eggs. These birds are considered fair to good at mothering and excellent at foraging. They are an endangered species.

Cayuga ducks have average weights of 8 lbs for males and 7 lbs for females. Hens have a yearly egg production of 100-150 eggs. These birds are considered fair to good at mothering and good at foraging. They are a common species.

Crested ducks have average weights of 7 lbs for males and 6 lbs for females. Hens have a yearly egg production of 100-150 eggs. These birds are considered fair to good at mothering and good at foraging. They are a common species.

Orpington ducks have average weights of 8 lbs for males and 7 lbs for females. Hens have a yearly egg production of 150-220 eggs. These birds are considered fair to good at mothering and good at foraging. They are a fairly common species.

Swedish ducks have average weights of 8 lbs for males and 7 lbs for females. Hens have a yearly egg production of 100-150 eggs. These birds are considered fair to good at mothering and good at foraging. They are a fairly common species.

Heavy

Appleyard ducks have average weights of 9 lbs for males and 8 lbs for females. Hens have a yearly egg production of 35-125 eggs. These birds are considered poor to fair at mothering and fair at foraging. They are a rare species.

Aylesbury ducks have average weights of 10 lbs for males and 9 lbs for females. Hens have a yearly egg production of 200-270 eggs. These birds are considered fair to good at mothering and good at foraging. They are a rare species.

Muscovy ducks have average weights of 12 lbs for males and 7 lbs for females. Hens have a yearly egg production of 50-125 eggs. These birds are considered fair to excellent at mothering and excellent at foraging. They are an abundant species.

Pekin ducks have average weights of 10 lbs for males and 9 lbs for females. Hens have a yearly egg production of 125-225 eggs. These birds are considered poor to fair at mothering and fair at foraging. They are an abundant species.

Rouen ducks have average weights of 10 lbs for males and 9 lbs for females. Hens have a yearly egg production of 35-125 eggs. These birds are considered poor to good at mothering and fair to good at foraging. They are a common species.

Saxony ducks have average weights of 9 lbs for males and 8 lbs for females. Hens have a yearly egg production of 190-240 eggs. These birds are considered fair to good at mothering and good at foraging. They are a rare species.

Caring for Ducklings

PURCHASING DUCKLINGS

First, consider purchasing from local farms or from community members. Make sure the ducks are freshly hatched with 2/3 of the yolk remaining on them for them to eat. At this time, they will not need any food or water for several days, so this is the best time to transport them.

WATERING DUCKLINGS

Once the ducklings are ready for water, they will need to be taught how to drink. To prepare suitable water, add 1 tsp of honey to 1 gallon of lukewarm water. Dip the duckling's beak into the mixture. Do not use a dish because it can be dumped.

BROODING DUCKLINGS

Ducklings need to be in a brooder. Their needs are much like chicks. Ducklings need brooding for four weeks. The brooder should have 1 sq ft of space per duckling. The brooder should be kept at 90 degrees Fahrenheit for the first week and then dropped 5 degrees at a time until the outside temperature is 55 degrees Fahrenheit or higher.

TEMPERATURE

During summer weather, when temperatures are warm, hang a light bulb in the ducklings' shelter at night. For 20-40 ducklings, suspend a 250 watts heat lamp 18-24 in. above the brooder area. If possible, use two bulbs in case one burns out in the middle of the night.

DUCKLING FEATHERS

Do not allow ducklings to get soaked prior to 4 weeks of age. They should not be allowed to swim until after six weeks of age due to natural oils not being fully distributed over the feathers. Ducklings are susceptible to chills or sickness until the oils have been fully distributed.

Handling Ducklings

Never catch a duck by its leg or legs. Instead, pick up a duckling by resting the hands in front of its neck and gathering it into the arms.

Caring for Ducks

Housing

A simple shelter is typically efficient for ducks, such as a hutch with a dry floor and protection from severe weather and predators. The shelter should have 5-6 sq ft of space per adult duck. South-facing doors allow sunlight during winter, but be sure that its orientation is not the same as the wind direction. The floor will stay warmer and produce heat via decomposing manure if deep litter is kept in the shelter.

Yard

The outside yard should have 10-25 sq ft per adult.

Fencing

Fencing requirements for ducks are the same as for chickens.

Nesting Boxes

Nesting boxes should be 15 in. by 15 in. and there should be one box per 4-5 adults. Nesting boxes should be set on the floor without a roof.

KEEPING A DRAKE

There should be one drake, or male duck, per up to six females. As with chickens, drakes are not necessary for egg-laying. They are only needed for fertilizing eggs for breeding. Drakes are more colorful than females.

EQUIPMENT

Basic feed and water dishes are sufficient for ducks. Old pans, buckets, and/or chicken dishes work well. Kiddie pools, ponds, brooks, etc. for swimming are also recommended.

FEED

Starter/grower feed should contain 20-22% protein. Use starter feed for the first eight weeks of life.

Developer feed should be used from 8 weeks old to maturity.

Layer or maintenance feed should be used for 2-3 weeks prior to a duck reaching egg-laying age.

Breeder or development feed should be used for two to three weeks prior to a duck reaching breeding age. It should also be used during breeding season for ducks who are of breeding age.

Ducks will eat most table scraps as well, including vegetable scraps, stale bread, and garden scraps.

WATER

Fresh, clean water should be available at all times. A cleaned-out plastic pool refilled daily works well. Ducks require three to four times more water than chickens. Ducks' beaks need to be immersed in water to drink, so water needs to be deep enough to allow for this action.

Sexual Maturity and Production

Ducks reach sexual maturity at 5-7 months old and remain productive for three or more years.

LIVESTOCK

Choosing what livestock to raise will depend on several important factors, such as traits, uses, breeding, cost, and regulations.

TRAITS

Size may be a deciding factor for some farms and programs. Raising animals for meat will typically make breeds that are larger more preferable, while animals being raised for other purposes may not require a specific size. Consider miniature and small breeds if space is an issue, or if handling skills make smaller animals preferable.

When considering size, it is best to use the average weight of a mature male, as females are typically smaller. For cattle, a bull's average weight ranges from less than 1,000 lbs (very small), to 1,000-1,200 lbs (small), to 1,200-1,500 lbs (medium), to over 1,500 pounds (large). For goats, a buck's average weight ranges from less than 100 lbs (small), to 100-150 lbs (medium), to more than 150 lbs (large). For sheep, a ram's average weight ranges from less than 140 lbs (small), to 140-170 lbs (medium), to more than 170 lbs (large). For pigs, a boar's average weight ranges from less than 400 lbs (small), to 400-800 lbs (medium), to more than 800 lbs (large).

Animals being raised for show or for materials will have specific desired traits, such as fiber type, attractiveness, or trainability.

COST

The cost of livestock includes more than the price per head. It is also important to consider the average cost per head to price at market and the costs associated with raising an animal.

The cost of feed may also contribute to decision making, as some animal feeds must be given a certain type or quality of feed to produce a desired size, product, or level of health. Other animals may only need basic feed or can have their diet supplemented by scraps or forage, reducing the cost of feed. For grazing animals, proper acreage must be available for the size of the animal group. This may be an added cost if additional space is needed to maintain healthy animals.

Medical care costs are also an important factor to consider. Most animals need regular vaccines and checkups, but some animals or species are more prone to illness and need more frequent care or medical intervention. Keeping male animals often necessitates neutering services, which usually involve veterinarian fees.

Maintenance costs also vary by animal and breed. Show animals may require more grooming-associated costs, as well as fees and travel expenses. Ungulates, large animals with hooves, require regular hoof trimming by a trained professional.

BREEDING

When breeding is the main goal of raising livestock, several additional factors should be considered. Consider breeding ratios of species and breeds. Know how many males are needed to service a certain number of females and if that ratio is appropriate for the farm setup. It is also important to know the expected birthrates of specific species and breeds to determine which will meet the goals of the farm's breeding program.

Lineage may be an important consideration as well, depending on breeding program goals. Origins of a breed may impact decision making for some, while preservation of heritage species may be more important to others. Homesteading versus large-scale commodity breeding plans may help determine which species and breeds are most appropriate as well. Homesteading goals may be maintaining a small, stable group, while commodity breeding will expect higher rates of growth.

Regulations

Certain animals, or how they are used, are more heavily regulated than others. Animals raised for fiber, such as goats or alpacas, must meet certain fiber standards to be sold under specific labels. There are also strict FDA and USDA regulations regarding meat and dairy production.

Livestock Uses

Livestock may be used for basic needs such as meat, dairy, and other materials, but it is also important to consider an animal's functionality and versatility. Certain breeds may be preferred for their "best known" features, such as egg production or size, hides, training abilities, or reproductive capabilities.

Some livestock are chosen particularly for how they may be used for production of items for sale or use, therapy, or companionship.

Below is a list of common, useful animals to be raised as livestock on a farm. Animals with an * are considered good options for first attempts at raising livestock. Animals marked with a + can be utilized as therapy animals.

+* Cattle
+* Sheep
+* Goats
* Pigs
* Ducks
Geese
* Chickens
Quail
* Fish (aquaponics, consumption)
Pheasant
+* Rabbits
+ Llamas
+ Alpacas
* Turkey
+* Dogs
+* Horses
* Mules

Other Considerations

The acidity of manure may be another factor influencing what animals to keep as livestock when there are multiple species, which will contribute to compost. Acidity levels should be compatible for easier management of composting production.

Grants may be available from certain conservation organizations for specific breeds, which may make them more attractive options. It may also be important to consider USDA pastoral rotation or grazing plan recommendations for aquaponics, hydroponics, and hydro fodder.

Goats

Goats are primarily raised for meat, milk, fiber, and skin. Goat farming must be balanced between animal care and production.

Common Homesteading Goat Breeds

Golden Guernsey goats are raised for dairy. Their color varies from light tan to golden red, with golden skin. Small, white markings may be present on the head and long hair is common. They are small to medium in size and are usually polled. Horned goats are possible as a recessive trait. Their conservation status is under study. Golden Guernsey goats come from the Channel Island of Guernsey. They are known for their beautiful coats and their excellent dispositions.

Nigerian dwarf goats are raised for dairy and as pets. They have a wide variety of colors and the males may be bearded. A small breed, they can be horned or polled. When horned, the horns are upright. Their conservation status is recovering. Nigerian dwarf goats are from West Africa. They have excellent milk production relative to their size and have a pleasant disposition.

Pygmy goats are raised for meat and as pets. They are short, less than 23 in. at the withers, but very stocky. They have full coats of straight, medium-length hair, with perky ears which stand upright or just above horizontal. They may be bearded and have recognized color patterns. Common patterns include Agonti black (mainly black, occasionally mixed with white hairs), brown (mainly brown, occasionally mixed with white hairs), dark brown (brown hairs mixed with fewer white hairs, but still a pronounced dark brown, with a salt and pepper appearance), dark grey (predominantly grey, ranging from light to dark, with some white hairs), black and brown solid, and caramel (varying shades of brown). Pygmy goats are small with small, upright horns that are straight or sweep slightly to the back. They are from Africa and are known for being affectionate and loving, making them a favorite amongst pet breeds.

Pygora goats are raised for fiber and as pets. They are muscular but not blocky. Their coloring and patterns are similar to pygmies and they have ears that are usually horizontal but can be erect or slightly dropped alongside the head. They are small, with small, upright horns that are straight or slightly swept back. Pygora goats come from the United States. They are known for their quality fleece, including the ability to produce colored mohair.

San Clemente goats are feral. They are typically colored brown, reddish brown, or tan with black markings. They are fine-boned and agile, with ears perpendicular to the head. They are a small breed with medium horns that sweep to the back and sides. Their conservation status is critically endangered. They are from San Clemente Island, California.

RAISING GOATS

Successfully raising goats requires preparation and understanding the basics of goat care. Goats need adequate shelter, grazing pastures, water, and proper fencing. Care of goats requires regular health checks, vaccinations, and knowledge of what health issues can be dealt with by the caretaker and which require veterinary intervention.

SHELTER

The type of shelter needed for goats depends on the temperature of the location. In warmer climates, a lean-to is typically adequate to provide protection from the elements. Colder climates will require an enclosed barn, possibly with artificial heating.

GRAZING

A benefit of raising goats is that they can be raised on low-quality grazing lands. A few acres are typically sufficient for a medium-sized herd. Any trees in the pasture should be protected with wire or fencing. Goats enjoy eating bark and will strip leaves and branches from the trees as well.

While grazing will provide most nutrients for goats, supplementing with hay, grain, feed, and herbs is often necessary for optimal health.

WATER

Goats require fresh water at all times. Goats often will not drink from water that is not fresh and can become dehydrated, especially on hot days.

FENCING

Goats require sturdy fencing and training to remain in their enclosure. Goats tend to rub against posts, so posts need to be very sturdy and fence posts should be outside the fencing so goats cannot climb them. Fencing should be of a type with small enough gaps that the goats cannot fit their head through the spaces. Latches on gates should be installed high enough that goats cannot reach them, as they are intelligent enough to figure out how to open many types of latches.

BUTCHERING

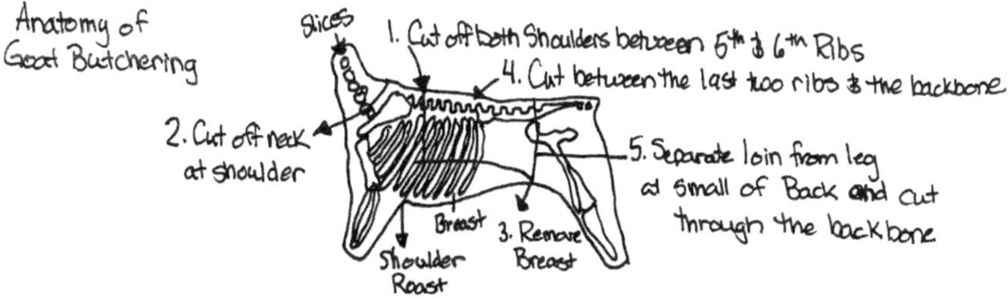

HEALTHCARE

It is important to monitor young goats' weight gain. The rate of gain is calculated by taking their current weight and subtracting their start weight then dividing by the number of days.

Example:

(Current weight – Start weight)/Number of Days = Rate of Gain

(75 lbs – 43 lbs)/90 days = 0.36 lbs/day

Preventative Care

Preventative care for goats is critical for raising a healthy tribe. Vaccinations and deworming protocols are especially important, as well as watching for signs of illness. Knowledge of common illnesses and issues with goats, along with a well-stocked supply of medicines and equipment, can help ensure proper healthcare.

NORMAL VITAL SIGNS

The normal heart rate range for goats is 70-80 beats per minute, though it will vary depending on environmental temperature and activity level.

The normal body temperature for goats is 101.5-104 degrees Fahrenheit. Temperature is typically lower in the morning. It is recommended to take healthy goat's temperatures to establish a baseline.

Respiration rates for goats are generally in the range of 12-15 breaths per minute.

Rumen motility will normally occur at 1-4 movements per minute, but will be faster after a meal and slower if the stomach is empty.

Rumen pH normally ranges from 5.5 to 7.0.

HEALTH CHECKS

Along with vital signs, it is important to observe goats for signs of health or illness, beginning with appetite and water consumption. Healthy goats will eat and drink the expected amount. Potentially ill goats will either not eat or drink, have too much interest in food, or drink an above average amount of water.

A goat's attitude and alertness are also indicators

of health or disease. Healthy goats will be bright and alert, inquisitive, and demonstrate normal goat behaviors. Unhealthy goats will have a hunched back, moan or cry, have little or no interest in their surroundings, stare at nothing, have drooping tails, experience tremors or shaking, or be unresponsive.

Healthy goats will have an overall good body condition while ill goats will either be overweight or too thin.

The ears of a healthy goat will be clean and appear normal. Unhealthy goats' ears may have brown or white discharge, a foul odor, or debris from mites or parasites. Goats with ear infections often shake their heads and their ears may droop.

Healthy goats will have clear and bright eyes with no discharge, and will be able to see clearly. Unhealthy goats may have cloudy or discolored eyes, or the eyes may be sunken, squinting, or shut. Infected eyes may have discharge or tearing. Goats may also experience blindness.

Observe the feet, hooves, legs, joints, and gait of goats. Healthy goats will stand comfortably, move easily, and be able to put weight on all feet. Pain, swelling, limping, lameness, or an unwillingness to stand indicates injury or disease.

Lymph nodes should be checked regularly. Normal lymph nodes are indicators of health, while swollen or lumpy lymph nodes indicate illness or disease.

Manure produced by healthy goats will be formed pellets. Goats who are not well will have manure that is too dry, watery or mucousy, or contains blood.

The mucous membranes of the eyes and gums of a healthy goat will be pink and moist. Pale, dry, red, or off-colored tissues indicate illness or disease.

A healthy goat should have clear respiratory sounds with no abnormalities and either clear or no nasal discharge. Rasping breath, rapid breathing, abnormal coughing, and green or cloudy nasal discharge may be signs of upper respiratory infection or another illness.

The skin and coat of a goat can be an indicator of health as well. Healthy goats will have supple skin and a smooth and silky coat. Unhealthy goats will have dull coats, possibly with hair falling out, or wounds or lumps.

Teeth and mouths of goats should be checked regularly. Goats who are healthy will have strong teeth, normal smelling breath, and no abnormalities of the mouth or tongue tissues. Broken or missing teeth, unusually worn teeth due to grinding, bad or unusual smelling breath, scabs or sores on oral tissues, or a swollen tongue are indicators of illness or disease.

Female goats' udders should be checked regularly for signs of disease or infection. Healthy udders will have a normal shape and texture and the goat will have expected milk production, with white and sweet milk. Abnormally swollen or hot udders may indicate infection. A sudden drop in production, blood in the milk, gassy or watery milk, or off-tasting milk are also signs of illness or infection.

Healthy goats will have normal urine produced at the expected rate. Blood or crystals in the urine, visible dribbling or discharge, and straining to urinate are indicators of illness or disease.

Medical Supplies and Equipment

When providing routine care to goats, it is important to have a supply of medical equipment on hand. Below is a list of recommended supplies.

Alcohol or alcohol preps
Bandage materials
Drench gun or syringe
California Mastitis Test (CMT) kit
Castrating supplies (surgical scissors, bander, or Burdizzo)

Clippers and supplies for clipping
Collars and leads
Disbudding iron
Eye puffer or ointment
Electrolyte replacement powder or fluid
Fecal test kit and microscope
Feeding tube for kids
Leather gloves
Surgical gloves, long and short
Hoof trimmers
7% iodine solution
Needles: 21- or 22-gauge by 1 in.
Measuring tape or weight tape
Novalsan (residuals are said to last for 2 days) or disinfectant
Obstetric lube (J-Lube powder)
Peroxide
Scissors, bandage and surgical
Splints
Stanchion and head gate
Stomach tube for adults
Syringes: 3 cc and 12 cc
Thermometer
Udder infusions
Veterinarian wrap
Wound ointment and/or spray
Weak kid syringe and stomach tube
Dewormer

Important Homemade Compounds

Electrolyte replacement fluid can be made from 1 gallon of warm water, 2 tsps table salt, 1 tsp baking soda, and 0.5 cups honey, karo syrup, or molasses. Never use cane sugar.

Wound ointment can be made from one medium

container of petroleum jelly, one large tube of diaper rash ointment, one tube of women's yeast infection medication (Monistat), one tube of athlete's foot medication, ¼ cups Nolvasan or betadine liquid, and one tube of triple-antibiotic wound ointment. Warm ingredients with low heat to liquefy, then blend and allow to cool.

A commonly used compound called "Magic Supplement" can be made from one part molasses, one part corn oil, and two parts karo syrup. Goats should be dosed at 120 cc twice daily.

Vaccinations and Deworming

Having a vaccination and illness prevention plan in place will help reduce illness in the tribe. Vaccine schedules and prevention plans should be based on current research and veterinarian recommendations.

Vaccination management plans may be conventional, sustainable, or organic. It is also important to consider what the risk tolerance for disease is for the farm, the known risk of exposure versus the risk of adverse reactions, the effectiveness of the vaccine, the safety of the vaccine, the benefit of the vaccination versus the expense, and whether the vaccine requires a yearly booster.

Injections should always be given behind the front leg, with the exception of penicillin, which can cause nerve paralysis.

When developing a parasite prevention plan, select medications and dosages based on herd observation and worm load testing. It is recommended to treat goats with medications based on need or FAMACHA scores, dosing only goats with high parasite loads. Treat parasitic infections with medications to prevent dehydration and secondary complications. Withhold feed for 12 hours prior to administering oral wormers.

Adverse Reactions to Vaccines

Lumps and swelling can occur at the injection site. It is possible to confuse injection site lumps with caseous lymphadenitis (CLA) lumps. Goats may also experience pain at the injection site. Gently massage the injection site to help relieve swelling, lumps, or pain. Icing the swelling or giving anti-inflammatory medication will also help alleviate symptoms.

Lameness may occur after injection. It generally resolves with time and the aid of anti-inflammatory medication.

Dragging leg can be caused by paralysis of the nerve. It is usually associated with penicillin injected in the hind leg. It can be treated with anti-inflammatory medication. It is recommended to avoid injecting penicillin in the hind leg or rump.

A rash or raised bumps that looks like little spots of raised hair over the goat's body is an allergic reaction response or mild anaphylaxis. This can be treated with an antihistamine such as Benadryl.

Difficulty breathing, trembling, or sudden collapse are signs of anaphylactic shock. Immediately give epinephrine. An injection under the tongue will work the fastest and is recommended in cases of severe, immediate reaction.

Common Health Concerns

Diarrhea

Diarrhea can be caused by bacteria, parasites, protozoa, or viruses. Common bacterial culprits are *E. coli*, *Salmonella* sp., and *Clostridium perfringens* and *tetani*. Common parasites include stomach worms, or *Haemonchus contortus*, which are commonly known as barber pole worms, and *Giardia* sp. The most common protozoa which cause diarrhea are *Cryptosporidium* and *Coccidia* (*Eimera* sp.). Viruses that cause diarrhea include *Rotavirus* and *Coronavirus*.

Goats most often become infected through soil, water, or food contaminated with feces. Infections can also originate from poor quality colostrum or not enough colostrum within the first 24 hours after birth or poor quality or improperly mixed milk replacer. Rich, wet pasture, especially when suddenly exposed to it, can also cause diarrhea. Too little or not enough roughage, toxins, or allergies can also cause bouts of diarrhea.

Stress is another potential cause of diarrhea. Common causes of stress include changes in or extreme weather, changes in routine, traveling or being shipped, and weaning. Reducing stress can help minimize intestinal upset.

Preventing diarrhea requires managing herd size so the tribe is not overcrowded or the area is not overstocked. Maintain low stocking rates to promote health. No more than 6-8 small ruminants should be housed per acre. Alternate grazing of species animals, as well as rotating grazing areas and pens can help reduce contaminant loads as well. Sanitize kid-rearing pens and equipment between batches of kids to ensure as clean of an environment as possible.

It is also important to correct any instances of poor sanitation. Avoid contamination of water buckets by animal or bird droppings. Place feed off the ground to keep feet and manure out of the feed sources.

BREEDING

There are several options for breeding systems and methods of breeding which can be utilized on a farm. It is important to consider the different elements of each to determine which will be the best fit.

Types of Mating Systems

OUTCROSSING

Outcrossing is breeding two animals of the same breed, but with no common ancestors for the past four to six generations. The advantages of this system are that it brings out strong, dominant breed traits and hides unwanted traits by keeping them recessive. It creates hybrid vigor, including longevity, better growth, and improved reproduction. One of the disadvantages of the system is that it produces greater variability in offspring. Improvement is based on the selection and availability of superior genetics.

LINE BREEDING

Line breeding is breeding two animals with a relationship in the pedigree for a low level of selective inbreeding. The advantages of this system are that there are fewer risks than continuous inbreeding, greater uniformity of type, increased prepotency, and it helps lock in strong traits. Disadvantages include an increased chance of recessive defects and slow improvement of line, especially if the line is mediocre.

INBREEDING

Inbreeding in the breeding of two animals who are directly related, such as mother, father, or siblings. The advantages of this system are that carrier animals can be identified and culled, it helps detect inferior genetics, it increases homogeneity of type in offspring, and it increases prepotency. Disadvantages of the system are that it creates inbreeding depression, which results in a loss of size and fitness. Other disadvantages include a higher risk of kids with defects, reduction of available genetics in future relationships, and a need for rigid culling.

Methods of Breeding

Pen Breeding

The advantages of pen breeding are that it is easy because it does not require tracking of heats. It is good for short-cycling does and good for hard-to-detect heats. It is also useful for off-season breeding.

Disadvantages include the inability to know exact breeding dates, which may make it difficult to perform prenatal care on does. This method may also require additional pens, depending on the number of goats being bred and the number of bucks being used.

Raddle Harness

The main advantages of the raddle harness method are similar to pen breeding, with the additional benefit of having a visual indicator of breeding.

Disadvantages include the expense of the raddle harness and markers, the difficulty of attaching the harness, the fact that the buck may remove the marker, and the possibility of false markers due to aggressive bucks or passive does.

Hand Breeding on the Farm

The two main advantages of hand breeding are knowing the exact breeding dates and that it requires fewer pens.

The disadvantages are that heat detection methods are needed, it requires close monitoring of does several times a day, it is more time-consuming, and handling the buck may be difficult.

HAND BREEDING OFF THE FARM

The advantages to this method are similar to home breeding, but there is a wider range of bucks to choose from and it eliminates or reduces the cost of owning bucks.

Disadvantages are also similar to home breeding, with several additions. Off-farm breeding may require multiple trips, adding more travel distance and time. It may be difficult to locate offsite breeders offering service. Breeders may require certain health tests, which may be an added cost, and it is possible for does to bring diseases back to the tribe.

ARTIFICIAL INSEMINATION

The advantages of this method include having a wider range of bucks to choose from, the possibility of faster genetic improvement, and the elimination or reduction of the cost of owning bucks.

Disadvantages include the initial investment in equipment, the fact that it often must be done by the goat owner, the necessity of good heat detection, the variability of conception rates, and the importance of technique on conception rates.

Heat Signs in Does

Allowing other does or wethers, a castrated buck or buckling, to mount her

Calling out or crying frequently for no reason

Exhibiting a drop in milk production

Fighting

Flagging (holding the tail high and frequently wagging)

Acting more affectionate

Losing interest in feed

Mounting other does

Exhibiting mucus discharge from vagina

Standing by the fence closest to the buck pen

Exhibiting a swollen or pink vulva

Exhibiting tail hair that is wet, sticky, or clumped together

Managing Bucks

Aggression is exhibited when bucks rear up, butt, attack fences separating him from does, challenge other animals, and mount other bucks or animals. Aggression attracts does by establishing the buck's position in the herd. The negative aspect of aggression in that it can be hazardous to caretakers or pen mates, it requires strong fencing, and may require the need to separate horned and dehorned bucks to avoid injuries.

Frequent erections are exhibited by the end of the penis being exposed. The buck may also insert the penis into its mouth. This exerts dominance and attracts does. It can be disconcerting for some caretakers or embarrassing for visitors.

Increased verbalization in bucks includes moaning and "talking" to does. Bucks may also wag their tongues or blubber. These attract does and encourage them to stand. The increased sound can carry a great distance and disturb neighbors.

The Flehmen Reaction, or lip curling, is when a buck lifts its upper lip into a grimace. It usually accompanies urine tasting. This exposes a sensory organ in the upper lip which detects estrus pheromones. It creates an odd appearance, but has no other drawbacks.

During mating season, bucks can give off a strong "goaty" odor, which often rubs on anything or anyone within reach. The scent attracts does and stimulates the doe to come into heat. This scent can be difficult to remove from skin and clothing. It may also affect milk quality if the bucks run with does. It is also offensive to some people or to downwind neighbors.

Stamping and pawing are also common behaviors of bucks. Bucks will paw at the air with their front hooves or use the foot to hit does or fencing. This encourages the doe to stand for service, but it is painful when directed toward people.

Bucks will also urinate on their front legs and face, spray urine into its mouth, or spray urine indiscriminately. This attracts does by increasing pheromones. Urine can scald skin and may leave the buck's skin raw and irritated, and may require the caretaker to frequently change clothes if the buck sprays people.

Sexual Maturity and Production

Goats reach sexual maturity at seven months and remain productive for 10-12 years.

Delivering Kids

In preparation for delivering kids, it is important to have a basic delivery kit on hand. Below are recommended items to include for the delivery and care of kids.

Basic Delivery Kit

7% iodine
Scissors
Frozen colostrum or fresh from another doe
J-Lube or other lubricant
Long, disposable surgical gloves
Nipples and bottles
Warm water for does
Novalsan or other disinfectant
10 cc and 20 cc syringes
20-/21-gauge syringes

Additional Delivery Kit Items

Baby monitor
Calendar or notebook for records
Dental floss and/or navel clamps
Goat serum concentrate
Kid puller or leg snare
ID bands or kid tags
Landry tub or kid basket
Nasal bulb
Nutridrench or energy supplement
Probiotic and/or yogurt

Weak/Chilled Kid Kit

Kid coat
Heating pad
Blow dryer
Feeding tube and syringe

Pregnancy Clip

Clipper lube
Small animal clippers
#10 and #30 blades

CAPRINE VENIPUNCTURE

Livestock clippers
Alcohol pads and/or alcohol
Vacutainer and holder
18- and 21-gauge needle(s)
Specimen tubes (usually with a red top for serum testing)
Pens/markers and labels for tubes

OVER-THE-COUNTER (OTC) MEDICATIONS

CMPK or calcium gluconate
Di-Methox
50% gluconate
Preparation H (for vulva swelling)
Uterine bolus
C&D antitoxin

PRESCRIPTION MEDICATIONS

Dexamethasone or Estrumate (for labor induction or preemies' lung development)
Oxytocin (to stimulate contractions)
Dopram (an under-tongue lung medication)

Additional Equipment

TATTOOING SUPPLIES

Tattoo ink
Tattoo pliers and characters
Restraining device
Toothbrush
Baking Soda
Alcohol pads

HAND-MILKING EQUIPMENT

Milking stand
Stainless-steel milking pail
Stainless-steel strainer and milk filters
Dish soap and/or dairy soap
Bleach or sanitizer
Acid detergent
Clean-up brushes
Strip cup
Mastitis indicators
Paper towels and/or dairy towels
Teat dip (to fight against bacteria)

DAIRY-CLIP EQUIPMENT

Large clippers and small clippers
Blades
Blade wash
Clipper lube
Brushes for blade cleaning (toothbrushes)

Culling

Culling is the process of reducing an animal population through selective slaughter. Culling is practiced to improve reproduction, remove weak or diseased animals, and for basic tribe management.

Criteria for culling include a bad bite, broken/ missing teeth, problems eating, bad teats (too big or too small), bad testicles (split, too small, infected), bad udders especially in dairy goats (lopsided, poorly attached), does who have not settled for two seasons, evidence of abscesses or other diseases, poor body condition due to illness or old age, poor-quality fiber on fiber goats, and structural defects, such as bad feet, legs, and back.

Wethering

Wethering, or neutering goats, is the process of removing a buck's ability to reproduce. It is an important part of buck management within a tribe. There is a limit to how many in-tact bucks should be kept each season in order to control reproduction and for overall tribe management. There are four main methods of wethering.

BANDING

The main benefit of banding is that it is inexpensive and bloodless, however it is also the least humane method and has an increased risk of tetanus. There is also a risk that an error in technique could leave a testicle intact and fail to sterilize. Banding is performed using an elastrator, bands or rings, and tetanus antitoxins if the buck is not vaccinated. Banding may be performed after the testicles have descended. The larger the testicles are, the more traumatic it will be for the buck.

CUTTING

Cutting is an inexpensive method and is the most reliable method. Drawbacks of this method are that it creates an open wound which puts the buck at risk for tetanus, it is bloody and may be disturbing to the caretaker, and there is a risk of excess bleeding in older kids. Cutting is performed using disinfected surgical scissors or a scalpel. Tetanus antitoxin should be used if kids are unvaccinated. Pain medication may also be used. Cutting should be performed after the testicles descend. The process is more traumatic the larger the testicles are at the time of cutting. Kids with scrotal hernias should not be cut. Bucks older than 6-8 weeks should be cut by a veterinarian using anesthesia.

EMASCULATION

Emasculation has a quick recovery time and there is no blood or cutting involved. There is also no chance of infection and it is relatively humane. The downside to this process is the high initial investment in equipment. Technique errors may result in incomplete castration as well. Emasculation is performed using a Burdizzo or nipper. Pain medication may be used. Emasculation can be performed on kids older than 4 weeks and on full-sized bucks.

VASECTOMY

Vasectomy is useful if a kid is to be used as a teaser buck. It is a very reliable method of wethering. It is, however, expensive and leaves breeding traits intact. Vasectomies are performed by a veterinarian under anesthesia and it can be performed at any age.

Horn Prevention and Removal

Horn prevention and removal can be a controversial subject. Some argue that the practice goes against the natural biological makeup of the species and others argue that horns pose an unnecessary danger to the animal, tribe mates, and caretakers.

Disbudding is the process of destroying the horn-producing cells, the corium, of the horn bud. Dehorning is the process of removing the horns and the horn-producing tissues after they have formed from the horn bud and attached to the skull. Dehorning exposes the sinus and has a greater risk of infection. Either process should only be completed by a veterinarian or a highly experienced caretaker.

Disbudding is the most recommended method of horn prevention. It should be performed when kids are 3-7 days old, or when the horn buds are found. Disbudding is performed using a disbudding iron. It is critical not to overheat the brain. Tetanus antitoxic should be given if immunity is at all questionable.

Banding can be used to remove small to medium horns. Insect control is critical, especially during fly season, as they can lay eggs in the wounds. The process requires a disbudding iron or heated rod for cauterizing, and can be bloody. Pain may also occur when the nerve is severed. Scurs may replace the horns if the bud is not completely removed. The process is effective on some goats and not on others.

Veterinary horn removal is costly, but generally very effective and humane. Veterinarians used anesthesia or blocks to manage pain. It is, however, difficult to find veterinarians experienced in horn removal.

The method of sawing can be bloody. It requires cauterizing bleeds with a disbudding iron or heated rod. Scurs may replace horns if the bud isn't completely destroyed. The process tends to be traumatic and painful and can be dangerous to the person performing the sawing if the wire blades slip.

Caustic paste is one of the least reliable methods and

can be dangerous to goats. The paste is also hazardous to the goat's eyes. Kids may rub or lick the paste off pen mates, causing burns. Caustic paste is more commonly used on cattle and is not recommended for goats.

Gouging is also a bloody method of removal. A gouging device is used to scoop out the horn buds. It is more commonly used on cattle and is not recommended for goats.

DISBUDDING KIT

Disbudding iron
Wire brush
Small hair clippers (optional)
Disbudding box (optional: homemade or purchased)
Gloves (optional)
Tetanus antitoxic (optional)
Burn relief spray such as Solarcaine (optional)

Showing Goats

While this guide does not include information on showing goats, it is helpful to have a basic idea of scoring and to know what equipment is needed to participate in showing goats.

BODY CONDITION SCORING

Body condition is scored on a scale of 1 to 5, with 1 being the lowest and 5 being the highest. The chart below is a general guideline and may vary slightly by breed.

A score of 1 has a very lean body condition, the backbone and ribs are easy to see and feel, the judge can feel under the ribs, and the loin has no fat.

A score of 2 has a lean body condition, the backbone and ribs are easy to feel but smooth, the judge needs little pressure to feel the ribs, and the loin has smooth fat.

A score of 3 has a good body condition, the backbone and ribs are smooth and rounded and have an even feel, and the loin has smooth fat.

A score of 4 has an overweight body condition, the backbone and ribs can be felt with firm pressure, there are no points on the spine, the ribs cannot be felt, the indent between the ribs can only be felt with pressure, and the loin has thick fat.

A score of 5 has an obese condition, the backbone and ribs are smooth with no individual vertebrae felt and no separation between the vertebrae felt, and the loin has thick fat that is lumpy and mobile.

GOAT SHOWING EQUIPMENT

Feed
Hay
Hay and grain feeders
Fasteners for feeders and display
Bedding, straw, or shavings
Rake and broom
Milking equipment
Milk stand
Pasteurizer
Clippers
Hoof shears or knife
Grooming supplies
Shampoo and conditioner
Tools
First-aid kit for goats

SHOW SUPPLIES

Health papers
Display items
Registration papers
Farm sign
Show collars
Business cards
Show whites

PERSONAL GEAR

Tent
Coffee pot and supplies
Cot
Street clothes
Sleeping bag
Black shoes
Pillow
Buckets
Toiletries
First-aid kit for people
Food and snacks

Herd Management Calendar

This is a general management regiment. It should be adjusted for the specific needs of a particular breed, personal management style, and environment.

SPRING

Bucks who are available for breeding should be assessed. Begin looking for replacements for bucks who are no longer fit for breeding. Administer vitamin E and selenium (BoSe) in selenium-deficient areas.

Does who are non-fiber goats should have their udders clipped at least one week prior to her due date. Freeze heat-treated colostrum for emergency use and caprine arthritis encephalitis (CAE) prevention and perform CAE prevention as necessary. Does' teats should be taped one week prior to delivery. CAE-positive does should be separated from the herd. Remove kids from does immediately after birth and feed heat-treated colostrum, pasteurized milk, CAE-free milk, or milk replacer. Shear or comb fiber goats for three to six weeks prior to kidding. Supplement lactation does to maintain milk. Supplement non-dairy goats for at least four weeks post-kidding. Deworm does at freshening, or one to two weeks following kidding.

To ensure kids are nursing easily, check the does' teats and start the milk flow. Feed kids colostrum within the first few hours after birth. Identify kids and keep records of each freshening. Neuter males who will not be raised for breeding and disbud kids. Monitor kids raised on the dam to ensure each one is getting enough to eat. Pen kids with individual does for dam-raising when possible. Send in registrations for new animals. Some registries such as ADGA have lower fees for early registrations. Start coccidia prevention or test feces by three weeks old. Supplement weak or slow-growing dam-raised kids with bottle feeding.

Monitor the herd for internal parasites by testing stool samples. Treat for worms before cleaning the barn or moving the goats to a new pasture when testing shows high levels of worms. Shear non-pregnant fiber animals.

Clean and bed kidding areas several days before the does' due date if this was not completed in the fall. Renew trailer licensing and affix the tabs. Clean the trailer or hauling equipment for market and show season. Order fly-control products. Sort show supplies and tack to be sure everything is in order.

Check and repair fencing around pastures. Check all outside pens before moving animals.

SUMMER

Assess bucks who are available for breeding and continue looking for replacement bucks as needed. Market excess bucks and cull those who do not sell. Administer vitamin E and selenium (BoSe) in selenium-deficient areas in late summer.

Cull does who have reproductive problems or ill health. Discontinue supplemental feeding for does who are at least four weeks post-partum and are not being milked for dairy.

Clip or bathe goats to remove dead skin. Check for external parasite and ringworm. Keep animals hydrated and cool with water and ventilation during hot-weather hauling. Maintain adequate shade for animals during hot weather. In consideration of show season, do not over fill the udder on does to prevent mastitis, make feed changes gradually, double-check show supplies, and send show entries on time. Test stool samples for internal parasites and treat for worms, if necessary. Trim goat's feet, if necessary, and watch for foot rot in wet conditions. Make sure clean water is available at all times, as water usage increases due to lactation and hot weather.

Continue fly-control measures in goat housing. Keep pens well-bedded or clean frequently to prevent illness.

Rotate pastures every several weeks, if possible. Repair fencing and pens before moving animals. Watch pastures for poisonous plants and remove if present.

FALL

Clip excess belly hair from bucks. Examine the penis and testicles for injury or inflammation. Shorten or remove scurs before breeding. Treat as recommended by semen processor if the buck's semen will be collected. Turn out bucks with does at a ratio of 1:25 to 1:50. The use of a raddle harness on bucks before pasture breeding will improve tracking of breeding dates.

Continue to flush does for two to three weeks after they are penned with a buck. Culture milk to pick up subclinical mastitis. Examine udders for signs of mastitis or injury. Plan dry treatment if mastitis has been a persistent problem. Treat dry does when kids are weaned or milking stops. Reduce grain for does who are too fat. It is easier and safer to change body conditions before dry-off.

Evaluate the final kid crop and choose replacement does and bucks for breeding. Wean kids.

Treat any lice or skin disorders found among the herd. Cull unsound or inferior animals. Determine body condition scores. Increase grain for two to three weeks before and after breeding.

Give supplemental selenium and/or copper, if necessary, for two to four weeks before breeding. Record breeding dates. Monitor internal parasites by testing stool samples. Perform any dehorning procedures after the frost if the season permits. Plan a winter supplemental feeding program. Test herd for diseases of concern. Cull or isolate test-positive animals from the clean herd. Treat for intestinal parasites as necessary after a hard freeze or before moving to new housing. Trim feet and monitor for foot rot before the rainy season. Vaccinate for tetanus and enterotoxemia (CD/T) unless a different schedule is recommended by a veterinarian.

Clean and disinfect pens and barns before the start of bad weather. Evaluate housing and repair as necessary, paying special attention to leaky roofs and drafts.

Evaluate range and forage conditions. Move the herd to fresh green pastures, if available, before pasture breeding begins. Soil-test pasture and supplement as needed.

WINTER

Remove bucks from the breeding pen or pasture once does have settled. Supplement bucks' diets to regain body condition lost during rut.

Delouse fiber goats at shearing, if necessary. Dry off and dry-treat udders sixty days before the does' due dates. Give vaccine boosters three to five weeks prior to the does' due dates. Gradually increase the quality of hay and the amount of grain fed to late pregnancy does. Perform pregnancy testing. The best window for ultrasound evaluation is forty-five to sixty days post-breeding. Shear or comb fiber goats three to six weeks prior to kidding. Sort pregnant does from open does. Supplement with selenium, if necessary, prior to due date. Pen unbred does with bucks for cleanup breeding.

Breed late kids at seven months old or at 75 lbs body weight. Castrate any late bucklings to be raised for meat. Tattoo and/or tag late kids. Vaccinate late kids according to schedule.

Check for lice amongst the tribe and delouse if found. Monitor the body condition of all goats and adjust supplemental feeding as required. Prepare sales materials and distribute sales lists. Cull unsound or inferior animals. Stock kidding supplies. Trim feet as needed. Clean equipment such as clippers so they are ready for kidding and show seasons. Watch older, younger, and other vulnerable animals for chilling.

Ensure kidding pastures have adequate shelter for freshening does. Evaluate forage and pasture conditions. Select the kidding pasture if range kidding is planned.

Fiber

CASHMERE

Cashmere is defined by the Wool Products Labeling Act of 1939 and the Cashmere and Camel Hair Manufacturers Institute as "the fine (dehaired) undercoat fibers produced by a cashmere goat (*Capra Hircus laniger*). Fibers have an average diameter of 19 microns, with no more than 3% by weight over 30 microns in diameter. Cashmere fibers are protected by long coarse outer guard hairs which must be removed from the shorn fleece to preserve the quality of the cashmere. Adults produce 4 oz of cashmere fiber per year. A single cashmere sweater requires the fiber of three cashmere goats.

MOHAIR

Mohair is the long, silky hair of the angora goat. Angora kid fiber is 4 in. long at shearing and finer than adult fiber. Yearlings produce 3-5 lbs of mohair. Adults produce 8-16 lbs per year.

CASHGORA

Cashgora is the hair of large-breed (cashgora) and small-breed (pygora and nigora) fiber crosses. This type of fiber has limited uses. It is typically not as fine as mohair or cashmere. Hair falls into three types. Type A hair is similar to mohair. It is smooth and cool to the touch, and requires shearing one to two times per year. Type B hair is airy, light, fluffy, soft, and warm to the touch. It is harvested once per year by combing, plucking, or shearing. Type C hair is creamy, suede-like, and warm to the touch. It shows no luster and is often commercially acceptable as cashmere in type. It is harvested once per year by combing, plucking, or shearing.

KEMP

Kemp fibers are long, straight, brittle, hollow hairs that can show up on the thighs and backbone of any fiber goat. These fibers break easily and do not take dye well. The presence of kemp is a criterion for culling a goat from a fiber herd.

Sheep

DIFFERENCES BETWEEN GOATS AND SHEEP

Male goats are called bucks and female goats are called does. Goats are bearded and hold their tails upright. Goats have 60 chromosomes. Goats are browsers, and individual goats maintain some independence within the tribe. Goats are more susceptible to illness and disease associated with rain and damp conditions. Goats butt downward after rearing on their hind legs.

Male sheep are called rams and female sheep are called ewes. Sheep are beardless and their tails hang downward. Sheep have 54 chromosomes. Sheep are grazers and flock closely together. Their fleece protects them from rain and they butt charging straight ahead without rearing.

Care and raising of sheep is similar to goats in many ways. There are several important differences to consider. Sheep tend to be less high-strung than goats and need less exploring area. They are not as prone to escaping and do not need as high of fences. Sheep are better uniform grazers and mainly stick to grasses rather than eating shrubs and bushes. They are less noisy than goats, which may make them preferable to neighbors. Lastly, sheep tend to have stronger digestive systems and are less prone to digestive problems.

COMMON HOMESTEADING SHEEP BREEDS

Black Welsh Mountain sheep are raised for fiber and

meat. They have no wool on their faces or on their legs below the knee. They have a very thin layer of fine wool on the underbelly and the tail. Long tails must remain undocked for registration. Coloring can be solid black or dark brownish-black. They do no grey with age like most sheep. This is a small breed. Males have medium horns that curl, but females are polled. Their conservation status is recovering. They originally come from Wales and are best known for their small size, hardiness, low maintenance, and true-black wool.

Brecknock Hill Cheviot sheep are raised for fiber and meat, and as pets. They have perky, upright ears with wool-free faces and a smudge of dark skin around the eyes and nostrils. They are a small, short breed, but are well-proportioned. Coloring can be white, which is most common, or black, tan, or grey. Rams may be polled or have curling horns that stay close to the head. Ewes are normally polled. This breed comes from Wales and is known for its small size, fiber production, and preference as pets.

Jacob sheep are raised for fiber and meat, and as ornamentals. Their appearance is almost goat-like, with a badger-colored face and body spots that may be black and white or lavender and white. Lavender coloring appears as a bluish-grey to brownish-grey. Jacob sheep are small and both males and females are polycerate, or multihorned. Their conservation status is threatened. They come from England and are best known for being polycerate and having unusual coloring.

Scottish Blackface sheep are raised for meat and fiber. Their legs are long in proportion to their size, and are wool-free with possible spots. They have wool-free faces with Roman noses, usually prominent in rams and slight in ewes. Their ears are large and horizontal. They are a small to medium breed, with rams having large, curling horns. Originally from Scotland, they are known for their strong, long fleece, which is used in carpets, Harris tweeds,

Scottish tartans, and hand spur.

Southdown sheep are raised for fiber and meat, and as pets. They commonly have white fleece, but other colors are possible. There are three types with distinguishing characteristics. Standard Southdown sheep are medium in size. They are tall relative to their weight with long, straight backs and upright heads. They have light wool with a brownish tint on the face, and dark nostrils and ears. The ears sit slightly above horizontal. Baby doll or miniature Southdown sheep are small and boxy, but proportional in size. Toy Southdown sheep are similar to miniatures, but even smaller. All types are naturally polled. Standard Southdown sheep's conservation status is recovering. They are originally from England. The standard is known for being an efficient meat breed, while the baby doll, miniature, and toy types are mainly pets.

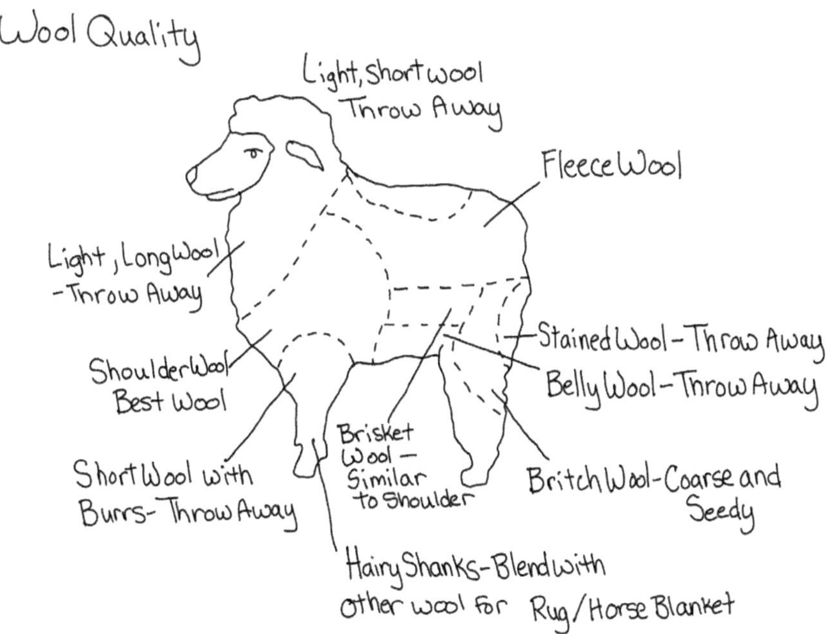

BUTCHERING SHEEP

Rabbits

Proper care of rabbits requires adequate housing, proper feeding and watering, and regular healthcare. Rabbits are not suggested for inexperienced caretakers, as they are more challenging to raise than many people expect due to being more physically delicate and have digestive systems which are prone to problems. Careful preparation is integral for success.

BASIC INFORMATION

Mature or immature male rabbits are called bucks while females are called does. A litter of rabbits is called a kindle. Rabbits are often raised for meat on homesteads. A 10 lb doe can produce 120 lbs of meet per year through producing offspring.

A block of wood should be added to rabbit cages during the winter so rabbits do not freeze to the wire floor. Rabbits also like to chew on the wood to keep their teeth sharp. Rabbits typically molt twice a year in spring and fall. They should be brushed when molting to minimize stress and discomfort.

HOUSING

An average-sized hutch measures 36 in. by 36 in. Rabbits do not require sunlight to remain healthy, so they can be raised indoors without issue. Woodchips, sawdust, or peat moss under hutches helps absorb moisture and minimize odors.

Feed

Rabbits are only fed once per day. Their diet consists of alfalfa hay, phosphorus, calcium, trace minerals, and salt. A salt lick is typically necessary to maintain health. Self-feeders and water tube bottles are ideal and sufficient in most cases. Alfalfa hay should also be put in cages to keep rabbits occupied because they like to chew and it acts as a good supplement during the winter.

How much feed a rabbit requires is determined by weight. Small breed bucks require 2 oz of pellets and does require 3 oz of pellets. Medium breed bucks require 3-6 oz of pellets and does require 6 oz of pellets. Large breed bucks require 4-9 oz of pellets and does require 9 oz of pellets.

Green vegetation, such as carrots, can be offered in small portions. Rabbits also like cabbage, lettuce, and other garden scraps. Nursing does like apple slices.

Water

As with all animals, fresh clean water should be available at all time. Nursing does drink a gallon of water per day to produce enough milk for her litter

Breeding

Does sexually mature at around 6 months old and can produce eight to twelve babies every thirty-one days. For breeding, does should be taken to the buck's cage to prevent fighting. Does will often attack a buck if it is brought to her cage.

When choosing a buck for breeding, good conformation is important. It should have a shiny coat, bright eyes, a healthy weight, and a full and large scrotum with two fully descended testicles. Bucks become sexually mature at around 8 months old. One buck per ten does is adequate. Bucks should not be used for breeding more than every 4-7 days.

BUTCHERING

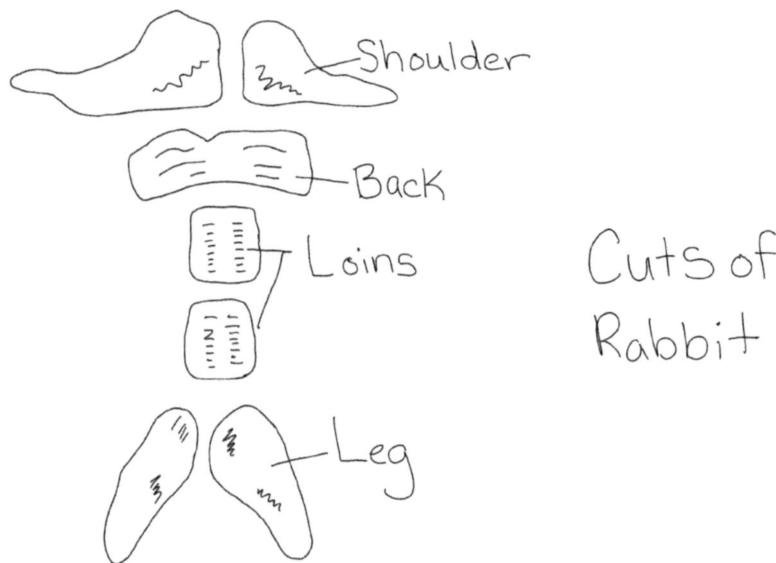

Cattle

A main component of sustainable cattle farming is managing pastures so animals can move and graze more freely. This method is labor intensive and can be expensive due to the need for large plots of land, but is more environmentally friendly, creates better quality of life for the cattle, and produces high-quality and often healthier products. The ratio of pasture to livestock is 1:1, meaning for every one cow, one acre of land is needed. Rotation of pasture is also necessary to prevent overgrazing or over-foraging, and to spread out the nutrients of the manure, which helps rebuild the soil over time.

COMMON HOMESTEADING CATTLE BREEDS

Canadienne cattle are raised for dairy. Their coats are dark brown to brownish black and they tend to have feminine lines due to their light bone structure. The typically have well-proportioned udders. They are small in size and are naturally polled, having no horns. Their conservation status is critical. Originally from Quebec, Canada, they are known for their hardiness and good production on pasture.

Corriente cattle are raised for beef. They are an athletic breed, with a lean but muscular build. They are small, with medium to large horns. They originally come from Mexico and the United States from Spanish stock. Corriente cattle are best known for their speed as rodeo roping stock.

Milking Devon cattle are mainly raised for dairy, but are considered a good multipurpose breed. Their coats are a deep mahogany to ruby red color, with long to moderately long horns. They are a fined-boned, small to medium breed. Their conservation status is critical. Originally from England, this breed has strong multipurpose traits with good production on grass.

Dexter cattle are a dual-purpose breed raised for both beef and dairy. They are compact animals whose coats are usually black, but are occasionally red or dun. They are a very small breed. Dexter cattle are naturally horned, but polled strains do exist. The breed is considered to be in recovering conservation status. They are originally from Ireland where they generally worked well for homesteads because of their scaled milk production.

Florida Cracker or Florida Scrub cattle are raised for beef. They are a compact, athletic-looking breed with a lean yet muscular build. They are a small breed with medium to large horns in a variety of shapes. Their conservation status is critical. This breed is originally from Florida, descended from Spanish stock. They are best known for their heat tolerance and disease resistance, as well as early puberty.

Mini Jersey cattle are raised for dairy. The breed is known for its feminine appearance, having a fine bone structure, doe-like eyes, and long eyelashes. They are brown in color, ranging from light to dark, with occasional white markings. They are a small to medium breed and are naturally horned. Jersey cattle come from the British-ruled Channel Island of Jersey. They are known for their good production of rich, creamy milk relative to their body weight and feed.

Kerry cattle are raised for dairy. The breed is petite, with a dairy-type body structure, whose appearance is usually black, with the possibility of white markings. Red is the recessive color of the breed. They are small to medium with medium upright horns that are white with black tips. Their conservation status is critical. Kerry cattle come from Ireland. They are known for good production of milk with a high percentage of butter fat and protein relative to their size and feed, even when raised on poorer-quality pastures.

Lowline cattle are raised for beef. They are small, black, and naturally polled. They are from Australia and are considered a low-maintenance breed. They are known for easy calving, good growth, good meat-to-bone ratio, and high-quality, well-marbled meat. They typically produce well on grass.

Pineywoods cattle are raised for beef. Their appearance is varied, with many different colors and patterns. They are small to medium and most are horned. Their conservation status is critical. Pineywoods cattle come from the southeastern United States and are known for their adaptability to humid conditions as well as excellent parasite and disease resistance.

CARE OF CATTLE

Feed and Water

Water for cattle may come from natural sources such as ponds or creeks, or through engineered sources. Cattle require about 10 gallons of water per day during the winter and up to 27 gallons per day during hot summers. Having water strategically located in pastures can increase the efficient use of pastures. If there is not a fenced pasture, the area can be staked with a large bucket of water and moved three times daily.

Cattle need grass or hay, water, and salt as part of their regular diet. They have four stomachs and eat with their heads down. During the winter, cows require higher calorie diets. Green hay is higher in sugar and is a good source of calories. It should be cut just after it blooms. Cattle require 2-3 lbs of hay per 100 lbs of body weight, which comes out to about 2 tons of hay per cow per winter.

Do not give dairy cows more feed than can be consumed between milkings because the old feed will not be eaten. Quality hay and grass will produce better milk. For dairy cows, the ideal pasture is lush with clover, alfalfa, grasses, and herbs such as lavender, mustard, rosemary, and sage.

After a cow gives birth, it is necessary to supplement with grains in order to increase milk production. Give cows oats, barley, corn, wheat, peanuts, soybeans, sorghum, peas, and legumes. Start off slow and increase as milk production also increases, then taper off as lactation slows. Use a ratio of 1 lb grain to 3 lb. milk production (about 0.5 gal). Quality grass and a half pound of grain equals 90% milk production. Cornstalks, washed and sliced root vegetables, and whole sunflower heads are great as a supplement when mixed together and chopped or ground. If cows are fed alfalfa, additional grain may not be needed due to its protein content.

CATTLE HEALTHCARE

Cattle, like any other livestock, require regular health checks and awareness of common health concerns which may require veterinary intervention. Below are common health concerns that may arise in cattle.

Downed cow is when a cow cannot get up from the position they are in or are injured. To help a downed cow, pull the legs out and to a level surface. If it appears to be injured, make sure it is watered and fed until moved.

White Muscle Disease presents as a calf with joints that are stiff to the point that the animal cannot follow the mother and dies of starvation. Calves should be immunization against this.

Scours is when a calf has diarrhea. Do not change the calf's diet. Administer Kaopectate, a mixture of pectin and kaolin clay.

Heel fly is when a fly lays eggs in the heel of a cow, which then hatch and crawl through the cow's blood vessels. They then bore holes through the skin and fly away. Medication is required for prevention.

Bang's disease results in a stillborn calf. Humans can get this disease as well. It presents with undulant fever. Prevent this disease by vaccinating heifers at 4-8 months old.

Udder cuts and other udder-related problems are common to both goats and cows. It can be treated with antiseptic ointments.

BUTCHERING CATTLE

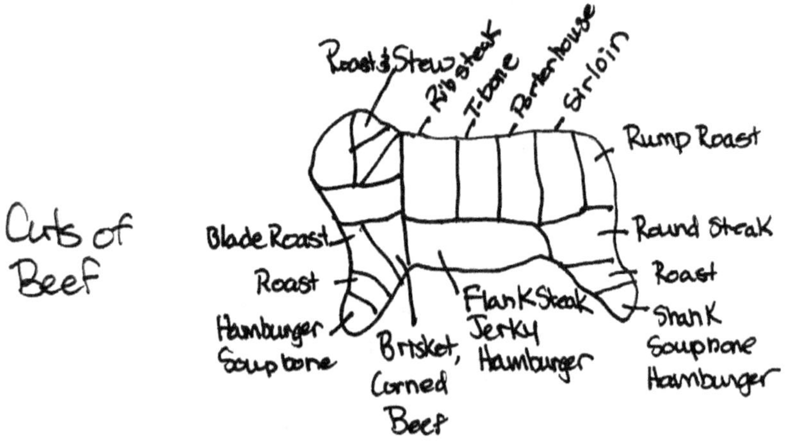

Breeding Cattle

Dairy cows can calve every year and give milk up to 10-16 years old. Cows should not be bred until at least 13 months old. Carefully track ages to avoid early breeding, which can happen as early as 3 months of age. Adhere to a yearly schedule. Allow cows to breed and dry up for 2-3 months before birth or gestation. The pregnancy term for cows is 285 days or 9.5 months. A cow's normal period of being in heat is 18-24 day, but can begin 30-60 days after calving. Cows can be bred immediately after calving.

Cows in heat are restless, stamp their feet, twitch their tails excessively, and are very vocal. Their vulvas become red and swollen and other cows, both male and female, may attempt mounting them and may try mounting caretakers.

When cows are close to calving, it is important to bring them into the barn. Put down thick bedding. Cows are close to calving when their udders swell with milk and the skin around the tailbone loosens. Call the veterinarian if labor goes beyond 3-4 hours without birth.

When the calf is born, clean it with a towel and make sure it gets milk soon after birth. A cow may hide her calf and go away to feed it during the day. Check on the calf and determine if it needs to be moved. If it does need to be moved, pick it up gently and the cow will follow. Milk the cow daily to avoid milk being held inside the udders, which can cause mastitis, inflammation or infection of the breast tissue. Calves should be vaccinated as soon as possible after birth. Chilled calves should be taken inside to a warm place and given a warm bath. Keep the calf wrapped up and dry after its shivering stops.

Handling Cattle

Cattle are colorblind with 360-degree vision. Their lives are based on habit and they utilize their herd instinct for survival. If one is taught something, the herd will follow. They will usually come when called if food is the reward. Cows with calves are very protective, and if a cow is in labor, she can become very violent. Cows in labor should be tied up. It is also important to be careful around cows in heat. Bulls under 18 months old do not breed. If a bull becomes aggressive it should be culled.

Feeding Calves

Nursing and Bottle Feeding

Calves can be separated from their mothers immediately after birth. This is often the best way to ensure proper nutrition. The cow can be milked and the milk can be bottle-fed to the calf. For the first four days, the cow will give colostrum, which should all go to the calf only. Once the colostrum is gone, humans may consume the milk.

If the cow does not produce colostrum, mix egg yolk with milk for several feedings or until the calf thrives. If milk cannot be mixed with yolk, use fresh goat's milk and water at a 50:50 ratio.

At birth, calves should intake about 1 qt of milk per day. From birth through two weeks, work up to feeding calves 2 qts per day. Increase intake to 3 qts per day over the next two to three weeks. Bottle feed five times per day initially, then four times per day, then morning, noon, and night. Gradually decrease to twice per day until weaned.

In cases where the calf cannot or will not bottle feed, pan-feeding is an alternative. To pan feed, make the calf lie down, dip the fingers in the milk, and allow the calf to suck on the fingers then slowly lower the fingers to the pan.

Milking Problems

If the milk does not let down, first try washing the udder with warm water and wait. If the milk still will not let down, massage the udder with a cloth or bag balm, or gently pat the udder similar to a calf butting. Lastly, try sucking on the teat to stimulate let down.

A cow's milk will dry up about ten months after birth to allow for calving every year. If the cow is allowed to nurse her calf, this will happen naturally. If the cow is being milked, slowly decrease the amount of milking over time, allowing some milk to remain in the udder. Allowing milk to remain in the udders causes an increased risk of mastitis. A bruised udder or drying out a cow too quickly can also lead to mastitis.

Mastitis presents with flaky, lumpy, or stringy milk. Monitor milk on a weekly basis by squirting milk into a cloth. Palpated the udders for tumors, large hard areas, or abscesses. The flesh may become red and swollen on one side of the udder and the udder will feel warmer than normal. The udder will be more difficult to milk, as well. If mastitis worsens, the milk may turn yellow, brown, or pink and there may be pus or blood in the milk. When mastitis is present, discard the milk where no human or animal will be exposed to it. Wash the udder thoroughly and wash hands or instruments that came in contact with the infected area.

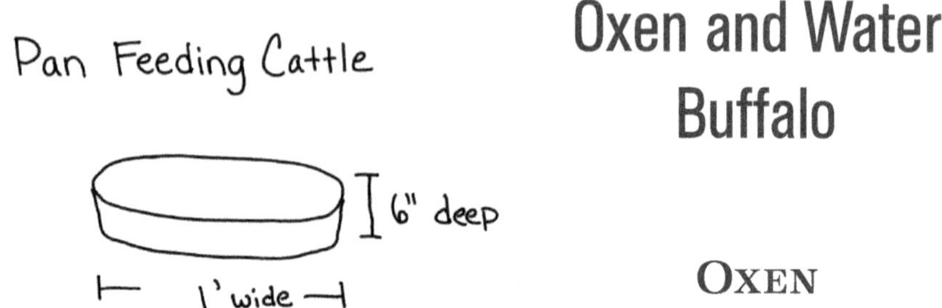

Oxen and Water Buffalo

OXEN

An ox is any breed of the bovine family, male or female. The terms bull, cow, or steer may be used but ox and steer are preferred. Oxen may be trained to be guided entirely by voice commands, body language, and whip pointing.

Oxen usually take four years to fully train and for the animal to reach full strength. It is typically cheaper and simpler to use oxen then horses because they do not need shoes or harness, typically require less medical care, and are gentler.

Oxen have excellent draft power and are very useful on the homestead for completing farm work. They can endure higher workloads than cattle or horses. Oxen can also be used for meat if they become too old or weak.

WATER BUFFALO

Water buffalo are social animals who prefer to live in mixed-gender herds. They are herbivores who feed mainly on grasses and herbs and will not eat aquatic plants. Cool climates are preferrable, as they do not dissipate heat well.

Water buffalo milk is thicker than cow's milk and has 6-8% butterfat compared to 3-5% butterfat. It is ideal milk for making butter, soft cheeses, and yogurt. Buffalo meat is very flavorful and has less fat and cholesterol than beef, making it desirable in the marketplace. Buffalo also produce more meat on less feed than cattle, which makes them very profitable to raise. Another benefit of buffalo is that they are highly disease resistance and can be raised with cattle, even using the same equipment for both species.

Pigs

Raising pigs successfully requires research and preparation. Pigs are generally considered fairly low-maintenance animals to raise, however they do still need suitable space and shelter, fencing, healthcare, and appropriate feed. Many of these considerations are similar to other livestock.

Space is one aspect that may differ, and depends on a homestead's goals and preferences. Required space varies based on the weight of the pigs. Pigs weighing 25-50 lbs need 3 sq ft per pig, 50-100 lbs need 4 sq ft per pig, 100-150 lbs need 6 sq ft per pig, and 150 lbs and larger need 8 sq ft per pig. Smaller pens allow for less exercise and quicker growth, but will more quickly destroy the ground of the pen. Rotation of pens is often necessary when smaller pens are used.

What pigs are fed and how they are fed are also frequently debated topics. Whether feeding commercial or homemade feed, pigs need a balance of carbohydrates, protein, fiber, and minerals to remain healthy and produce quality meat. Ratios of each depend on weight, age, and function. Protein needs are highest at 18-20% when creep-feeding piglets prior to weaning. Young and growing pigs need 15-16% protein, and finishing and older pigs need 13-14% protein.

COMMON HOMESTEADING PIG BREEDS

Berkshire pigs are raised for modern meat and as terminal sires. They are a medium breed that is black in color with six white points, one each on the tail, snout, and four white socks. They are short with erect snouts and ears. Berkshire pigs come from England originally and are known for their flavorful meat, hardiness, and good production on pasture.

Chocktaw pigs are raised for lard. They are a small breed that is black with possible white markings. Their ears are medium in size and are normally upright but may droop. They may have wattles and their toes are fused, similar to a mule's foot, and they have long legs relative to their size. Their conservation status is critical and they are originally from the Unites States. They have historical importance as the earliest breed descended from Spanish descent.

Guinea hogs are raised for lard and kept as pets. They are a small breed that is typically black but can be red on occasion. They have large, upright ears and are medium- to big-boned. They can have short or long legs. Their hair is long and dense, and may be curly. Their conservation status is critical. They are originally from the United States and are best known as homesteading hogs.

Hereford pigs are raised for modern meat. They are a medium breed that is red with white points on the snout, ears, and feet. They have a slightly dished face, large jowls, and a long neck. The ears are floppy, but medium in size. Their conservation status is recovering. They are originally from the United States and are known for their unique coloring, pleasant disposition, suitability for pasturing and homesteading, and flavorful meat.

Vietnamese potbelly pigs are a small breed mainly raised as pets. The Vietnamese variety are predominately black while the North American variety are black and white. They have fine bones, short legs, upright ears, and long snouts. They are originally from Vietnam and are best known as pets.

Kunekune pigs are raised for meat. They are a medium-sized breed whose coats vary in pattern and color, ranging from solid to speckled or blotchy, and their hair may be short and silky or coarse and curly. They may or may not have wattles and have short snouts. They are originally from New Zealand. Their conservation status is rare. Kunekune are known for their pleasant temperature, friendliness, and ease of raising. They are a popular breed for beginning homesteaders.

Horses

Horses may be kept as companions, for work, or for show. Regardless of why a homesteader chooses to raise horses, the responsibility of their care includes appropriate feed and water, shelter, space and exercise, and healthcare. What breed of horses are being raised will determine the specifics of care and maintenance.

For all horses, in order to prevent medical and behavioral problems, basic standards should be followed. Stables and horse stalls should be cleaned regularly. Feed and water should be clean. Do not introduce unpleasant smells into water or feed. Use only fresh or non-moldy hay and make feed changes gradually. Feed horses based on weight and monitor for behavioral changes.

COMMON HOMESTEADING HORSE BREEDS

Belgian horses mature early and are relatively low maintenance. Their dominant color is chestnut or bay with white socks and a blaze or stripe. Their average height is 17.3 -18.2 hands. Their average weight is 2,100–2,800 lbs.

Clydesdales are gentle and enjoy people. Their most common color is bay and the preferred markings are a blaze and white socks. Their average height 16.2-18 hands. Their average weight is 1,600-1,800 lbs. Stallions may weigh up to 2,200 lbs.

Fells are black, brown, bay, or gray with very little white. Their average height is 13.2 hands.

Fjords are very gentle, long-lived, agile, and intelligent horses. Their common colors are brown or dun-colored with zebra-like stripes on the back. Their average height is

14-14.2 hands. Their average weight is 900-1,200 lbs.

Haflingers are known to be cooperative. They typically have chestnut coloring. Their average height is 13-14.75 hands. Their average weight is 800-1,300 lbs.

Percherons have calm dispositions and are considered intelligent. Their coloring is usually black or gray with no markings. Their average height is 16.2 -17.3 hands. Their average weight: is 2,000–2,700 lbs.

Shires are high endurance and patient. Their coloring is black, brown, bay, or grey with a blaze and white socks with feathers on the legs. Their average height is 17.2 hands. Their average weight is 1,200–18,00 lbs.

Suffolk horses are gentle, with high endurance. They are chestnut in color with white on the face and feet. Their average height is 16.1 hands.

Welsh horses are reliable and small. Their coloring may be any color. Section A ponies are no taller than 12.2 hands, while section B ponies no taller than 14.2 hands.

BASIC CARE OF HORSES

Feeding and Watering

WATER

Horses should always have access to clean water. The ideal temperature for drinking water is 45-75 degrees Fahrenheit. Horses require 5-15 gallons of water per day per horse. Adequate water helps avoid colic and dehydration. A well-hydrated horse will have moist gums and its skin will immediately bounce back into place after pinched. Limit the amount of water given after horses are exercised. Wait until the horse has cooled down, if possible.

FEED

A horse's main calories typically come from hay and fresh pasture. Forage comprises the bulk of a horse's meals. Forage can be almost any plant material, including grass, hay, or straw. Alfalfa is a great source of energy, but it does require a grain supplement. Bahiagrass withstands heavy grazing and is one of the most recommended warm-season grasses for horse pastures. Grass hay can be used as the only source of feed. Green hay should still be green when cut so it contains grains. Yellow hay is straw and contains no grain. It is the stem of any type of grain without seeds. It can also be used as bedding. The best kind of straw for feed is oat. Chopped forage mixed with molasses, such as alfalfa and molasses (A&M) and oat hay and molasses (O&M) are good options as well. On average, a horse needs 1 ton of good hay per winter. Protein needs are met from hay and forage feed.

Horses need 5 lbs or less of grains per meal. Grains add extra nutrition and vitamins. Working horses may need up to 15 lbs of grain per day. Grains are another important part of a horse's diet. Corn is the most common grain fed to horses. It must be cracked, flaked, or rolled for easier digestion, but should not be ground. Oats should be fed by weight of the feed, not by volume. It is easiest to calculate feed amounts needed per horse. Barley should be fed in between corn and oats to improve healthiness and should be processed similarly to corn. Grains can be fed in a large, smooth stone feed box for slower eating.

Horses also require various vitamins and minerals for a complete diet. Calcium needs are usually met through alfalfa and nutritional supplements. Phosphorous can be attained from timothy grass, hay, grain, and supplements. Calcium and phosphorous should be given in a 1:1 ratio. Copper and zinc come mainly from supplements. Vitamin D is gained though sunlight. Vitamin C is needed by pregnant horses and comes from supplements. Salt is essential to a horse's diet and should be freely available in the form of a salt block or loose in the pasture or feed box.

Alfalfa provides 2 calories per kg, 17% protein, 23.4% fiber, 1.24% calcium, 0.24% phosphorous, 16.1 ppm copper, 28 ppm zinc, and 1,810 UI per kg vitamin D. 1.75 calories per kg, 8.5% protein, 28.1% fiber, 0.45% calcium, 0.2% phosphorous, 2.1 ppm copper, and 6 ppm zinc.

Bluegrass provides 1.58 calories per kg, 8.5% protein, 28.1% fiber, 0.45% calcium, and 0.2% phosphorous.

Clover provides 1.9 calories per kg, 20% protein, 18.5% fiber, 1.35% calcium, 0.3% phosphorous, 8 ppm copper, and 15 ppm zinc.

Orchard grass provides 1.95 calories per kg, 7.6% protein, 33.9% fiber, 0.24% calcium, 0.3% phosphorous, 16.9 ppm copper, and 34 ppm zinc.

Timothy grass provides 1.77 calories per kg, 8.6% protein, 30.9% fiber, 0.43% calcium, 0.2% phosphorous, 14.2 ppm copper, and 1,736 UI per kg of vitamin D.

Whether horses are fed mainly on hay, alfalfa, or a mixture of hay and grazing will determine their dietary needs. Horses fed mainly on alfalfa will need to be supplemented with 50% oats, 45% cracked corn, 3% molasses, 1% bone meal or dicalcium phosphate, 0.5% ground limestone, and 0.5% salt. Horses fed on hay or grazing will need to be supplemented with 40% oats, 40% corn, 15% soybean meal, 3% molasses, 0.75% ground limestone, 0.75% bone meal or dicalcium phosphate, and 0.5% salt.

If horses are allowed to feed on roughage, it is important to be aware of certain dangers. Some hybrid sorghum grasses can cause Cystitis Syndrome or prussic acid poisoning, which can lead to death. Fescue can contain endophyte fungus, which can cause a mare's milk to dry up (agalactia) and cause early foal death. All pregnant mares should avoid fescue for at least 90 days prior to foaling.

Estimating Calorie Needs

Calories provided are estimated by weight. Hay adds 1,000 calories per pound. Oats add 1,500 cal. per lb. Vegetable oil adds 4,000 cal. per lb.

How much a horse is fed is based on body weight. The feed should be equal to 1.5% of body weight. This includes weanlings. Two-thirds of that amount should be forage. Breeding stallions, mares, pregnant and lactating mares, and foals all have special feed requirements. Any changes in feed should occur gradually over two weeks.

A 2,000 lb horse will require 22,500 calories for maintenance. When working at farming or light logging, it will require 33,750 calories. A horse working in heavy logging and plowing will require 45,000 calories. Broodmares in the last three months of pregnancy will require 26,000 calories. Lactating mares require 39,000 calories. Lactating mares engaged in heavy work will require 62,000 calories.

Laminitis

Laminitis is a foot disease, most commonly found in the front feet. Without treatment, it leads to problems such as sinking or founder. Laminitis can be classified as mild, moderate, or severe. Mild cases will exhibit signs such as horses having a sawhorse stance, shifting of their feet, and a reluctance to move. Moderate cases will exhibit signs such as a pounding pulse above the feet, painful foot soles, and irregular hoof growth. Severe cases will exhibit signs such as a horse being unwilling to stand, loss of appetite, and separation of the hook from the sole.

To prevent laminitis, do not give large quantities of grain suddenly, suddenly change from sparse pasture to lush green pasture, work on hard surfaces, allow horses to drink large quantities of very cold water, allow horses to eat black walnut shavings or beet tops, or have high or prolonged doses of anti-inflammatory medication. Proper hoof care is a must, including correct filing, cleaning, and shoeing.

Grooming

Grooming horses not only keeps their coats clean and neat, it provides opportunities to assess a horse's health and condition, acts as preventative health care, and aids bonding. While grooming, take the time to inspect the horse's overall health and conditioning. Brushing increases blood flow, massages large muscle groups, and performs preventative maintenance that can help avoid health problems. Engaging in quiet, relaxing time with a horse during a grooming session helps create a bond between humans and animals as well.

CLIPPING

A thick winter coat will make a working horse sweat. Clip coats according to work being done and/or the tack being worn.

A tracer clip is where the hair is removed from the underside of the neck and the belly, but it is left intact on the head, back and legs. This style is used for horses who regularly wear harnesses.

A blanket clip is where the hair is removed from the neck and flanks, but left on the back, hindquarters, and legs. This style is used in extreme weather and for horses engaged in outdoor work.

A hunter clip is where hair is left only on the legs and the saddle area. This style is used for hunting and/or horses working in wet or muddy conditions.

A full clip is where the whole coat is clipped off. This

is mainly used for showing horses.

GROOMING EQUIPMENT

Dandy brush
Body brush
Small, soft face brush
Rubber currycomb – Raises dust and loose hair from coat
Metal currycomb – For cleaning brushes.
Mane and tail comb
Hoof pick with brush
Hoof dressing
Kitchen towel
Show sheen or detangler (Mane and Tail)
Fly repellant
Bot knife

It is a good idea to keep the kit in a basket or container with the horse's tack. Each horse should have its own kit. Keep to the same routine when grooming, whether head first or hooves first. Feet first is usually best due to the hooves being very important to health.

FLY PREVENTION

Flies and gnats can cause itching, hives, and other skin irritations. In more serious cases, they can cause abrasions and ulcerations. Several natural mixtures can be made to keep flies away from horses.

Myrrh spray: Mix ½ tsp oil of myrrh, 2 c water, ½ c cider vinegar, and ¼ tsp citronella oil

Eucalyptus spray: Mix 2 c apple cider vinegar, 2 c cold tea (sage or chamomile), 20 drops eucalyptus oil, 20 drops citronella oil, 10 drops lavender oil, 10 drops tea tree oil, and 10 drops cedar oil.

Hoof Shoeing and Trimming

Hoof shoeing and trimming is important for protecting and strengthening the hooves and feet and for maintaining structure and function. Regular trimming keeps the hoof balanced, which helps horses move better and have less strain on the body. Properly trimming hoofs requires training or hiring an experienced veterinarian or farrier. During the summer, horses should be trimmed or shoed every 6-8 weeks. Hoofs grow more slowly in the winter, so trimming or shoeing may only be needed every 6-12 weeks. Show horses may require more frequent trimming and shoeing.

Hoof Trimming Equipment

Apron/chaps: a leather cover protecting the legs from hooves and legs, and helps grip.

Hoof knife: A knife used to trim away loose, dried-out soles, and the loose, ragged frog. Be sure not to cut live flesh.

Nippers: This trims the growth of the hoof wall. An adult will have a 3-3¾ in. hoof wall.

Rasp: A tool like a file. It is used to level the bottom of the hoof wall.

Hoof gauge: A tool that matches the pairs of hoofs in their angle to the ground so the front and back are the same. The front is usually at 50-58 degrees; and the back is 2 degrees steeper.

Parts of a Horseshoe and Horseshoe Terms

Nails: Made of soft steel with four sides and tapered

shafts.

Frost nails: Nails made with a head that provides temporary traction on hard surfaces.

Borium: A coating for horseshoes that provides traction on pavement or ice and increases the life of the shoe.

Calk: Projections attached to the ground side of the shoe to increase traction, alter movement, or adjust the horse's stance.

Clinches: Parts of the nails that are visible outside of the hoofs, which are then folded down against hoof-like clamps.

Clips: Flat projections extending upward from the outer edge of the shoe to prevent it from shifting, to stabilize the hoof wall, and to reduce the number of nails needed.

Hot fitting: Holding a hot shoe against the bottom of the hoof until it burns high spots of the horn so the farrier knows what should be removed.

Scotched: A shoe with the outer edge sloped down and out from the hoof at the same angle as hoof-scotch-bottom shoes. They are commonly used with draft horses.

Rock toe: A shoe that has been bent upward at the toe to ease and direct the breakover, for which the hoof should be specially prepared.

Rolled toe: A shoe that has been rounded or beveled on the outer edge of the ground surface at the toe to ease the breakover, for which no hoof preparation is needed.

MEDICAL CARE

This section will cover information about the basic medical care of horses.

Vaccinations

All horses require regular medical care, including vaccinations and deworming. Below is a general vaccination and deworming schedule suitable for most horses.

February: Five-day Fenbendazole interval or daily dewormer

March: Tetanus, EEE/WEE, intranasal flue, West Nile virus, VEE (optional)

April: Ivermectin interval dewormer

May: Ivermectin or Moxidectin daily dewormer

Jun: Potomac and rabies (optional), Moxidectin interval dewormer

August: Pyrantel pamoate (double dose) interval or daily dewormer

September: Intranasal flu

November: Ivermectin or Moxidectin daily dewormer

October: Ivermectin interval dewormer

December: Moxidectin interval dewormer

Taking a Horse's Pulse

First, squat down next to the left front leg. Then, place the index finger around left side of the fetlock joint at the lower edge. Apply pressure with the finger and run it from side to side around the joint until a cord-like bundle snaps beneath the touch of the finger.

Next, apply pressure to the bundle (a vein, an artery, and a nerve) for 5-10 seconds until a pulse is felt. If there is too much pressure, blood flow will stop. If there is not enough pressure, the pulse will not be felt. This takes practice to become proficient.

Usually, a healthy horse's pulse is difficult to find. If it is easy to find, there may be a problem and the veterinarian should be called.

Cleaning a Horse's Sheath

Male horse's sheaths need to be cleaned, in and around the penis, every 6-12 months. Use disposable gloves that reach to the elbow, old towels, warm water, sheath cleaner, and an ample supply of paper towels or clean, old towels. Put a dollop of sheath cleaner into the gloved hand and reach up into the sheath with a wet towel. It will take several towels to clean it out the smegma from the sheath. Remove the whitish residue that forms in a small pocket at the tip of the penis, also called the bean. Rinse the area with clean warm water and towels until clear.

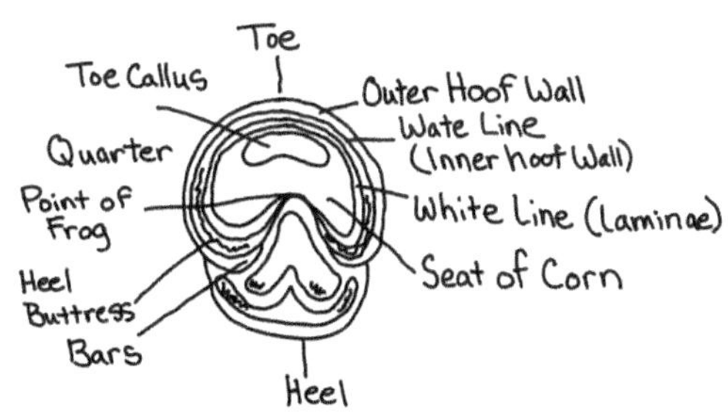

Choking

Choking in horses is when an item gets caught in the throat, not the windpipe. It is normally non-fatal, but it can happen when eating, from not chewing, or when drinking too fast. Horses who eat pelleted grain, dry hay cubes, and unsoaked beet pulp are more susceptible to choking.

Signs of choking include a horse standing still in the stall, not eating nor drinking, large amounts of green discharge draining from the nose, pain, and a horse exhibiting signs of panic.

To treat choking, take all food out of the stall and muzzle the horse. Continuing to eat may cause pneumonia. If a bump is felt on the left side of neck below the throat latch, it is possible to massage the blockage out or rinse it down with a garden hose, which will make the horse swallow to dislodge the blockage. The chance that choking will recur within 72 hours is very high. Give the horse anti-inflammatory medication to reduce swelling and feed gruel instead of hay.

Tying Up

Tying up is an exercise-related muscle degeneration with an unknown cause. The horse will suddenly be unable to move, or will not want to move, will sweat significantly, will have an at-rest heart rate over 60 bpm, have tense hindquarter muscles, have a swishing tail, and will show signs of pain, especially on the hindquarters.

To treat tying up, discontinue all exercise immediately and do not take the horse back to the stall. Do not walk the horse anywhere, either. Give the horse a dose of xylazine/butorphanol to relax the muscles and relieve muscle cramps, and also administer phenylbutazone for inflammation and pain. Give the horse water if it is away from the barn or an immediate water source. Wait until all symptoms are gone, then slowly walk (not ride) the horse home, stopping every 30 minutes for a 10-minute rest. Watch for urine discoloration for 1-2 days after being tied up. If the urine is dark, there may be kidney damage. Consult a veterinarian for further treatment.

Foundering

Foundering occurs when a horse or goat is given too much rich food too quickly. To avoid foundering, the animal should be eased into a new diet. Any sudden diet changes can cause bloating. The belly will swell and the animal will have excessive burping. The animal can die from excess gas building up, so the animal needs to be kept moving. If the animal begins to swell, raise the front feet 6 in. higher than the back feet by standing it on something elevated. Call the veterinarian right away.

If a veterinarian is not immediately available, more substantial measures may need to be taken. Get a rubber garden hose about 4 ft or less in length and a piece of black pipe big enough for the horse's mouth. Put the pipe in the horse's mouth and feed the hose through it and down the throat. The purpose of the pipe is to keep the animal from biting down. Thread the hose until it reaches the gas. Stand aside from the hose, as the gas will release from the hose, or loop the rope around the horse's bottom jaw and push back until the horse gags.

If the gas has still not been released using the hose and pipe method, and the animal is on the ground and unable to rise or is gasping for breath, an emergency measure may need to be taken. Insert a pocketknife into the left side of the animal behind the ribcage and below the spine at the point at the middle of the dipping spot which caves in naturally. This is the location of the gut. The knife should point toward the right front knee of the animal. Turn the knife slightly to allow the gas to escape. Do not stand directly in front of the incision area, as gas will be released there.

Poisoned Water

There are several naturally-occurring ways water may become poisoned, including algae, salt, and fluoride.

Watch for blue-green algae when it is blooming. It can cause convulsions and sudden death to all animals when ingested.

Water contaminated with too much salt, or water deprivation, can cause blindness, deafness, or paralysis to most poultry and ruminants.

Prolonged exposure to feed, water, or airborne factory waste with fluoride can cause abnormalities to the skeleton and teeth.

Poisoned Soil

Soils that are highly alkaline contain selenium, which causes blindness, staggering, lameness, and cracked hooves.

Imbalanced soil is soil with higher levels of copper and molybdenum. Soil may be ingested when animals are foraging on imbalanced soil. This can cause severe scours and emaciation to ruminants.

Poisoned Feed

Feed can become poisoned by a variety or compounds, including natural substances, farm supplies, and household supplies. Carefully monitor what feed may be exposed to and avoid contamination. Below is a list of common poisons.

Cotton seed food coloring contains gossypol. High levels of cottonseed feed food coloring can cause weight loss, weakness, and loss of appetite in young ruminants.

The sudden addition of urea or ammonium salts

in feed can cause muscle tremors, weakness, difficulty breathing, and death to mature ruminants.

Moldy feed contains mycotoxins, which can cause lameness, paralysis, listlessness, jaundice, and internal bleeding to all livestock, especially horses and poultry.

Fluoride in feed causes the same symptoms as in water, abnormalities to the skeleton and teeth.

Eating too much copper can cause liver damage, diarrhea, pain, dehydration, jaundice, and blood in the urine for sheep.

Eating paint, batteries, grease, oil, etc. which contain lead can lead to dullness, lack of coordination, blindness, and convulsions to all animals, especially dogs.

If unsweetened baker's chocolate, which contains theobromine, is ingested by animals, it can cause nervousness, vomiting, diarrhea, seizures, and, at times, comas to all animals, especially dogs.

Eating poisonous houseplants can cause vomiting and neurological symptoms to many animals, but mostly dogs and cats.

Eating blister beetles, which are found most commonly in the southwest United States, contains cantharidin, which causes oral ulcers, abdominal pain, shock, and blood in urine in horses and sheep. The prevent beetles in feed, do not crimp hay when cutting.

Cleaning supplies and medications ingested by animals can cause severe vomiting and diarrhea. Tylenol, Advil, Aleve, etc. causes death to cats and dogs.

CARE OF STALLIONS, DRAFT HORSES, MARES, AND FOALS

Care of Stallions

Stallions never need their sheaths cleaned. Only geldings need to have their sheaths cleaned. The best way to prevent infection is to not breed stallions with questionable mares.

Breeding stallions need additional carbs, but not additional protein. It is important to check a stallion's body condition weekly during breeding season and to adjust its diet accordingly.

While in the stall, a stallion will relieve himself in the same spot continually if there is a small amount of urine already there. Leave a small amount of urine in the stall for easy cleanup.

Stallions need a good amount of exercise and should not get stressed during breeding season. Fevers decreased sperm count, so their health should be watched carefully and vaccinations should be kept up to date. If concerns arise, consult a veterinarian.

Care of Draft Horses

Draft horses should be on the same general care plan as other horses, however regular farrier care is very important because of their heavier workloads. Along with regular care of shoes and hoofs, draft horses should be monitored for signs of shivers. Shivers is a neuromuscular disease that affects the hind legs. Symptoms include a trembling hind end, difficult raising the hind legs, trembling of the tail when raised, and muscle atrophy. The cause is unknown and the only treatment is working with the animal long-term.

Draft horses should also be monitored for common health conditions specific to draft horses, such as Equine Polysaccharide Storage Myopathy (EPSM), which is the inability to properly metabolize starches and sugars. EPSM can cause muscle weakness, intense sweating while engaged in work or exercise, intolerance of physical activity, and recumbency, the inability to get up after lying down. Draft horses experiencing EPSM should be fed a diet significantly reduced in sugar and carbohydrates.

DRAFT HORSEPOWER

Draft horsepower is important to calculate in order to determine what type and the amount of work a horse can perform. If weighing a horse is not possible, the weight can be estimated by measuring the girth. The girth is measured around the horse's abdomen just behind the forelegs. This is an estimate only.

An 80 in. girth estimates about 1,540 lbs weight.
A 75 in. girth estimates about 1,320 lbs weight.
A 71 in. girth estimates about 1,100 lbs weight.
A 65 in. girth estimates about 880 lbs weight.
A 53 in. girth estimates about 660 lbs weight.
A 41 in. girth estimates about 440 lbs weight.

Based on weight, or weight estimates, determine what amount of work a draft horse can be expected to complete.

A 1,200 lb. horse can perform 180 lbs work for 10 hrs with 1,800 lbs bursts.

A 1,600 lb. horse can perform 200 lbs for 10 hrs. with 2,400 lbs bursts.

A 2,000 lb horse can perform 220 lbs. for 10 hrs with

3,000 lbs bursts.

A 1,600 lb horse is more efficient than any other size. It typically has enough overload ability to break loose logs, about 2,400 lbs.

A 1,500 lb team of daft horses can plow 1.5 acres. When in peak condition, a team can perform in one day of work: single-row cultivation of seven acres, harrow eight acres, mow seven acres, drill eight acres, rake fourteen acres, plant eight acres, or haul a wagon with 1.5 tons for 20 minutes.

When buying a draft horse, age will largely determine the price. Weanlings (under 1 year old) are about $500-$2,500. Yearlings (1-2 years old) are about $1,000-$6,000. Two-year-olds (2-3 years old) are about $1,500-$10,000. Riding horses (3 years old and older) are about $2,000-$20,000. Draft teams (matched with harnesses) are about $6,000-$20,000. Thoroughbred foals (racing) are about $5,000-$50,000. Two-year-old thoroughbreds are about $50,000-$3 million. Thoroughbred studs are about $100,000-$3 million.

Draft horses may be bought by way of private treaty, a breeding farm, or auction. Private treaty is a purchase direct from seller to buyer. More research is required and a higher price is usually paid. Purchase from a breeding farm may be through direct sales or auction. Auctions are a way to sell off stock quickly. This may be good or bad. Carefully read all terms and conditions of sales prior to purchase.

Care of Mares

Mares kept in stalls or dry lots need 1 lb of hay to 100 lbs of body weight. A healthy horse should have a level back, ribs that are easily felt but not seen, some fat felt around the tail head, and some boney areas without looking obviously thin.

PREGNANT AND LACTATING MARES

Pregnant and lactating mares need more feed than normal. During the first stages of pregnancy, mares will get the needed nutrients from pasture feeding, if it is quality pasture. If the pasture is not of good quality, it will be necessary to substitute with high-quality hay from 1.5-1.75% of body weight. Mares also need ample water and a mineralized salt block. If a mare is not in optimal condition, add supplements to her diet.

Daily feeding of pregnant mares is based on weight. For a 1,100 lb mare fed on alfalfa hay, she should be fed 13-14 lbs of hay supplemented with 4-5 lbs of grain. A 1,100 lb mare fed on good quality hay or grazing, should consume 11-12 lbs of grass hay supplemented with 5-6.5 lbs of grain.

Once a mare reaches late-term pregnancy, its dietary needs change. When fed on alfalfa hay, supplement with 50% oats, 45% cracked corn, 3% molasses, 1% bone meal/dicalcium phosphate, 0.5% ground limestone, and 0.5% trace mineralized salt. When fed on another type of quality hay or grazing, supplement with 40% oats, 40% corn, 15% soybean meal, 3% molasses, 0.75% ground limestone, 0.75% bone meal/dicalcium phosphate, and 0.75% trace mineralized salt.

In addition to a good diet, over the 340 days of gestation, mares may be vaccinated 2-4 weeks before her due date so the foal carries the same vaccinations. Scheduled dewormer should also be given during pregnancy. Mares will not look obviously pregnant until the final months of the term, the 10th or 11th months.

Lactating mares also require more feed. Her pounds of feed should be 2-3% of her body weight, which is typically about 11-12 lbs of roughage or 13-14 lbs of grain. Allow seven to ten days for her to adjust gradually to the increased diet. By four months postpartum, her feed should be decreased back to normal while foals are creep feeding.

Vaccinations for pregnant mares include:

Tetanus: Tetanus is fatal to horses, so it is critical that all horses receive this vaccine. New foals may also be vaccinated with two doses thirty days apart.

Encephalitis: There are three types of encephalitis vaccinations: eastern, western, and Venezuelan. Encephalitis is spread by mosquitos and infects the nervous system, including the brain.

Potomac horse fever: This vaccine is recommended for horses raised on coasts or rivers in moderate climates. Consult a veterinarian on whether the vaccine is recommended for a specific area.

Rabies: All animals should receive this vaccine. Rabies is fatal and can be spread to humans.

Rotavirus diarrhea: A virus carried by mothers which can kill newborn foals. Consult a veterinarian on its administration.

Influenza: This vaccine will help lessen the symptoms of equine flu in young horses. It is not 100% effective.

Rhinovirus: This virus can cause abortions. Only Pneumabort-K +1B is approved for use in pregnant mares in prevention of abortion due to the virus. Symptoms are similar to a common cold.

Strangles: This is a highly contagious virus. Symptoms include fever, nasal discharge, and abscesses near swollen lymph nodes. The vaccine is typically administered prior to a mare going to a breeding farm.

Pregnancy Due Date Signs:

Two months prior to labor, the fetus will move into delivery position. The mare's belly looks much bigger and she will take bigger steps. The udder and milk veins will enlarge.

One month prior to labor, the mare will experience loss of appetite and may want to be alone.

Two weeks to two hours prior to labor, sticky, clear yellow drops will drip from the teats and harden, often referred to as waxed teats. The tailhead, croup, and perineal areas will become relaxed as hormones are released in preparation for delivery.

Hours prior to labor, the udder will fill with milk and become warm. The waxy buildup will drip off. Delivery should be expected at any time.

Care of Foals

New Foals

New foals should be able to walk, stand, suck, and nurse within two to three hours after birth. They should pass their first meconium, a dark, hard manure, within six hours. For constipated foals, use a mild soap and water enema or foal laxative.

Administer all routine vaccines and dewormer at two months old, with boosters after four to six weeks. Administer dewormer every eight weeks to control parasites.

Small weak foals may appear to be fine at first, but may weaken within twenty-four hours. Monitor closely for signs of fading.

Always keep foals in a sturdy, warm, and dry shelter. Allow them to run in a small pasture in good weather.

A foal should weigh about 10% of the dam's weight

at birth. From 7-28 days, measure heart girth by using a cloth tape at the barrel just behind withers. Subtract 25 and divide by 0.07. From 29-90 days old, use the same formula, but at 10% of the result.

ORPHANED FOALS

Newborn foals should receive two to three liters of colostrum every hour for the first six hours after birth. Divide the colostrum into doses and bottle-feed foals, or have a veterinarian use a stomach tube. It is vital that foals receive the antibodies contained in colostrum to protect against disease or they may die.

About 200-300 ml of colostrum may be milked from a mare without robbing a new foal of what it needs, or it can be milked from a mare right before death. If frozen, colostrum may be kept up to one year. It should be thawed at room temp before use.

Foals should nurse every one to two hours during the first week and every four to six hours the second week after birth. A few weeks later, foals may be introduced to solid feed. Use a nurse mare, if she accepts the foal, or a goat, placed on hay, or manually bottle feed orphaned foals. Orphaned foals may be kept with other orphans, a pony, a goat, or another horse. Use mare's, goat's, powdered mare's milk or foal formula if bottle feeding. Do not use straight cow's milk or a big calf nipple.

Foal's formula can be made in several ways.

Cow's milk recipe: 24 oz cow milk, 12 oz saturated lime water, 4 tsp dextrose

Evaporated milk recipe: 4 oz evaporated milk, 4 oz warm water, 1 tsp white corn syrup

CREEP FEEDING

Creep feeding is when foals are fed separately from adult horses to allow foals to begin eating solid food before being fully weaned. This should begin within the first two months of life. Foals should gain 2.5-3 lbs per day.

Creep feed foals through a small fence that the foal can get under but the adults cannot. If there are more than four foals using the trough, it should be designed so the foals can stand on both sides with their tails toward the exit.

The height of the creep should be 4 ft when the mare's weight is between 1,000-1,300 lbs. Install the foal feeder trough low to the ground with the bars closely spaced enough to keep the mare out. The size of the creep should be proportional to the number of foals being fed.

1 foal = 8 ft x 8 ft
2 foals = 10 ft x 10 ft
3 foals = 12 ft x 12 ft
4 foals = 14 ft x 14 ft
5 foals = 16 ft x 16 ft
6 foals = 18 ft x 18 ft
7 foals = 20 ft x 20 ft
8 foals = 24 ft x 24 ft

The creep size should be increased 2 ft by 4 ft per additional foal.

WEANING FOALS

Foals should be at least four months old and be used to pasturing with the herd before weaning. They should also no longer be dependent on the mother for food. Foals should have been creep-feeding for at least two months before weaning as well. The mother and foal should be pastured in parallel fields so they are able to see each other. If a foal or mare loses weight or begins to become thin, separate at a slower pace.

Equipment for Foaling

Bright flashlight with extra batteries
At least 8 ft cotton strings
Scissors
1 cup of betadine/iodine solution
Clean towels
Enema tube, mild soap, and lubricant or foal laxative
A veterinarian's or knowledgeable person's phone number in case of complications

Problems During Delivery:

If a mare pushes for 45 minutes and the foal's feet do not emerge, call a veterinarian right away or the foal may not get enough oxygen.

If the foal's feet are upside down, stand the mare up. If the foal is upside down, this may turn it. If the foal does not turn and remains breech, call a veterinarian right away. Walking the mare may slow down labor until a veterinarian arrives.

If labor stops completely, call a veterinarian. If the placenta is too thick, the mare's water may not break, and no labor will occur. If the mare feels threatened for some reason labor may stop.

If the mare's water breaks but nothing happens after 20 minutes, or if the foal is not moving, the labor hormone has likely not been released. Tug on the foal's leg and the foal should tug back, stimulating labor. If it does not, call a veterinarian.

If the shoulders of the foal are out, but the mare cannot pass the hips, call a veterinarian. The pelvises of the mare and the foal are locked.

If the mare stands up quickly after birth and blood hemorrhages, call a veterinarian immediately. If the mare is still lying down, but the placenta has already been delivered, cut the umbilical cord and tie it off.

Blood will drain from the umbilical cord no matter what, but if it is coming from foal's navel, pinch and tie off the cord with a cotton string.

POTENTIAL PROBLEMS WITH NEWBORN FOALS

If a foal has not nursed within six hours, show the foal the mare's nipple and halter the mare to hold her still while the foal nurses. If the foal cannot or will not nurse, call a veterinarian.

If a mare does not let the foal near her, there may be too many distractions around her. Rub fluid from the foal's body on the mare's nostrils and leave the immediate area. However, if the mare appears to be a threat to the foal, restrain her and call a veterinarian.

If the foal appears to be weak, is making barking sounds, wanders, convulses, or walks unsteadily or drunkenly, these may be signs of brain damage. If symptoms persist for more than one hour, call a veterinarian.

If a foal has frequent, watery bowel movements, it may have a virus. Call a veterinarian.

If the whites of a foal's eye are yellow, it is possible that the foal has jaundice, a ruptured bladder, or there are milk problems. Call a veterinarian.

If a foal's legs are deformed and do not straighten when it is let out to pasture the day after birth, call a veterinarian. Swollen joints may be a sign of infection and will require veterinary care.

If a foal has a swollen navel, drips urine, has enlarged testicles, or a filly appears to have testicles, it may have a hernia. Call a veterinarian for further examination.

A foal who is solid white with blue eyes may have lethal

white syndrome, which can cause various abnormalities. Call a veterinarian to assess whether the foal should be euthanized to prevent suffering.

Imprinting and Haltering Foals

Imprinting foals is a process of focused and specific handling believed to create a less reactive horse and improve long-term handling. The first few days of life are critical learning periods for foals. Foals do not instinctively fear humans, and imprint training is believed to program foals to better tolerate handling and improve the foal's attitude and personality.

To imprint a foal, use the hands and clean towels to rub the neck, body, and legs of the foal until it is completely relaxed. Then run the hands over ticklish spots, gums, ears, tail, hooves, girth, and teats. Then take the halter and run it over her body before slipping it over the head. Remove and replace the halter several times to acclimatize the foal to its feel and the process of haltering. This process takes 20-25 minutes. Make sure mare can see her foal and is comfortable throughout this process.

Training and Handling

Basic Handling

When handling horses, it is integral to respect the horse and be willing to learn from the horse. If a horse does not respond to a method, try a different one and be patient. The handler is the leader when training, but should remain positive and confident even when facing challenges.

Remain aware of signs and warnings that a method is not working or that something is wrong. Think critically to work around problems when possible. The horse is always going to be stronger than the trainer, so staying aware of potentially dangerous situations or reactions can help prevent injury to the horse or the handler. Always be aware of the surroundings and what the horse is doing during a training session. Only use quick-release knots when working with horses. It is dangerous to the horse and the handler to use any other type of knot.

Knowing basic information about how horses experience the world can help tremendously when training. Horses are not colorblind and can see everywhere around themselves except right in front of their feet and the space directly behind them. Horses hate to step on unstable ground or unreliable surfaces. Using such surfaces during training may hinder progress. Mares are more sensitive and prone to mood changes when in heat, but they are also more sensitive to the handler's feelings as well.

When training, do not be afraid of the horse. Set aside any preconceived ideas about training and be open to learning new methods. Maintain a mindset that the horse can do no wrong because the handler influences everything the horse does. Learn horse body language and communication to interpret their responses better. Do not use negative reinforcement such as hitting, jerking, pulling, tying, or restraint. Engage in training that teaches the horse what to do rather than what not to do.

When attempting to lift a horse's hooves, run the hand down the leg to the bottom of the cannon bone just above the fetlock. Put pressure on either side of the leg with the thumb and the forefinger. The horse will lift the foot if the right spot is found. To lift the rear leg, keep the hoof turned upward and support it with the handler's legs. If the horse will not pick up its leg, lean against it to shift its weight and encourage lifting of the leg.

Horses have a variety of vocalizations. Neighing can communicate greeting, fear, or anger, depending on the tone. Nickering is used for greeting, calling foals, and courtship. Squealing communicates excitement, warning, and resentment. Alarm or playing at being scared can be indicated by snorting. Grunting or groaning usually indicated great effort or pain.

BODY LANGUAGE OF HORSES

Becoming familiar with equine body language can help improve training efforts and general handling. While one gesture, movement, or vocalization can communication something specific, it is often important to evaluate multiple factors to fully understand what the horse is attempting to communicate. Below are common body language elements and their basic interpretations.

High-held tail: Excitement

Clamped-down tail: Fear and submission

Ears pricked and forward: Startled or the horse saw something in the distance

One ear back, one ear forward: The horse's attention is split

Droopy ears: Lack of attention or the horse is bored

Ears back: May indicate submission, sleepiness, fear, or anger depending on the rest of the horse's body language

Nose high and top teeth exposed: The horse smells something unexpected

Tense, tight mouth: Upset or confused

Head lowered, moving the tongue and teeth around: Submission

Nudging: Friendliness or seeking attention

Thrusting with the head: Aggressiveness

Jerking the head back: Startled

Shaking the head vigorously: Getting rid of an annoyance

Pawing with the hooves: Warning, investigation,

frustration, or anger, depending on the rest of the horse's body language

Equine Equipment and Equipment Care

Care and use of horses requires various equipment depending on what the horses are being used for, such as farm work, pleasure riding, show, etc. This section outlines common types of equipment needed for raising and working horses, as well as care of equipment.

Types of Harness:

A buggy harness is used for pleasure driving or training.

A farm harness is used for practical work.

A logging or plowing harness is used for lightweight work, such as skidding, dragging, or plowing.

Harnesses come in all sizes. Harnesses for ponies are for animals weighing 800 lbs or less. Harnesses for horses are for animals weighing between 800 and 1,400 lbs. Draft harnesses are for horses weighing more than 1,400 lbs.

Plow harnesses have multiple components. Proper use and care require knowledge of its parts. The parts and their purpose are listed below, moving from head to tail.

Bridle: Lays over the forehead and nose and holds the bit in place

Bit: A cylindrical piece of metal in the mouth used to direct the head

Check rein: Tack that goes from the bit over the housing to the other side

Leading rein: A chain from the bit to the strap, connected to the trace chain

Collar: A ring of leather that sits around the neck for

pulling

Hames: Two pieces of wood or metal on either side of the collar that are held on by a top strap

Top strap: A strap that holds the hames together

Housing: Covers the top of the hames and the top strap

Meeter: Connects the hames to the crupper

Tug hook: Holds the chain that goes from the hames to the trace chain

Martingale: A strap that connects the collar to the girth

Crupper: A strap that runs along the back of a horse and under the tail, known as the backbone of the harness

Lead guide: A strap going from the crupper to the leading rein behind the housing

Backstrap: A strap that goes over the horse behind the lead guide to connect to the trace chain

Girth: A strap that goes from the ends of the backstrap under the horse's belly

Loin strap: A strap just in front of the tail connecting to the traces

Trace chain: Traces that go from the backstrap to the spreader to pull the plow

The parts of a shaft harness are listed below, moving from head to tail.

Blinker: A blinder that sits on the bridle over the eyes so the horse can only look forward

Saddle: Tack that sits just behind the housing and holds the chain carrying shafts

Saddle cover: Sits under the saddle and adds support

Ridge tie: Sits beneath the saddle cover and connects to the ridger

Ridger: A strap beneath the ridge tie that connects over the back to the girth

Staple: Tact connected to the chain going to the harness which holds the shaft

Shaft: A long pole for pulling a cart or a wagon

Loin strap: Three straps over the back, behind the saddle, to help carry the shafts

Quilter: A piece of wood on the shaft connected to the ends of the loin straps and the chain from the staple

Types of Collars

Collars come in three shapes. Full-face collars are for thin-necked horses, such as buggy horses. Half Sweeney collars have less stuffing by the withers for muscular necks, such as draft horses or thick-necked horses. Full Sweeney collars are for very thick-necked, heavy draft pullers. The collar should have enough gap at the bottom for the four-finger test.

Equipment Care

Leather components of tack must be dressed regularly. Leather dressing can be made rather than purchased. A common leather dressing formula is 5-6 oz beeswax, 8 oz lanolin, and 8 oz cedarwood or other oil. Combine components and heat to 160 degrees Fahrenheit in a double boiler. Mix thoroughly and pour into smaller containers for storage. Use as a leather conditioner and waterproofer.

CROPS

Choosing what crops to grow depends on several factors. Assess the location planned for growing crops to determine the amount of sunlight it will receive daily, its level of protection against harsh weather and storms, and whether the area is prone to flooding. Not all geographic areas experience seasons for the same length or intensity. Evaluate the typical seasons of the area and what plants will be most appropriate for the length of the season and the hardiness needed. Spacing is also an important consideration, as some crops require more or less space than others. Conduct soil testing to determine the quality of the soil and what plants will do well in specific soil types, or what remediation may be needed to improve the soil.

The following sections offer suggestions on herbs and crops common to homesteading and sustainable living.

HERBS

Herbs are an important component of homestead living due to their many uses and functions. Herbs may be used in teas, cooking, for medicinal uses, and for ornamental purposes. Below is a list of common useful herbs, followed by a more detailed description of specific culinary, fragrant, medicinal, and decorative herbs.

Anise
Anise hyssop
Basil
Bay laurel
Borage
Cacao

Chamomile
Chervil
Chives
Cilantro
Dill
Fennel, Florence fennel is less common
Garlic
Horseradish
Lavender
Lemon balm
Lemon grass
Milk thistle
Mint
Mexican pepperleaf (root beer plant)
Mustard
Nasturtium
Oregano
Parsley
Pineapple mint
Pineapple sage
Rosemary
Sage
Sweet marjoram
Tarragon
Tea: orange pekoe, black, green, etc.
Thyme
Vanilla verbena

Culinary Herbs

Basil is a tender annual that grows 12-15 in. tall, with dwarf varieties that grow 6 in. tall. It is easily germinated and should be planted outdoors when it is consistently warm. Basil requires medium-rich soil in partially shaded areas. Pinch off main shoots to make bushy growth. Basil also makes good edging plants.

Chives are hardy perennial that grows about 12 in. tall. It germinates slowly, but can be sown outdoors in the spring or the fall in medium rich soil. Chives increase rapidly by bulb division and should be split every few years.

Dill is a hardy annual that grows up to 3 ft tall. It germinates easily and will often self-sow the following season. Do not transplant plants. Instead, thin and weed around plants and stake after the plant reaches18 in. height. It grows best in fertile, sandy soil.

Garlic is a semi-hardy perennial that grows 1-2 ft tall. They should be planted in single cloves 2 in. deep in early spring in moist, rich soil. Soil should be hoed at intervals and harvested as soon as the leaves die in the fall. Garlic is a great companion plant and repels many insect pests.

Mint is a hardy perennial that grows 2-3 ft tall. There are many varieties of mint, but spearmint is the usual culinary variety. Apple mint and peppermint are the most popular varieties. Plant 6 in. pieces of the root in the spring or the fall at 2 in. deep in rich, moist soil in semi-shaded areas. Water plants thoroughly, to prevent spreading. It is recommended to sink 12 in. boards around the planted area for containment.

Oregano is a hardy perennial that grows 2-3 ft tall. Oregano looks similar to marjoram, but it is more pungent and spicy than marjoram.

Marjoram, also called wild marjoram, should be sown as seeds in the spring or the fall in medium-rich alkaline soil. It spreads rapidly.

Parsley is a semi-hardy biennial that grows up to 12 in tall. In cooler climates, it grows as an annual. Sow plants in spring or fall, in full sun or semi-shade, in medium-rich soil. Do not transplant. Parsley has slow germination and can be soaked to improve speed germination. Pinch out or clip new growth to produce bushier growth.

Rosemary is a tender perennial shrub that grows 2-6 ft tall. It is often grown for decorative, aromatic, and culinary purposes. It can be used for hedging, as well. It has very slow germination, so it is best to buy starters and propagate by cutting or layers. Rosemary needs sandy, alkaline soil and a sheltered, sunny growing area. Add chalk or lime to the soil around the plant regularly.

Sage is a hardy perennial that grows 2-3 ft tall. It is a small evergreen shrub with several varieties, including common or garden sage, which is generally used for cooking. Pineapple sage is a good aromatic, but is not good for cooking. It has easy germination and should be planted in moist, sunny soil. Do not grow near annuals, as sage inhibits their root growth.

Summer savory is an annual that grows 12-18 in. tall. It is a fine-leafed aromatic herb that spreads rapidly. Sow in medium-rich soil and allow four weeks for germination. Summer savory is generally preferred over winter savory

Tarragon is a hardy perennial that grows 2-3 ft tall. It does not seed, so it is best to buy starters or propagate from cuttings or layers. Plant in slightly sandy soil. French tarragon has a much better flavor than Russian tarragon.

Thyme is a hardy perennial that grows 4-10 in. tall. It grows slowly, so it is best to use starters and propagate by cutting and layers. Seeds can be sown in rows in the spring. Lemon and common or garden thyme are the most useful varieties for cooking. Plant in sandy soil with a small amount of lime added. Thyme produces fragrant purple blossoms which yield prized honey, as well.

Fragrant Herbs

Bergamot is a hardy perennial that grows 2-3 ft tall. It is a native American species that produces showy, fragrant flowers that are often used in potpourris. Use starters for planting, and propagate by root division. It spreads rapidly if not restricted.

Geranium is a tender perennial that grows 2-4 ft tall.

Lemon, rose, and peppermint scented varieties have highly fragrant leaves often used for potpourris and culinary flavorings. Use starters for planting, and propagate by stem cuttings, as seeds do not grow true to type. Plant in dry, sandy soil. Transplant and bring in at the start of winter.

Iris Florentina, also called White Flag, is a hardy perennial that grows 18-24 in. tall. The dried root, called orris root, makes a useful scent fixative for potpourris and sachets. Plant rhizomes horizontally with the topside just above the soil surface. It produces showy white flowers in early spring. Plants should be divided every few years due to rapid multiplication.

Lavender is a semi-hardy to hardy perennial that grows 1-3 feet tall. The fragrant flowers and leaves are used for potpourri and sachets. The seeds are slow to germinate, so it is best to propagate from cutting and layers. Plant in sandy, alkaline soil and fertilize with lime occasionally.

Lemon balm is a hardy perennial that grows 2-4 ft tall. It is highly fragrant and attractive to bees. Seeds are extremely slow germination, so it is best to use starters and propagate by splitting and cutting. Lemon balm grows best in sandy, semi-shaded soil.

Rose is a hardy perennial that grows 2-5 ft tall. The old varieties of cabbage, damask, dog, and apothecary's rose are the most fragrant. They are often used for potpourri, sachets, and medicinal purposes. To plant, use starters in a root-free, established bed in clayey soil that has been enriched with compost and manure.

Medical and Decorative Herbs

Chamomile is a hardy perennial that grows 4-15 in. tall. Roman chamomile is used for soothing, sleep-inducing teas, as well as hair conditioners and lightening. It is also used for headache relief. Propagate plants from seed or by root division. Chamomile thrives in well-drained soil.

Comfrey is a hardy perennial that grows 2-3 ft tall. It is rich in allantoin and vitamin B-12. It is renowned as a healing herb and is often steeped as tea. Plant in rich, moist soil in sun or semi-shade. Propagate by root cuttings or division.

Feverfew is a hardy perennial that grows 1-2.5 ft tall. It should be planted in rich, heavy soil in sun or semi-shade. Propagate by seed or root division in the spring. Infusions of this ornamental herb can be applied externally to insect bites and used as a repellant.

Wormwood is a hardy perennial that grows 2-4 in. tall. Propagate by root division or seeds sown in the fall. It creates a decorative contrast in any herb garden due to its silvery foliage. It received its name from when it was used to remedy worms. It is also an ingredient in absinthe.

VEGETABLES

Below is a list of vegetable crops to be considered for homestead gardens.

*Artichoke: common, Jerusalem
Asparagus
Beans: pole, lima, pinto, kidney, soybean, *yard-long, etc.
Beets
Broccoli
*Brussels sprouts
Cabbage: red, purple, green, etc.
Carrots: purple, orange, red, etc.
Cauliflower: white, green, orange, etc.
Chard, Swiss chard
Celery
*Celeriac

*Chinese cabbage, bok choy
Chrysanthemum (edible)
Coffee
Collard
Corn: sweet, white, multicolored, blue
Cucumbers
Eggplant
*Horseradish
Kale
Kohlrabi
*Leeks
Lettuce: romaine, iceberg, oak leaf, red, etc.
*Mushroom
New Zealand spinach
Okra
Onion: Vidalia, purple, green, etc.
Parsnips
Peas: snow, sugar snap, chick, cow/black-eyed, etc.
*Peanut
Peppers: bell (red, green, yellow, orange), jalapeno, chile (red, green), banana, cayenne
*Popcorn
Potatoes: redskin, gold, red, sweet, etc.
Purslane
Radish
Rhubarb
Rutabaga
*Salsify
*Scallion
Sorrel
Spinach: New Zealand variety is less common
Squash: summer (zucchini, yellow, patty pan), luffa, crenshaw, winter (butternut, buttercup, pumpkin, acorn, etc.)
*Sunflower
Swiss chard

*Tampala
Tomatillo
Tomato: heirloom varieties, cherry, Roma, etc.
Turnip
*Vegetable spaghetti
*Watercress

*Less common crops

Fruit

Below is a list of fruit crops to be considered for homestead gardens and orchards.

* Apples (Granny Smith, gala, grapple, etc.)
+* Banana (plantains, Lady Finger, etc.)
Blackberry
Blueberries
Cantaloupe
* Cherries (rainier, black, choke, tart, sour)
+* Citrus (orange, lemon, grapefruit, lime, etc.)
+* Coconut
Cranberries
Currant
Gooseberry
Grapes
Honeydew
Mulberry
Nectarines
* Pears (bartlett, canning, etc.)
Peaches
+* Pineapple
Plum
Pumpkin

Raspberries
Strawberries
Watermelon

*Require 3-5 years for edible production
+Require a tropical climate
*Grow in pairs for edible production.
Some varieties of fruit trees are also available as miniature trees

OTHER USEFUL PLANTS

Below is a list of useful plants to be considered for homestead gardens.

+Aloe Vera
Bamboo
*Catnip
+Cactus
Daisies
Gardenia
Geraniums
+Hibiscus
+Honeysuckle
Horseradish
*Hyssop: attracts bees
+Jasmine
Kudzoo
Marigolds
Marmalade
Nicotiana
+Passionflower
Petunias
+Poppy

Roses
Statice
Stock
*Stinging nettle
Summer savory
+Sunflower
Sweet Pea
Thornapple
Venus flytrap

*Attracts small beneficials
-Attracts aphids
+Edible (some part of the plant)

Average Crop Yield Chart

Crop	Yield lbs per row foot	lbs needed per adult	Row foot per adult	Rows per 4 ft wide bed	Bed ft length per adult
Potato	5	50	10	2	5
Asparagus	.25-.33	7	28-21	7	3-4
Beans: bush, snap	.8	8	10	2	5
Beans: pole	1.5	10	6.67	2	3.34
Beet: greens	.4	4	10	3	3.34
Beets	1	10	10	3	3.34
Broccoli	.75	15	20	2	10
Brussels sprouts	.6	5	8.34	2	4.17
Cabbage	1.5	12	8	2	4
Cantaloupe	1	10	10	1	10

Carrot	1	20	20	3	6.67
Cauliflower	.9	10	11.11	2	5.56
Chard	.75	6	8	4-5	1.6-2
Collard	.75	6	8	3	2.67
Corn	.96	30	31.25	2	15.63
Cucumber	1.2	10	8.34	1	8.34
Eggplant	.75	10	13.34	2	6.67
Kale	.75	5	6.67	2	3.34
Leek	1.5	6	4	3	1.34
Lettuce	.5	30	60	3-7	8.6-20
Onion	1	20	20	3	6.67
Parsnip	.75	10	13.34	3	4.45
Pea, English or shell	.2	5	25	3-4	8.34-6.25
Pea, snow	2	6	3	3-4	1.0-75
Pepper	.5	10	20	2	10
Rhubarb	.8-1.2	8-12	6.67-15	1	6.67-15
Spinach	.75	8	10.67	3	3.56
Squash, Summer	2	8	4	1	10
Squash, winter	2	20	10	1	15-3.34
Tomato	1.5	20	13.34	2	6.67

Companion Plant Influences

Species	Attracts	Repels/Inhibits	Common Companion Crops
Alliums (onions, leeks, garlic, scallions)		Aphids/peas	Roses, daffodils, tulips
Amaranth			Sweet corn
Apple			Chives, clover
Asparagus		Onion, garlic, gladiolus, asparagus beetle	Parsley, basil, tomato, nasturtium
Basil		Rue	Tomato, asparagus, nasturtium, pepper, and most other plants
Bean: bush		Onions, pole beans, marigolds, wormwood, fennel, garlic	Carrots, cabbage family, corn, cauliflower, beets, cucumber, celery, lettuce, peas (improves growth), spinach, strawberry, eggplant, mustard, potato, rosemary
Beet			Bush beans, cabbage, lettuce, onion, kohlrabi, lima beans, radish, celery
Borage			Tomato, squash, strawberry
Broccoli/ Cabbage		Tomato	Dill, celery, chamomile sage, beets, onions, potatoes, sage

Cabbage family		Dill, pole beans, strawberry, tomato	Sage(deters pests and improves growth), celery, beets, onion family, chamomile, spinach, chard, peas (improves growth), anise, beans, cucumber, tansy (deters cutworm and cabbage worm), bush beans, hyssop, mint, cabbage, rosemary, thyme
Carrots		Dill	Peas, onions, leeks, herbs, leaf lettuce, parsley, tomato, sage (deters rust/carrot flies, improves growth), beans, chives, bush beans, flax, rosemary, chervil (deters Japanese beetles), peas (improves growth), radish (deters disease, rust flies, cucumber beetles)
Catnip	Small beneficials	Catnip tea repels fleas and beetles	
Celery			Leeks, tomato, cauliflower, cabbage, bush beans, onion, spinach
Chamomile	Small beneficials		Onions, cabbage family
Chard			Cabbage
Chervil			Radish, lettuce, carrot, grape, rose, tomato
Chives			Carrot, tomato, apple, grape, rose

Clover			Apple
Collard		Tansy	
Corn			Onion, pole and bush beans, sunflower, radish, amaranth, squash, pumpkin, potato, peas (improves growth) snap or soybeans (improves growth), cucumber
Coriander			Anise
Cucumber		Sage, potato; deters cucumber beetle, rust flies, disease	Bush beans, cabbage family, corn, peas (improves growth), radish, dill, lettuce
Dill	Small beneficials	Carrot, tomato, cabbage	Cabbage, beets, lettuce, onion, cucumber
Eggplant	Potato bugs	Potato, pepper	Potato, 4 o'clock flowers, bush and pole beans, spinach
Fennel		Many species	Plant by itself
Flax			Carrot, potato
Garlic		Repels, aphids, Japanese beetles, mites, deer, rabbit; asparagus, bush and pole beans, peas	Roses, many vegetables
Grape		Deters Japanese beetles	Tansy, radish, nasturtium, hyssop, chives, chervil
Hyssop	Bees	Cabbage moth/ radish	Grapes, cabbage

Kohlrabi		Potatoes, beans	Onions, beets, cucumbers, cabbage family
Lettuce		Chrysanthemum	Carrot, cucumber, onion, radish, beet, chervil, dill, peas, bush and pole beans, strawberry
Marigold		Nematodes, Mexican bean beetles	Tomatoes, beans, potatoes
Mint			Cabbage, strawberry
Mustard			Beans
Nasturtium	Aphids	Squash bugs	Trap crop with cabbage family
Nicotiana	Potato bugs		potatoes
Onion		Asparagus, peas, bush and pole beans; with carrots, deters rust flies, nematodes	Beets, cabbage family, lettuce, tomato, dill, celery, cucumber, pepper, squash, strawberry, carrot
Orach		Potato	
Parsley	Small beneficials		Tomato, asparagus, carrot, rose
Peas		Garlic, onion, potato, wormwood	Carrot, corn, cucumber, potato, radish, turnip, lettuce, spinach, cabbage, bush and pole beans, peas, squash
Pepper		Potato, eggplant, tomato	4 o'clock flowers, onion
Pole Beans		Garlic, onion, beans, wormwood, cabbage, beets	Marigold, radish, carrot, corn, cucumber, eggplant, lettuce, peas, radish

Petunia		Mexican bean beetles	Beans
Potatoes		Deters Mexican bean beetles, Colorado potato beetle; Peppers, eggplant, pumpkin, cucumber, tomato, squash, sunflower, raspberry	Beans, corn, cabbage, eggplant, marigold, horseradish, flax, peas (improves growth), tansy
Pumpkin		Potato	Corn
Radish		Hyssop	Beets, carrot, spinach, squash, corn, peas (improves growth), chervil, cucumber, lettuce, pole and bush beans, grapes
Rose		Deters Japanese beetles	Parsley, garlic, chives, chervil
Rosemary			Cabbage, beans, carrots, sage
Rue		Japanese beetle	Inhibits many plants
Rutabaga/ Turnip			Peas (improves growth)
Sage		Deters cabbage moth, carrot flies; cucumber, rue	Cabbage family, carrot, broccoli, cauliflower, rosemary, strawberry, tomato, beets
Savory			Beans, onion, cabbage

Spinach			Strawberry, eggplant, celery, radish, cabbage, peas (improves growth), beans, tomato (improves growth, shade)
Squash		Deters rust flies, disease, cucumber beetle	Onion, corn, borage, tansy, nasturtium, radish
Stinging nettles	Small beneficials		Almost all plants beneficial
Strawberry		Cabbage; Deters aphids and ants when planted with mint, deters rust flies and disease when planted with borage or sage	Spinach, onion, lettuce, bush beans, mint, borage, sage
Sunflowers		Potato; Deters nitrogen-fixing bacteria/potatoes	Corn, cucumbers
Summer savory		Mexican bean beetle	Beans
Tansy		Collards	Cabbage, potato, squash, grape
Thornapple		Japanese beetle	Plant near grapes, roses, pumpkins

Thyme		When grown with tomato and cabbage, deters flea beetles, cabbage maggot, cabbage butter flies, Colorado potato beetle and cabbage worm	Cabbage family, tomato, borage
Tomato		Deters asparagus beetle; Fennel, potato, pepper, fill, corn, cabbage family	Roses, asparagus, gooseberry, basil, garlic, marigold, parsley, spinach, carrot, chives, sage, thyme, celery, onion

BERRIES

Blueberry and Huckleberry

Blueberries are native to North American and huckleberries are native to eastern North America. It is best to grow two varieties, but it is possible to yield a large crop from a single variety block. Their hardiness depends on the variety, but they usually do best in USDA zones 3 through 10. They grow best in full sun and can last eighty or more years. When planting, space plants the same distance as the expected height of the plant. Both plants propagate through softwood cuttings and can be difficult to root. The expected yield per plant is five to fifteen pounds.

Blueberry and huckleberry plants require acidic soil

with a pH of 4-5.5. Soil should be well-drained, but the plants can tolerate wet feet in the winter. If the natural pH is high, water the plant with 2 tbsp vinegar to 1 gal water. Blueberries are shallow-rooted, so do not cultivate deeply around the plants. Peat is an excellent addition to the soil. Plants should be well watered the first summer, and thereafter will need some moisture in arid (dry) summers. Light surface application of organic fertilizer or ammonium sulfate in spring is beneficial to the plants. Areas with alkaline or neutral soils should not only have peat added to the hole when planting, but should also have pine shavings added 1 ft deep and 3 ft wide, and blueberries should be planted higher. Be sure to keep plants well-watered, but do not over-mulch. More than 2-4 in. of mulch can suffocate the roots. When pruning, renew older branches to new shoots.

There is evidence that eating blueberries can reduce memory loss and possibly reduce the risk of cardiovascular disease. Cooked blueberries have greater levels of antioxidants than fresh berries. Among varieties testing high in antioxidants are Bluegold, Chandler, Darrow, Rubel, Elliott, and Maine wild blueberries.

These plants are well suited to edible landscaping because of their varied and beautiful appearance. Bronze new growth in spring is followed by pin-white, bell-shaped flowers. During summer, green leaves contrast with the blueberries. Leaves turn bright red or yellow in the fall. When the leaves drop, bright-colored red or yellow branches appear. The bushes can be used for hedges, screens, foundation plantings, accent shrubs, and espaliers. All blueberry varieties will thrive in a container. For best results mix 80% bark, 10% pumice, and 10% peat when utilizing container gardening.

Early ripening varieties include Earliblue, Bluecrop, Bluegold, Brunswick, Top Hat, Sharpblue, Spartan, Patriot, Misty, Polaris, and Reka. Mid-season ripening varieties include Chippewa, Emerald, Olympia, Rubel, Elizabeth, Blueray, Toro, Chandler, Hardyblue, Jellybean, Peach Sorbet, and Blueberry Glaze. Late-ripening varieties include pink lemonade, Darrow, Jersey, Legacy, Sunshine Blue, Liberty, Aurora, and Elliott.

Cranberry

Bogs are not required to grow cranberries, Vaccinium macrocarpon, but well-drained beds are a must. If natural drainage is not adequate, add peat or sand to plantings.

Cranberries are very high in antioxidants and are a great edible ornamental groundcover. Plants need very acidic soil and need to be well watered. If the temperature drops below 10 degrees Fahrenheit, plants require heavy mulch to protect the following year's fruiting wood.

When planting, space plants 1 ft apart in rows 2 ft apart. The evergreen foliage has a reddish cast with small, profuse flowers that are reddish pink. Cranberry plants are self-fertile and grow best in USDA zones 3 through 9.

Lingonberry

Lingonberry plants, *Vaccinium vitis-idaea*, are self-fertile, but having two varieties improves pollination. Plants reach an average height of 1 ft and should be spaced 1 ft apart in semi-shade or full sun in cool summer areas. Soil should be at a pH less than 5.8 and have good drainage. Be careful not to overwater plants. To improve the soil, mix well with peat. Plants should also be mulched with 3-4 in. of sawdust. The roots are shallow, so do not cultivate around the plants.

Berries are harvested in late fall, but plants take two years to produce their first fruit. Plants will yield an average of 0.5-1 lb per plant.

Extremely hardy plants can withstand arctic

temperatures, but in severe climates, the plants should be covered with sawdust or peat during the winter. They tend to grow well in USDA zones 3 through 8.

Strawberry

Strawberry plants are self-fertile, unless a specific variety notes otherwise. They are hardy up to -15 degrees Fahrenheit. Lipstick and Alpine varieties are hardy up to -30 degrees Fahrenheit. Plants should be planted in full sun, unless otherwise noted, and should be spaced 12 in. apart in rows 18 in. apart. Plants propagate through seeds or runners. The average plant lasts 2-3 years, but it is best to replant day-neutrals every two years. Alpine, Musk, and Lipstick varieties can last many years.

Strawberries are harvested June through July, with day-neutrals ripening June through early fall. The average plant will yield 0.5-1 lb per plant.

Soil should be rich, well-drained, and high in organic matter with a pH between 5 and 6. If the soil has poor drainage, plant on mounds. Plants may also be planted in planters, hanging baskets, as borders and groundcovers, and in raised beds. They are typically easy to grow for beginners.

Day-neutrals have additional requirements. They should be planted by April 15 in order to have a good crop the first year. Plants should be mulched with compost or manure and should be planted 1 ft apart. Remove the first blossoms and any runners during the first year. The pruning of runners will produce larger berries. Keep plants well-watered during arid summers and add soil amendments before planting. The first June crop will be light with small fruit. Crops from July through early fall will have heavy production.

Raspberries

Raspberry plants, *Rubus idaeus*, are self-pollinating and are hardy to at least -20 degrees Fahrenheit, depending on the variety. Ever-bearers are hardy in most areas of the Unites States if cut to the ground and mulched. Raspberries do best in USDA zones 5 through 9.

The average plant will reach a height of 4-6 ft, with Brazelberry and Strawberry Shortcake varieties on reaching heights of 2-3 ft. Raspberries should be planted in full sun, spaced 20 in. apart in rows 5 ft apart. It typically takes plants one to two years to reach bearing age. The fruitful life of plants vary from 1-15 years and should be replaced as they decline in productivity. Expect up to 2 lbs of fruit per row.

Soil should have a high amount of organic matter and good drainage. Plants cannot handle wet feet. In areas with poor drainage or consistently wet ground, plant on mounds 18 in. above water. Cascade Delight, Anne, and Autumn Britten varieties do better than others in wet sites. When planting, use well-rotted manure and fertilizer, adding more manure the following spring. Be sure to provide adequate moisture during the growing season.

When pruning July bearers, prune out second-year canes in the fall after they are done fruiting. Do not prune out new shoots because they will produce fruit the following year. Ever-bearers have specific pruning requirements. Caroline, Autumn Britten, Nantahala, and Rosanna Bear should be pruned on 1-2-year-old wood. Prune or mow the canes each winter to achieve freestanding fall crops, or prune similar to July bearers to produce a July and a fall crop.

Raspberries can be used for landscaping purposes as well. They make excellent hedges or fence rows and benefit from trellising. The colorful berries beautify landscapes and fruit salads. Three ever-bearing plants in a large pot do well on decks, as do potted dwarf Brazelberry and Strawberry Shortcake varieties.

Raspberries, as well as blueberries and black currants, contain especially high levels of antioxidants, which are known cancer-fighting agents. The Caroline variety contains about 50% more antioxidants than other varieties and is also 20-44% higher in beta-carotene, 27-43% higher in vitamin A, 16-77% higher in vitamin E, and 25-48% higher in vitamin C. The Meeker variety is the best source of ellagitannin-phytochemical, which is known to prevent cancer and inhibit the growth of cancer cells, and is found in naturally high quantities in raspberries. Black raspberries are rated 11% higher in antioxidants than blueberries and are rated very high in anthocyanin and vitamins A, C, E, and folic acid.

Planting and Planning Guide for Strawberries, Blueberries and Brambles

Type	Planting between Rows (ft)	Distance in the Rows (ft)	Planting Stock	Years from Planting to Economic Yield	Number of Bearing Years	Average Yield (lbs)
Strawberries						
Matted Rows	3.5- 4	1.5- 2	1 yr. runners	1	2-3	1 per row ft
Hill	4- 5	.5- 1	1 yr. runners	1	2-3	1.5/ plant
Blueberries						
High-bush	8- 10	4- 5	2 yr. plants	3	25+	6-8/ plant
Rabbit eye	10- 12	6- 8	2 yr. plants	4	30+	12-15/ plant

Bramble Blackberries						
Erect	8- 12	2-6	Root pcs.	3	10-12	1.5/row ft
Trail-ing	8- 12	6-8	Root Cane tips	2	5-10	9/plant
Raspberries						
Red	8-10	2-4	1 yr. suckers (virus free)	3	10-12	1.5/row ft
Black	8-10	3-4	Rooted Cane tips (virus free)	3	3-4	1.5/ plant

HIGHLY NUTRITIOUS GARDEN CROPS

Allium species

Spanish Roja garlic is a good source of allicin, which reduces the risk of cancer and cardiovascular disease. It is a hardneck garlic that is intense and spicy.

Southport Red Globe onion is an heirloom variety that keeps very well and provides anthocyanins and quercetin. Anthocyanins may have antidiabetic, anticancer, anti-inflammatory, antimicrobial, and anti-obesity effects, and it may help prevent cardiovascular diseases. Quercetin may help reduce the risk of heart disease and cancer.

Bonilla shallot provides more antioxidants than onions. They can be grown from seeds and harvested in the same year.

Apples

Akane apples are rich in phytonutrients. The Japanese variety is disease resistant and a great blend of sweet and tart.

Bramley's seedling apples have 3-4 times more antioxidants than many other varieties and are resistant to scabs and mildew. They are a large, late-season variety.

Liberty Spy apples have 2-3 times more phytonutrients than many other varieties. They are scab- and fire-blight resistant and produce a balanced blend of sweet and tart.

Northern Spy apples are 19th-century heirloom variety. They have nutritious skin and flesh, and they keep well and are great for pies.

Asparagus

Jersey Knight asparagus is healthier and more nutritious than other varieties.

Purple Passion asparagus is rich in anthocyanins. For max sweetness and health benefits, it should be eaten within one day of harvest.

Berries

Wild-Treasure blackberry has high antioxidant activity. It is a prolific, thornless blackberry that is tart and sweet. It is a cross between a trailing and an upright domestic variety.

Elliott blueberry has more anthocyanins than most other varieties. It is a large, late-season variety that is very flavorful.

Rancocas blueberry is a flavorful, medium-sized berry that is rich in anthocyanins.

Rubel blueberry is one of the most nutritious blueberries. It is smaller than other varieties and is an intensely flavored, semi-wild blueberry.

Caroline raspberry contains almost as many cancer-fighting antioxidants as the average blueberry. It is disease resistant and ripens in June and again in August. It is preferred by most chefs.

Ovation strawberry has two times the antioxidants of other varieties. It is larger than the Sweet Charlie variety and is late maturing, which extends the harvest season.

Sweet Charlie strawberry is higher in antioxidants than most varieties. It has a mid-season harvest.

Carrots

Deep Purple carrots are the richest in anthocyanins of all purple carrots. They are purple throughout. They are often served with orange carrots for contrast.

Comic Purple carrots are sweet and extra-nutritious. They are purple with an orange core.

Purple Haze carrots are a Nantes-type carrot, almost perfectly cylindrical. They are purple with an orange core.

Corn

Ruby Queen corn is super-sweet. It is a red variety that produces anthocyanins.

Crucifers

Packman broccoli is extra nutritious. It is a green variety whose seeds and starters are widely available. After harvest, it should be kept cold and consumed within 24 hrs to maximize health benefits.

Purple Sprouting broccoli is rich in anthocyanins

and cancer-fighting compounds. Small heads that are picked will regrow for months.

Graffiti cauliflower is a purple, large-head variety that is rich in anthocyanins and cancer-fighting glucosinolates. It should always be eaten raw or lightly steamed.

Grapes

Concord grapes are a blue grape that may lower blood pressure and enhance memory in people with early-stage dementia. A seedless variety is available.

Glenora grapes are a black, seedless grape that is rich in anthocyanins and ripens early.

Salad Greens

The top ten varieties of salad greens for high nutrition are Blackjack, Concorde, Concept, The Marvel of Four Seasons, Lollo Rosso, Merlot, Prizehead, Radicchio di Treviso, red iceberg, and red oakleaf. The most healthful choices are red loose-leaf, followed by green loose-leaf with a brown or reddish fringe.

Herbs for Tea

The seed of the anise plant is the source of flavoring for most licorice candy as well as many baked goods. It was known to the Egyptians and used to treat digestive disorders and toothaches. In the Middle Ages, the seeds were coated with sugar and taken after meals. Today, they are used to sweeten both tea and breath.

Basil became well-known during the 80s when pesto became popular. It is also used in tea. It contributes savory notes that blend well with other herbs. It is an annual member of the mint family that is easy to grow when planted in a sunny spot with moist, rich soil. The cinnamon and lemon varieties are best in teas.

Cardamon is a member of the ginger family. It contributes pungent notes to many teas, especially chai. Each yellow-green pod contains about twenty brown seeds. Some recipes will call for whole pods and others just seeds. It is also used to make perfume in Europe. It has also been used in digestive medicines for centuries. It figures significantly in both Scandinavian and Indian recipes. Indians call it the "Queen of Spices."

Catnip, the same herb that sends felines into comedic spasms of joy, can also be used by humans to assist digestion, and it is gently calming. It can even be used in children's tea. It is easily grown at home, but like other mint family members, it may need to be contained.

Chamomile is one of the most common tea herbs and has two main species: German (*Chamomilla recutita*) and Roman (*Chameamelum nobile*). Flowers of the German variety are annual, and are most often used for tea, because the Roman variety has a more bitter taste. It is a bright, daisy-like flower that has a light, floral taste. It has antispasmodic and mildly sedative qualities, which make it a sovereign remedy for stomach upsets due to nervousness. Those who are allergic to ragweed pollen are often also allergic to the related chamomile.

Cinnamon is native to Sri Lanka, India, and Southeast Asia. It is now cultivated throughout the tropics. The inner bark of an evergreen, it comes in dried sticks, chips, or ground. For teas, buy cinnamon sticks and crush them prior to use for a fresher flavor. Using the ground herb can yield a muddy, over-spiced tea.

Clove is an aromatic evergreen tree native to Indonesia; its unopened flower buds are dried to make the familiar, brown, peg-shaped spice that flavors pumpkin pies and other holiday recipes. Like cinnamon, it should be purchased whole and then coarsely crushed for tea. Cloves are strong, and only a small amount is needed in tea. Some people are allergic to cloves or find the flavor and smell irritating.

Dandelion root, the same long, tenacious taproot that is considered a weed, is also esteemed by herbalists as a diuretic and a general cleansing herb. Roasted, it has an earthy flavor that makes it a good coffee substitute. To roast, scrub the root well and roast at 200 degrees Fahrenheit for about 4 hours or until dark brown throughout. Grind and brew as a coffee.

Echinacea is one of the most popular herbal remedies to stimulate the immune system's defenses against colds and infections. There are two echinacea species: *E. angustifolia* and *E. purpurea.* Each one produces a root with a multitude of beneficial chemical components. Both varieties of bright purple wildflowers can be grown at home, but as the root takes up to four years to develop, many gardeners choose to simply enjoy the flower's looks and purchase echinacea root for tea.

Fennel is a relative of the same bulb used as a vegetable in Mediterranean cooking, it produces small, light green, ridged seeds that are good for digestion. The flavor is akin to basil and anise, but warmer. It is commonly used in sausage, curries, and pickling. Indian cooks sometimes candy the seeds to chew after a meal.

Ginger root is native to tropical Asia, it is now cultivated in the West Indies. It is a lumpy, brown root that gives a tangy bite to foods and beverages like stir-fries, ramen, gingersnaps, and ginger ale. It can be used fresh or dried. It is effective against upset stomachs due to indigestion, morning sickness, and travel sickness. The dried, chopped roots are used for tea and can be prepared in single-servings. Fresh root in roughly the same quantity can be used for a more intense flavor.

Hawthorn is a small tree or shrub whose berries and glowing tops have gained wide use both in the west and in Chinese herbalism as cardiac medicines. It is high in bioflavonoids and antioxidants. In the United States, hawthorns are extensively grown as ornamentals.

Hibiscus flower gives tea a tart flavor and bright reddish color. The leaves and seeds are also edible. It is rich in vitamin C and mildly antibacterial. It is often combined with rose hip, which is high in antioxidants.

Lemon balm leaves have a lemon scent. Fresh leaves are more flavorful than dried ones. The plant is easy to grow in moist soil and full sun. It is currently the focus of research for its antiviral properties. It is also a mood lifter, wound healer, and toothache soother.

Lemon verbena is a shrub that grows well in southern climates, but must be pampered in northern climates. It is native to South America, and it gives off a stronger, sweeter smell than lemon balm

Lemon and orange zest and peel can also be used for teas. Scrape off the colored part of a citrus peel with a grater, potato peeler, or zester to produce zest. Zest can be added to fresh teas, or dried and chop coarsely to add to dried tea blends. Other citrus peels, such as lime, tangerine, and grapefruit, can also be used in teas, but most are very astringent and tart and should be used sparingly.

Licorice root contains a substance that is 50 times sweeter than sugar. It has anti-inflammatory qualities that can be used to relieve upset stomachs from ulcers. Pregnant women and those with high blood pressure or heart or liver disease should not use this because it raises blood pressure and can decrease platelet aggregation.

Peppermint and spearmint are cooling and sweet. These herbs form the basis for many digestive teas. They can be added in smaller quantities to any tea for flavor and garnish. If growing at home, containment is advised.

Rose petals and rose hips are popular components of

many teas. Rose petals imbue tea with a soft, floral scent and a faintly sweet taste. Use only unsprayed petals or buy certified organic petals. Rosehips have high levels of vitamin C and are often combined with hibiscus flowers for a rosy-colored tea.

Rosemary gives a clean, refreshing, piney scent and flavor. It is believed to improve concentration and memory. Aromatherapists use it to ease stress and lift mild depression.

Sage and pineapple sage are two different species of mint. Garden sage is ubiquitous in turkey stuffing. Pineapple sage is a red-flowered, fruity-flavored herb that is often used in iced tea. Garden sage is valued as a remedy for sore throats and poor digestion, but it also makes a mineral-packed tea.

Scented geranium, *Pelargonium*, is related to the familiar, big-flowered bedding plants, pelargonium. It has modest, delicate blooms. It is highly scented with a wide variety of fragrances. Fresh leaves of various rose, mint, or citrus-scented cultivars are flavorful and fragrant when added to tea.

Siberian ginseng is not a true ginseng, but *Eleuthero senticossus* is a ginseng-like plant native to eastern Russia, China, Korea, and Japan. Herbalists use it to improve both physical and mental stamina. It is also thought to stimulate the immune system.

American skullcap, *Scutellaria lateriflora*, leaves, stems, and flowers can be used in teas to help calm nervous tension. In Chinese medicine, Baikal skullcap, *Scutellaria baicalensis*, or Huang qin is more commonly used.

Star anise is an eight-pointed, woody fruit from an evergreen native to China, India, and Vietnam. In China, it is known as eight-horned fennel, and it is used in five-spice powder. It has a pungent flavor that mixes well with chai.

Stevia is a tender, easy-to-grow member of the

verbena family. It can be grown as a house plant. It is used in teas because of its sweetness. It is eight times sweeter than sugar, and in powder form can be even more so.

Common thyme and lemon-scented thyme lend a pungent aromatic flavor to tea. Common thyme is more medicinal tasting. The essential oil from thyme is strongly antibacterial. Herbalists recommend teas with thyme for colds and coughs. It is easy to grow with lots of sun and excellent drainage.

Vanilla, Spanish for "little pod," is extracted by soaking vanilla beans, bruised or chopped, in alcohol. Vanilla varieties high in vanillin have antioxidants, as well as anti-cancer, anti-inflammatory, and neuroprotective properties.

Wintergreen's familiar flavor is found in candies and gum, as well as tea. It is a creeping, evergreen shrub native to North America, and is a popular herbal remedy of Native Americans. It was a common substitute for tea during the American Revolution. Today, it is mainly used for flavor and digestive benefits. It should not be consumed by anyone allergic or sensitive to aspirin.

PERENNIAL FOOD PLANTS

Vegetables

Jerusalem Artichokes (*Helianthus tuberosus*)
Scarlet runner beans (*Phaseolus coccineous*)
Radicchio (*Cichorium intybus*)
Early purple sprouting broccoli (*Brassica oleracea* var. italica)
Rhubarb (*Rheum rhabarbarum*)
Asparagus (*Asparagus officinalis*)

Fruits

Alpine strawberries (*Fragaria vesca*)
Raspberries (*Rubus idaeus*)

Herbs and Aromatics

Shallots (*Allium cepa* var. aggregatum)
Garlic chives (*Allium tuberosum*)
Bronze fennel (*Foeniculum vulgare* 'Rubrum')
German thyme (*Thymus vaulgaris*)
Sorrel (*Rumex acetosa*)
Spearmint (*Mentha spicata*)

Medicinal Herbs

Peppermint (*Mentha x piperita*)
Echinacea (*Echinacea angustifolia*)
Yarrow (*Achillea millefolium*)
German chamomile (*Matricaria chamomilla*)
Oregon grape root (*Berberis aquifolium*)
Goldenseal (*Hydrastis canadensis*)
Passion flower (*Passiflora incarnata*)
Lemon balm (*Melissa officinalis*)
American ginseng (*Panax quinquefolius*)
Blue vervain (*Verbena hastata*)

EDIBLE WILD PLANTS AND HERBS

Dandelion, *Taraxacum officinale*, is rich in vitamin E, calcium, iron, and potassium. It is native to the Mediterranean.

Red clover, *Trifolium pratense*, is known to be a

favorite of bees. It is edible, but may cause bloating and upset stomach.

Sheep sorrel, *Rumex acetosella*, is a grassy-looking herb with rust-colored tips and leaves. It has a tart, citrus taste.

Purslane, *Portulaca oleracea*, is rich in fatty acids. It has paddle-shaped leaves and rubbery pink stems. It has an oily texture with a crisp, faintly lemony flavor.

Acorns, the fruit of the oak tree, should only be eaten either cooked or roasted and can be made into flour.

Camas bulbs, *Camassia quamash*, can be eaten fresh, boiled, or roasted, or they can be dried and stored.

Wapato, *Sagittaria latifolia*, is an aquatic tuber that is also used for environmental cleanup work due to its ability to absorb heavy metals.

Huckleberry, *Vaccinum spp.*, can be tart or sweet, depending on their color, and tend to have a mild flavor.

Salal berry, *Gaultheria shallon*, ripens in late summer. They are a dull blue-black and are slightly hairy.

Pineapple weed, *Matricaria matricarioides*, also called wild chamomile, has a tropical fruity aroma that gets stronger with touch, i.e., scratch and sniff.

Lemon balm, *Melissa officinalis*, is known for its anti-anxiety effects. It has a citrus flavor and can be dried to be used in tea. It is part of the mint family, and is antimicrobial and acts as a mild sedative.

Plantain, *Plantago major*, has hairless leaves with coarse, stringy parallel veins on the underside. It can be eaten, as well as chewed and placed on bug bites to stop itching or to draw out a splinter. The seed can be used in tea as a laxative.

Wild carrot, *Daucus carota*, also called Queen Anne's Lace, has a stem that is very hairy, even stubbly, lending itself to the saying "Queen Anne forgot to shave her legs." It looks very similar to poison hemlock.

Wild Rose, *Rosa nutkana*, has five pink petals with a

bright yellow center.

Ground ivy, *Glecoma hederacea*, has a pungent mint flavor suitable for tea.

Miner's lettuce, *Claytonia perfoliate*, can be eaten as a salad green.

Chickweed, *Stellaria media*, can be eaten cooked or raw. The whole plant is edible, with the exception of the roots.

Stinging nettle, *Urtica dioica*, grows in partial shade in moist forest habitats. It tastes like spinach and is full of fatty acids, iron, calcium, potassium, and vitamins A, C, and D. It can contain up to 25% protein. It has a humid green tea-like smell resembling a mint plant. The fibers in the outer layer of the stem make sturdy cordage. The leaves are brewed as tea, it creates an astringent hair rinse to treat dandruff. The above-ground portion of the plant can also be steeped in alcohol to make an extract to treat allergies, which can be taken regularly.

Elderberry, *Sambucus racemosa*, has leaves in groups of 5-9 leaflets and flowers that grow in disc-like clusters with tiny, star-shaped blossoms. There are forty ornamental varieties. An elderberry extract, made from the flowers and berries, can be used to treat cold and flu symptoms. The leaves and twigs contain compounds that produce cyanide and should not be used. All parts of the plant are potentially toxic, with the exception of the flowers and fruits. Black, blue, and red are the most common varieties.

Black elderberry, *Sambucus nigra*, grows up to 19 ft tall with black fruit. It is used for jams, syrups, and wine.

Blue elderberry, *Sambucus cerulea*, grows up to 40 ft tall in dry, open habitats with dark blue berries. It is used for jams, syrups, and wine.

Red Elderberry, *Sambucus racemose*, are prolific in forests, meadows, and stream banks in the pacific northwest. It has red or orange berries, which must be cooked to neutralize the toxins they contain.

Hazelnut, *Corylus cornuta*, is rich in monounsaturated fat, vitamin E, copper, and magnesium.

Red huckleberry, *Vaccinium parvifolium*, is quite tart, but often used in jams, jellies, and wines.

Burdock, *Arctium minus*, has large, fuzzy, ruffled leaves shaped like elephant ears which are attached to smooth, thick, purple stalks that grow in a rosette shape from the root. Plants live 2-3 years. Once the stalks grow tall, the roots become too woody to eat and grow as deep as 3 ft.

Pine trees, *Pinus ponderosa*, have needles that can be steeped into tea. The needles grow in clusters of three. The ponderosa bark smells faintly of vanilla.

Cleavers, *Galium aparine*, also called bedstraw, has a texture that makes it challenging to chew. It is more commonly used as a tea, which tastes like cucumber water when cold. It can also be used as a tincture as an anti-inflammatory, antiviral, or antimicrobial action for swollen lymph glands. The leaves resemble star-on-a-string.

Bull thistle, *Cirsium vulgare*, has a stalk, midrib of the leaf that is celery-like in texture but less stringy. The roots are all edible, but it is an extremely thorny plant.

Yarrow, *Achillea millefolium*, can be drank as a tea to combat a cold or rubbed on the skin as an insect repellent. The leaves and flowers can be applied topically to stop bleeding and pain.

Jewel weed, *Impatiens capensis*, is an orange flowering herb that has leaves and stems which can be split and rubbed on skin exposed to poison ivy or poison oak to prevent a rash.

Chestnuts, *Castanea spp.*, have husks that are green with thin, sharp, prickly spikes. They are best when roasted, but can be boiled as well. Always remove the husk, or hull, before eating.

Horse chestnuts, *Aesculus hippocastanum*, are toxic

and only become edible after being leached. The husk is thicker, with wider-spaced spikes, like a medieval mace, than regular chestnuts. They are good for making soap and laundry detergent, due to the saponins they contain. Saponins are soap-like compounds.

Hawthorn, *Crataegus sp.*, has more than 200 species, which are all edible. Hawthorn, rose and apple, are all related in the rose family. The berries and leaves are edible. The berries are full of antioxidants. Extracts made from berries are used to strengthen the heart, lower blood pressure, and steady arrhythmias.

Yellow dock, *Rumex crispus*, is a common weed with long, smooth, arrow-shaped leaves that are flecked with purple splotches. The leaves are edible raw or boiled, and are high in vitamin C and zinc. The roots can be boiled and used as a detoxifying tea. Root extracts are used as an iron supplement and/or for chelation and removing heavy metals from the body. It contains oxalic acid, which can bind with calcium and prevent absorption. This is normally only an issue when consumed in large quantities or for those with kidney disease.

Mallow leaves, *Malva neglecta*, can be combined with other ingredients to make a tea with a thick, creamy texture.

Sumac fruit, *Rhus typhina*, is scarlet and oblong. They stay colorful throughout the winter and are high in vitamin C, potassium, calcium, and antioxidants. They may also be dried and ground up to be used as a spice in Middle Eastern cuisine. The red fruit grows in clusters.

Poison sumac, *Rhus vernix*, is toxic. Its white berries grow in clusters.

Cattail, *Typha latifolia*, grows in marshy areas and roadside ditches. It looks like a reed, with the top resembling a hotdog on a stick. The entire plant is edible, from the shoots in early spring to the powdery pollen in later summer, to the starchy rhizomes in winter. It is known to absorb pollutants. The leaves can be used for weaving.

Oregon grape, *Mahonia aquifolium*, has herbal antibiotic and antiviral properties. It is used internally and externally to treat strep throat, pneumonia, staph infections, pink eye, gonorrhea, and syphilis, as well as infections caused by *E. coli* and *Giardia*. It is also a liver stimulant. The plant has shiny leaves like holly and bright yellow blossoms, and is often found in conifer forests. Medicinal compounds are concentrated in the blue berries and the roots. The roots contain berberine, a bright yellow antibiotic. It reproduces via seeds in berries and horizontal shoots.

Meadowsweet, *Spiraea ulmaria*, contains salicin, which is what aspirin was originally made from.

Opium poppies, *Papaver somniferum*, are used in traditional Chinese Medicine. Morphine and codeine are derived from the milky white fluid harvested when the stem is cut.

Beard lichen, *Usnea lichen*, is used as a tincture for pneumonia.

California poppy, *Eschscholzia Californica*, is used as a tincture for insomnia.

Redroot, *Ceanothus velutinus*, is a leafy plant that can be eaten cooked or raw. Every part of the plant is edible, but should be harvested when the leaves are young because older leaves become bitter.

Osha root, *Ligusticum porter*, can be brewed as a tea, crushed into a powder, or drank as a tincture to boost immunity.

Western red cedar, *Thuja plicata*, has wood and leaves which do not rot, giving it multiple uses and making it one of the most important trees, especially in the pacific northwest. As a medicinal plant, it is a topical antifungal. Brew a strong tea from the leaves to use in foot baths. Essential oils can also be extracted for use.

Bleeding heart, *Dicentra formosa*, is a dangerous

plant due to its narcotic properties. It has delicate, bell-shaped pink flowers.

Comfrey, *Symphytum officinale*, is a common weed from the borage family which helps the skin regenerate very quickly. It is used topically to heal scrapes, burns, and cuts. The wound must be disinfected prior to application.

Great mullein, *Verbascum thapsus*, has a cooling, fluffy, smooth texture with a nutty taste. It is called the "Swiss army knife of plants." The leaves can also be dried and smoked, or brewed as tea for lung medicine. The flowers can be infused into oil and used as a remedy for ear infections. The roots can be pounded and used as soap or tossed into still water as a fish poison. The stalk can be used as a spindle to make a friction fire.

Russian sage, *Perovskia atriplicifolia*, is a menthol-flavored ornamental plant native to Pakistan which contains thujone, one constituent in absinthe.

Vanilla leaf, *Achlys triphylla*, is used for vanilla flavoring.

Pokeweed, *Phytolacca americana*, also called poke sallet, is being studied as a treatment for leukemia. The fermented juice of pokeberries makes a dark, purple-red stain. This type of stain was used to write The Constitution.

Bittersweet vine, *Solanum dulcumara*, is extremely poisonous to eat, but also contains anti-cancer compounds. The stem can be used to treat skin conditions and the leaves, fruit, and root have been used to treat warts and tumors and to relieve fever and nausea.

Cottonwood tree, *Populus balsamifera*, aka Balsam Poplar or Balm of Gilead, should be harvested in late winter and early spring when the bright orange-red buds are sticky with resin. They have antibacterial and anti-inflammatory properties and can be infused in olive oil and mixed with melted beeswax to create an antiseptic salve for cuts and burns.

Amaranth seeds, *Amaranthus spp.*, contain 15%

protein.

Goosefoots, *Chenopodium spp.*, is a close relative of amaranth. It is also called lamb's quarters. The leaves can be eaten raw or cooked in small quantities. Large quantities of the leaves or seeds can be harmful.

Magnolia buds, *Magnolia grandiflora*, are very fragrant. They can be inhaled via steam as a remedy for sinus issues.

Bittercress, *Cardamine oligosperma*, is a type of mustard green.

Cat's ear, *Hypochaeris radicata*, is identical to dandelion, except for its hairy leaves and multiple blossoms branching off a single stem. The leaves and root are edible.

Kudzu vine, *Pueraria lobata*, makes excellent weaving material for baskets. In traditional Chinese medicine, it is used to treat alcoholism, vertigo, and tinnitus. The flowers can be made into jelly. Its starchy roots are used in Vietnamese and Chinese cuisine.

Honey locust tree, *Gleditsia triacanthos*, have flat, black seedpods which contain sweet, gooey, golden pulp that tastes similar to a fig.

Horsetail, *Equisetum arvense*, is about 3 ft tall and very thin. It drops spores for reproduction. The stalk has a sandpaper texture which can be used to file nails or scour dishes.

Wild cherry bark, *Prunus avium*, can be used as a cough remedy.

Indian tobacco, *Lobelia inflata*, is used as an anti-asthma treatment.

Mugwort, *Artemisia vulgaris*, is used as a digestive stimulant. It is also used to bring on delayed menstruation.

10 Pollen-Rich Flowers for Gardens

Alyssum spreads along the ground and produces hundreds of tiny flowers which bloom all season. Combine the purple and pink varieties with eggplants, purple varieties of basil, bush beans, lettuce, and sprouting broccoli. White varieties will give a frilly, pleasant aesthetic setting for the stiff, dark kale, chard, bok choy, and red-leafed beets. It also fills in nicely between chives, leeks, onions, and shallots.

Orange, yellow, and apricot calendula flowers brighten cool-season vegetable beds filled with beets, broccoli, bush peas, cabbage, carrots, collards, lettuce, kale, and parsnips. Tall heirloom varieties grow up to 18 in. and are less prone to mildew than the 6 in. dwarf varieties. Calendula petals can be collected for use in tea and natural body care products.

Coreopsis is a perennial native to North American prairies. It furnishes a season full of sunny yellow flowers that are held well above its foliage. It works well planted near the edges of trellises built for beans, cucumbers, and tomatoes. The native variety, *Coreopsis grandiflora*, should be staked. Shorter varieties work well with basil, endive, eggplants, kale, peppers, and other short edibles in a smaller area.

There are two common types of cosmos. *Cosmos bipinnatus* is the familiar pink and white variety, often found in the old-time 'Sensation' mix. *Cosmos sulphureus* comes in orange, red, and yellow. Both attract beneficials. When the flowers are allowed to go to seed, they attract yellow finches. Combine 4 in. tall 'Sensation' cosmos with artichokes and cardoons. Plant the 2-3 ft tall *C. sulphureus* varieties, such as 'Diablo', in front of tomatoes and okra and next to trellises of cucumbers and beans.

Echinacea is a native plant prized for its healing

properties. It is also a favorite with bees. It is a perennial that forms clumps of upright leaves of pink-purple, daisy-like blooms off and on all summer. It can grow up to 4 ft and comes in numerous varieties. Plant at the end of mixed vegetable and herb beds, and combine it with tall herbs, such as dill, fennel, lovage, and sage.

Marigolds are annual flowers that come in shades of yellow, orange, and reddish-brown. They bloom from spring through fall. Tall, older varieties grow up to 4 ft and work best in front of trellises of tomatoes, beans, cucumbers, and other climbers. Dwarf marigold varieties range from 6 to18 in. and are ideal for creating a compact flowering hedge to border a bed of bush beans or peppers, for interspersing among kales and other greens, or bordering squash. Gem series marigolds have fine, citrus-smelling foliage and edible flowers.

Stately sages, such as 'Victoria' and other non-edible natives bear spikes of either red or blue flowers that are especially enticing to bees and hummingbirds. Varieties range from 18 in. to 3 ft. Some are perennials if grown in growing zones 5 through 8. Some native sages common to home gardens are often treated as annuals. Interplant them with okra, tall pepper varieties, and shorter tomato varieties.

Sunflowers are cheerful, towering plants that attract many beneficials, and several varieties offer edible seeds. Some varieties reach 8 ft and pair well with corn or a planting of large winter squash. Dwarf varieties can be used behind large zucchini plants, a bed of bush beans, or soybeans. Avoid varieties that have been bred to produce little to no pollen.

Violas are an edible, cool-season annual flower. Colors include purples, blues, and yellows. Their whiskered, up-facing, flat blooms make perfect fillers among members of the cabbage family. They also accent a geometric bed of lettuce and shine in colorful containers.

Zinnias attract butterflies and are suitable for almost any vegetable combination. Dwarf 'Mexican' varieties pair well with chiles. Tall, pastel varieties pair well with artichokes, brussels sprouts, or fennel. Edge an edamame bed with mixed dwarf varieties and combine petite varieties in a large container with a mix of basil.

GARDENING IN LIMITED SPACE

For those who would like to become engaged in gardening but do not have a large space to grow a traditional garden, it is still possible to begin raising small crops in a small space.

Crops that tend to do well in windowsill gardens include carrots, radishes, cress, spinach, lettuce, tomatoes, mustard, and zucchini. These also do well in balcony, rooftop, and window box gardens, as well as beans, peppers, broccoli, potatoes, brussels sprouts, squash, cabbage, corn, turnips and other roots, and cucumbers. Plants that do well indoors, under grow lights include beets, cucumbers, carrots, endive, celery, onion, Chinese cabbage, radishes, and watercress.

Many vegetables also do well when grown in containers. Below is a list of common container garden vegetables and how they are best grown.

Bush beans should be planted in a container with a capacity of at least 2 gallons. Plant up to six plants in a large container at 2-3 in. apart.

Pole beans should be planted in a container with a capacity of at least 4 gallons. Plant up to six plants per container.

Beets should be planted in a container with a capacity of at least 1 pint. Plants two to three plants in a large container at 2 in. apart.

Broccoli should be planted in a container with a capacity of at least 5 gallons. Plant only one plant per container.

Brussels sprouts should be planted in a container with a capacity of at least 5 gallons. Plant only one plant per container.

Cabbage should be planted in a container with a capacity of at least 5 gallons. Plant 1-2 plants per container at 12 in. apart.

Chinese cabbage should be planted in a container with a capacity of at least 1 gallon. Plant only one plant per container.

Carrots should be planted in a container with a capacity of at least 1 pint. Plant three to four plants in a large container at 1-2 in. apart.

Corn should be planted in a container with a capacity of at least 10 gallons. Plant four plants at a minimum of 4 in. apart. Twelve plants in total should be grown in multiple containers for pollination.

Cucumbers should be planted in a container with a capacity of at least 5 gallons. Plant two plants per container and train vertically.

Eggplant should be planted in a container with a capacity of at least 5 gallons. Plant only one plant per container.

Kale should be planted in a container with a capacity of at least 5 gallons. Plant three to four plants in a large container at 16 in. apart.

Lettuce should be planted in a container with a capacity of at least 0.5 gallons. Plant 1-2 plants in a large container at 10 in. apart.

Mustard greens should be planted in a container with a capacity of at least1 pint. Plant 1-2 plants in a large container at 4 in. apart.

New Zealand spinach should be planted in a container

with a capacity of at least 2 gallons. Plant only one plant per container, ideally in a hanging basket.

Onions should be planted in a container with a capacity of at least 0.5 gallons. Plant sixteen green onions at 2-3 in. apart. For full-sized onions use a large container.

Peppers should be planted in a container with a capacity of at least 2 gallons. Plant only one plant per container.

Radishes should be planted in a container with a capacity of at least 1 pint. Plant four to five plants in a large container at 1 in. apart.

Spinach should be planted in a container with a capacity of at least 1 pint. Plant 1-2 plants in a large container at 5 in. apart.

Summer squash and zucchini should be planted in a container with a capacity of at least 5 gallons. Plant only one plant per container.

Swiss chard should be planted in a container with a capacity of at least 3.5 gallons. Plant four to five plants in a large container at 8 in. apart.

Standard tomatoes should be planted in a container with a capacity of at least 1.5 quarts. Plant only one plant per container.

Dwarf tomatoes should be planted in a container with a capacity of at least 5 gallons. Plant only one plant per container.

NATURAL PEST CONTROL IN GARDENS

Many common garden plants can act as natural forms of pest control, either encouraging good insects or repelling harmful insects and diseases. Carefully choosing companion plants can provide a healthier overall garden that requires less intervention by the grower.

Attracting Beneficial Insects

Bees are attracted by bee balm, borage, and summer savory.

Hoverflies are attracted by buckwheat, German chamomile, dill, parsley, and morning glory.

Ladybugs are attracted by yarrow.

Predatory ground beetles are attracted by lovage and amaranth.

Predatory wasps are attracted by anise, borage, dill, German chamomile, and yarrow.

Detering Pests and Harmful Insects

Aphids are deterred by anise, catnip, chervil, coriander, dill, garlic, mint, peppermint, yellow nasturtium, petunias, and sunflower.

Ants are deterred by catnip, mint, tansy, and pennyroyal.

Asparagus beetles are deterred by parsley, petunia, and pot marigold.

Bean beetles are deterred by rosemary, tomato, and summer savory.

Black flea beetles are deterred by sage, catnip, and wormwood.

Blister beetles are deterred by horseradish.

Cabbage moths are deterred by hyssop, peppermint, rosemary, and sage summer savory.

Cabbage worms are deterred by borage and thyme.

Carrot rust flies are deterred by rosemary, salsify, wormwood, and sage.

Codling moths are deterred by garlic and mint.

Colorado potato bugs are deterred by flax, horseradish, and eggplant.

Corn borers are deterred by radish.

Cucumber beetles are deterred by nasturtium and radish.

Flea beetles are deterred by catnip, hyssop, mint, and peppermint.

Fleas are deterred by lavender and pennyroyal.

Flies are deterred by basil and rue.

Gophers are deterred by elderberry.

Japanese beetles are deterred by catnip, chives, white flowering chrysanthemum, garlic, rue, tansy, white geraniums, and larkspur.

Leafhoppers and Mexican bean beetles are deterred by petunias.

Mosquitos are deterred by basil.

Moths are deterred by costmary and lavender.

Potato beetles are deterred by coriander and horseradish.

Root maggots are deterred by garlic.

Root nematodes are deterred by chrysanthemums.

Slugs are deterred by comfrey and wormwood.

Snails are deterred by garlic.

Spider mites are deterred by coriander and dill.

Striped cucumber beetles are deterred by tansy.

Striped pumpkin beetles are deterred by nasturtiums.

Squash vine beetles are deterred by radish.

Squash bugs are deterred by catnip, dill, nasturtiums, and tansy.

Thrips are deterred by basil.

Tomato hornworms are deterred by borage, petunias, and pot marigold.

Weevils are deterred by catnip.

White cabbage butterflies are deterred by peppermint and wormwood.

White flies are deterred by nasturtiums and marigolds (*Calendula*).

Wooly aphids are deterred by clover.

Organic Pest Control Methods

Alfalfa weevils encourage parasitic wasps.

To deter aphids, spray plants with watered-down clay or soapy water and bring in ladybugs.

To get rid of asparagus beetles, place the beetles into a can of soapy water or spray tea on affected plants to deter them.

To deter black flea beetles, dust plants with soot and ashes, or place plants near shade and spray with garlic or hot pepper.

To remove blister beetles in a hay crop, cut the hay with a sickle bar or rotary mower and do not crimp or crush the hay. These beetles are toxic to horses and other grazing animals.

To remove cabbage loopers, sprinkle the worms with flour or salt

To deter cabbage maggots, apply wood ashes to the soil.

To deter cabbage worms, put sour milk in the center of the cabbage head and dust with 1 cup flour, or apply mint cuttings and mulch.

To deter carrot rust flies, sprinkle wood ash at the plant's base.

The deter codling moths, spray with soapy water.

To deter Colorado potato beetles, spray plants with wheat bran when the plants are wet, remove beetles and eggs by hand, and spray with a mix of basil leaves and water. Finally, cover the ground with 1 in. of clean hay or straw.

To deter corn earworms, put a small amount of mineral oil in the silk of each ear.

To deter cutworms, sprinkle wood ash around the plant and press a tin can with the bottom cut out around the stem 3 in. deep.

To remove Harlequin bugs, handpick the bugs from

the plant.

To deter Hessian flies, encourage parasitic wasps.

To remove hornworms, handpick worms from the plant and sprinkle dried hot peppers on the plant.

To deter leafhoppers, shelter the plants.

To deter Mexican bean beetles, spray plants with garlic, destroy the eggs, handpick the beetles from the plants, and plant earlier.

To deter mosquitos, empty out all standing water.

To deter moths, sprinkle dried sprigs of lavender around the plants.

To deter onion maggots, plant onions throughout the garden instead of in one place.

To deter slugs, handpick them from the plants, make borders of ashes or sand, and mulch with wood shavings or oak leaves.

To deter spider mites, spray cold water on the plant's leaves, or spray soapy water or coriander on the plants, and introduce predators. Another option is to spray a mixture of wheat flower, buttermilk, and water on the leaves of plants.

To remove squash bugs, handpick bugs from the plants. Growing plants on trellises and dusting with wood ashes is also effective for prevention.

To deter squash vine borers, pile up the soil as high as the blossoms.

To remove striped cucumber beetles, handpick bugs from the plants. To prevent this, mulch heavily around plants, dust with wood ashes, and grow on trellises.

To deter tarnished plant bugs, remove plants after harvest.

To deter thrips, spray plants with an oil and water mix or spray with soapy water.

To deter weevils, hill up soil around sweet potato vines.

To deter wire worm, plant green manure such as

clover.

To deter a variety of pests, sprinkle dried bay leaves on plants.

Catnip repels a variety of pests when sprigs are sprinkled around plants.

Chrysanthemum (*Pyrethrum*) can be mixed with water and sprayed on plants as a general insecticide.

Concentrated garlic spray deters fungus and insects, and can be used on livestock. Mix at a 5:1 ratio.

Horseradish root can be made into an insecticide spray, either raw or as a tea.

Hot peppers can be made into a spray from tea for most insects.

Kelp can be used as a powder or tea to spray or sprinkle on plants to kill insects and act as a fertilizer.

Lemon balm can be used as a powder and sprinkled throughout a garden to deter pests.

Scented varieties of marigolds can be planted throughout a garden to deter pests.

Steep petunia leaves into a tea and use as a potent insecticide spray.

Four o'clock flowers may help deter some beetles, but they are also poisonous to people, especially children.

Larkspur acts as a general insecticide, but it is poisonous to humans and animals.

Marigold (*Calendula*) also acts as a general insecticide, but it is poisonous to humans and animals, unlike pot marigolds.

Mole plants deter moles and mice, but they are harmful to humans.

Stinging nettle can be used as insecticide for powdery mildew, fungal diseases, aphids, mites, and other pests. The hairs on the leaves have formic acid, however, which stings and irritates skin. If properly prepared it can be ingested.

Tansy acts as a general insecticide, but it is toxic to

many animals. Do not let it go to seed or it will proliferate rapidly.

Wormwood is a medicinal herb used to create a botanical poison, but it should not be used directly food crops.

Do not kill or remove spiders from gardens. Allow them to act as natural pest control agents.

Do not remove or kill minute pirate bugs. They eat spider mites.

Introduce mite destroyer beetles to the garden to eat spider mites.

Introduce parasitic wasps into the garden to eat Hessian flies and other insects.

Introduce six-spotted thrips into the garden to eat spider mites.

Encourage toads by placing a flower pot upside down in the garden.

Encourage purple martin birds by setting up birdhouses with several apartments, or a group of birdhouses clustered together. Paint the houses white and put them on high poles away from trees and buildings. Remove any other bird nests, and take down the houses during the winter.

CHOOSING SEEDS

When choosing seeds, look for disease resistant varieties as well as those that have a long useable lifetime.

Useable Lifetime of Common Seeds

Properly stored seeds can last for more than one growing season. Choose seeds that will remain viable for more than a season, so if not all seeds are needed they can be kept for the following season. Below is a list of common seeds and their useable lifetime.

Beans: 3 years
Beets: 3 years
Cabbage: 4 years
Carrots: 1 year
Cauliflower: 4 years
Corn, sweet: 2 years
Cucumbers: 5 years
Eggplant: 4 years
Kale: 3 years
Lettuce: 4 years
Melons: 4 years
Onions: 1 year
Peas: 1 year
Peppers: 2 years
Pumpkins: 4 years
Radishes: 3 years
Spinach: 3 years
Squash: 4 years
Swiss chard: 4 years
Tomatoes: 3 years
Turnips: 5 years

Disease Resistance

Seed catalog descriptions often feature a string of letters denoting a variety's resistance to disease. Below is an example of disease resistance denotations for tomatoes.

Tomato Disease Resistance Abbreviations

Early blight resistance is denoted as EB
Fusarium wilt resistance is denoted as F, FI, F2, or F3
Late blight resistance is denoted as LB
Nematodes resistance is denoted as N

Tomato spotted wilt virus resistance is denoted as TSWV, TSW, or SWV

Verticillium wilt resistance is denoted as V

Plant Spacing Tip

When crops are closely spaced in a bed, the plant leaves come to rapidly touch one another, creating a beneficial microclimate. This canopy reduces weed growth, helps retain moisture in the soil, and protects the crop from wind damage.

Interplanting Formula

$A + B = C \div 2 = D$

A and B = spacing per plant in inches

Example: Growing cabbage and turnips together (A)15 in. cabbage + (B) 4 in. turnips = (C)19 ÷ 2 = (D)9.5 in.

MARKET GARDENING

Gardening for market is different from gardening only for homestead use, mainly in that the goals for production will differ. Market gardening seeks to produce more in order sell products at market for income. This section offers tips on developing a Consumer Supported Agriculture program, crop planning, evaluating land, getting the most out of available land, pricing, and more.

CONSUMER SUPPORT AGRICULTURE

Consumer supported agriculture (CSA) models are systems where consumers buy shares of the harvest in advance, becoming members who take on both the risks and benefits of that season's food production. Members pay an agreed upon amount at the beginning of the growing season. Members then receive a share of the produce throughout the season.

ADVANTAGES OF CSA

Guaranteed Sales

The main advantage of the CSA model is that production is prepaid at the start of the season, often before the first seed has been sown. This model allows farmer to budget with great precision. There is nothing better for a solid business plan than guaranteed sales.

Simpler Production Plans

Since members have already purchased the produce, the farmer can plan production based on sales. Once the number of customers has been determined, the contents of each share can be planned out beforehand. This is all the more important for growers who do not yet have a lot of farming experience.

Risk Sharing

The idea behind CSA is that the risks inherent to agriculture are shared between the grower and the members. When members sign up, they sign a contract where they agree to be tolerant in case of hail, drought, or any other natural catastrophe. If the season is good, the members will receive more than planned, but if the season is bad, they will receive less. It is similar to taking out an insurance plan on the harvest.

Customer Loyalty

CSA allows farmers to build not just customer loyalty, but tangible relationships between consumers and the farm. As its name suggests, CSA really does have the power to build community

Networking

CSA is even more advantageous when a third organization can play a coordinating role; such third parties who promote CSA through publicity campaigns or finds members for the farms in its network. Others may provide training on production planning for new farmers, link them with more experienced growers through mentorships, and organize visits to other operations. Such partnerships are very helpful and useful services for any beginning vegetable farmer.

Strategies for Commanding Good Prices

Focus on the quality and freshness of crops. Favor root vegetables that can be sold with their leaves, demonstrating that the crops are fresh. Avoid storage vegetables, such as potatoes, parsnips, winter squash, etc., which take up space in the garden for a long period of time and cannot be marketed as fresh. Develop expertise in just a few crops which can be deemed as most profitable.

Choose the most flavorful cultivars, different varieties of the same vegetables, to encourage members and customers to discover new tastes. Regularly try different or unusual cultivars in order to keep members and customers interested.

Supplement production with vegetables purchased from producers who specialize in crops not grown on the homestead.

Force early-season crops in order to be the first to offer them at market.

Change prices as little as possible and explain to customers and members the negative effects of "dumping," a tactic which drives grocery store prices down.

Always wash vegetables and display them neatly.

Always guarantee satisfaction with your products, no questions asked.

Take the time to design an eye-catching logo that clearly identifies products.

Setting up a Wash Station

A simple and economical washing station consists of

two tubs positioned side by side, each with its own garden hose. Ensure there is adequate water pressure so that both hoses can work simultaneously. The drain pipes should be designed in such a way that they can be drained at the same time without creating an overflow. Standard height for work surfaces is about 36 in. but installing the tubs at different heights to accommodate workers of different sized can increase comfort and efficiency. Cover the walls with waterproof materials in an indoor washing station to prevent mold growth. Water used to wash vegetable must be potable and drained in an environmentally responsible manner, preferably recycled.

Design the washing station area with enough space to accommodate a large table for weighing and bagging vegetables. A separate area for handling deliveries and assembling CSA boxes is preferrable. Good shelves are needed to store bags, elastic bands, and other market equipment. Harvest containers should be easy to stack for storage. Movable tables are helpful in order to move the work outdoors in nice weather.

Include a sink with a soap dispenser for hand washing. Sanitary norms generally require that hot water be available for hand washing.

Lighting and windows are also very important in a wash station for both lighting and making the area pleasant to work in. Floors should be smooth and easy to clean. The ideal floor is a level cement slab with one or more drains.

Design the loading area so produce can be loaded into the delivery truck without having to lift the harvest containers one by one. Either build the loading dock to the height of the truck bed or build a moveable loading ramp. Design the space to allow for work with a dolly and containers that stack easily.

Site Evaluation Checklist for Buying/Leasing Land

Determine which hardiness zone the site is located in and consider the implications of running a market garden in a zone that is harsher than others that may be available.

Determine the last spring and first fall frost dates.

Calculate the number of frost-free days in the region to determine the length of the CSA season. The number of frost-free days and the average temperature regulate both the length of the growing season and the production potential. For optimal growing potential, finding a site with the best climatic conditions is imperative.

Determine the earliest outside planting dates for early crops, as well as a feasible date for the first CSA/or market deliveries.

Determine whether there is there a good customer base for organic and local products in the area, such as restaurants, potential CSA members, farmers markets, etc. Determine whether other small producers have already saturated the market, or if there is room for new growers.

Check to see how far the site is from a central market. Estimate how much travel time the distance will be each week and what costs are associated with transporting produce.

Determine whether the plot is large enough to meet the needs of a market garden. Too small of a plot will be limiting, but too large of a plot might require unnecessary investment, both in capital, cost, and time.

Have the soil type tested or evaluated to determine its composition of clay, sand, and silt. Soil is rarely ever pure clay or pure sand, but is typically a mix of different-sized particles, such as clay, silt, sand, and gravel. To determine the proportions that are present, put 2 in. of soil in a mason jar and fill the rest with water. Add a teaspoon of dish detergent, which will act as a surfactant and help to separate the layers of soil. Shake the jar well and let it sit for a day. The separation of the soil into layers of different thicknesses will show the dominant characteristics of the soil.

Determine if the soil is healthy, or if it has been contaminated, if possible. This must be done by a certified laboratory test. If testing is not possible, attempt to research the site's history or collect anecdotal evidence when possible.

Determine the orientation and the slope of the site to see if they are favorable to growing.

Determine whether there are any topographic depressions on the site and, if so, can they easily be filled, leveled, or corrected with drainage tiles?

Determine whether the height of the water table will pose a problem for soil drainage. If underground drainage is needed, estimate the costs involved.

Determine whether the site has enough unpolluted water for proper irrigation of the crops. If a water reservoir needs to be dug, determine whether the proper permits can be easily obtained. Estimate the cost of such a project with a local and trusted contractor.

Evaluate any buildings on the property for their suitability, proximity to the proposed garden site, and stability. Estimate the cost for renovations if needed. Determine whether purchasing, and possibly renovating, an existing building is a better investment than constructing a new one that can be tailored to the needs of a market garden.

Determine whether the site has access to electricity and a source of potable water.

Determine whether the site is accessible by vehicles in all seasons.

Find out whether conventional crops are grown on any neighboring properties. If they are, determine whether the garden site can be protected from potential contamination, such as pesticides and chemicals.

Crop Planning

Setting Farming Objectives

Set an Annual Budget

Setting financial goals is a priority, because the farm or ranch supports the family first and foremost. Make sure production will generate the target revenue or at least cover needs and bills.

Translate financial objectives into sales objectives, which translate into production objectives for the season. The formula for this is the number of weekly shares multiplied by the average price per share multiplied by the number of weeks, which equals the revenue.

Formula: number of weekly shares * average price per share * number of weeks = revenue

The formula works for calculating production for both CSA and farmers market production.

Determine Type and Quantity

Decide the type and quantity of vegetables to grow in order to reach production objectives. In order to do this, roughly decide the content of the CSA shares for every week of the season. Then calculate the planting dates needed in order to harvest crops on time and in a quantity that will meet demand.

Plan Garden Layout

Regroup every seeding by species, making sure that everything fits into the garden space available. Develop a crop calendar and garden plan.

KEEP RECORDS

Keep records throughout the growing season, taking notes of what went wrong and/or what could have been planned more precisely. Notes will be crucial for the following season's planning. Make corrections or adjustments each year.

Deciding What to Grow

Create a table with the number of weeks of harvest and deliveries. For example, 21 rows = 21 weeks. Then define the CSA shares by making a list of assorted vegetables along with their values. Vegetables should be chosen based upon seasonal availability, customer preferences, and/or the farmer's preferences. Pin down the exact contents of the first three and last four shares of the season, because these shares are the most critical given the limited availability of crops grown at those times.

Shares four and onward are not calculated per weekly content as precisely. Instead, make a rough plan of all the vegetables that will be grown in succession. When the season is in full swing and many vegetables are ripening all at once, shares should be built with some vegetables that will store (either on the plant, in the ground, or in the refrigerator) and some that must be harvested and sold quickly (e.g., peas, bean, tomatoes). Needs are calculated differently according to the type of vegetable.

For single-harvest vegetables (root, lettuce, broccoli, celery root, etc.), determine the number of times to include these in the shares (e.g., eight times for carrots, five times for beets) which gives the number of seedings that will be needed.

For multiple-harvest vegetables (tomatoes, cukes, summer squash), the objective is to plant enough to produce a certain number of shares or units per week. For example, summer squash averages two fruits per plant, so to produce 220 shares per week, 110 plants should be producing at a given time.

Expected Crop Yield Per Acre

Alfalfa: 60lbs
Apples: 60lbs
Barley: 48lbs
Buckwheat: 50lbs
Clover: 60lbs
Field corn: 60lbs
Flax: 56lbs
Oats: 32lbs
Red clover: 50lbs
Rye: 56lbs
Sweet sorghum: 50lbs
Spelt: 40lbs
Wheat: 60lbs

* Measurement is per bushel

Square footage required to grow 1 bushel

Field corn: 500 sq ft
Grain sorghum: 600 sq ft
Oats: 600 sq ft
Barley: 900 sq ft
Wheat: 1000 sq ft
Buckwheat: 1300 sq ft
Rye: 1500 sq ft

Example of Share Plan for one Season

Share 1: June 13th

Spinach ($3), radishes ($2), cucumber ($4), summer squash ($4), kohlrabi ($2), garlic scapes ($2.50), kale ($2.50), arugula ($4), cilantro ($2). Total value: $26.00.

Share 2: June 20th

Lettuce ($2), turnips ($2.50), beets ($2.50), cucumbers ($4), squash ($4), green onions ($2), broccoli ($3), mustard greens ($2), bok choy ($2.50), dill ($2). Total value: $26.50.

Share 3: June 27th

Lettuce ($2), spinach ($3), radishes ($2), cucumbers ($4), squash ($4), kale ($2.50), garlic scapes ($2.50), kohlrabi ($2), basil ($2), snow/snap peas ($3). Total value: $27.00.

Shares 4-17: July 4th-Oct. 3rd

Lettuce (type subject to availability) ($2), carrots ($2.50), turnips ($2.50), beets ($2.50), cucumbers ($4), tomatoes ($4), summer squash ($4), snow/snap peas ($3), beans ($3), broccoli ($3), cauliflower ($3), garlic ($2), onions ($3), Swiss chard ($3), basil ($2), eggplant ($4), peppers ($3), cherry tomatoes ($4), leeks ($3), melons, tomatillos ($3), celery root ($2), hot peppers ($3), and herbs ($2). Total value varies depending on the vegetables included.

Share 18: Oct. 10th

Lettuce ($2), carrots ($2.50), turnips ($2.50),

cucumbers ($4), tomatoes ($4), garlic ($2), leeks ($3), arugula ($2), bell peppers ($3), cilantro ($2). Total value: $27.00.

Share 19: Oct. 17th

Spinach ($3), beets ($2.50), winter radishes ($2.50), cucumbers ($4), kale ($2.50), cauliflower ($3), celery root ($2), onions ($3), parsley ($2), broccoli ($3). Total value: $27.50.

Share 20: Oct. 24th

Spinach ($3), carrots ($2.50), turnips ($2.50), garlic ($4), Chinese cabbage ($4), kohlrabi ($2), leeks ($3), arugula ($2), potatoes ($3), thyme ($2). Total value: $28.00.

Share 21: Nov. 1st

Spinach ($3), carrots ($5), kale ($2.50), onions ($3.50), winter radishes ($2.50), celery root ($2), winter squash ($4), parsley ($2), potatoes ($3). Total value: $27.50.

Organizing Shares Contents

Vegetables that can be included frequently included: tomatoes, lettuce, herbs, cucumbers, carrots, summer squash, peppers, and onions.

Secondary vegetables include garlic, beets, turnips, radishes, snow/snap peas, beans, broccoli, cauliflower, potatoes, eggplants, Asian greens, arugula, spinach, basil, melons, cherry tomatoes, Swiss chard, and kale.

Occasional vegetables include fennel, hot peppers, tomatillos, chicory, kohlrabi, celery root, celery, winter radishes, winter squash, garlic scapes, sweet corn, and brussels sprouts.

When planning share contents, always consider the customer's needs, suggestions, wants, and the cultural regions surrounding the market.

General CSA Share and Garden Market Guidelines

Include 8-12 different items per share on any given week.

Include lettuce in every share (or spinach, early and late in the season).

Include one variety of greens per week, sometimes two to three types early in the season, if possible, but never give the same greens twice in a row.

Try to include two root vegetables in every share. Include carrots as often as possible.

Try to have fruits and vegetables ready as early as possible to add value to shares early in the season.

Include herbs in every share.

Production Calculation

Vegetable	Days to Maturity	Yield per 100 ft bed	Notes
Arugula	35	200 bunches	
Asian greens	60	300 units	
Basil	60	150 units/week	Assume one bunch (0.4 oz) per plant per two weeks
Beans	55	65 lbs/week	Assume 130 lbs. total per two weeks
Broccoli	75	120 heads	
Bulk spinach	40	75 lbs.	Assume 35 lbs. at first harvest, 40 lbs. at second and third

Cabbage	80	150 units	
Cauliflower	75	130 heads	Allow many more days for certain cultivars
Carrot	55	180 bunches	
Celery root	140	300 units	
Eggplant	100	65 units/week	Assume about 1 fruit per plant per week
Fennel	80	400 units	
Garlic	N/A	600 units	
Green onion	75	350 units	
Greenhouse cucumbers	50	115 unit/week	Assume 1.75 fruits per plant per week
Ground cherry	110	Undetermined	Two beds are enough on average per season
Kohlrabi	60	420 units	Allow many more days for certain cultivars
Lettuce	50	250 units	
Melon	80	100 units or less	Assume 1.25 fruits per plant
Onion	120	400 lbs.	
Pepper	120	102 units/week	Assume 1 fruit per plant per week
Radish	30	300 munches	
Snow/snap pea	55	25 lbs/week or less	Assume 75 lbs. every 3 weeks
Summer squash	50	100 units/week	Assume 2 fruits per plant per week
Swiss chard/kale	60	150 units/week	Assume 1 bunch per 2 plants per 2 weeks
Tomato	120	150 lbs./week	Assume 3 fruits per plant per week
Turnip	40	200 bunches	
Summer leek	120	175 units	Sold in bunches of 3-4

Days to maturity equals the number of days between seeding and the first harvest. It includes time spent in all flats. For vegetables transplanted early in spring or late in fall, days to maturity must be adjusted for slower plant growth.

Weekly yields are approximate and take account of intensive spacing on a bed measuring 30 in. wide by 100 ft long. Numbers must be modified in proportion to bed dimensions.

Example of Possible Sales

Projections based on typical annual sales at Les Jardins de la Grelinette

Vegetable	Total sales	Price	Number of beds per season	Garden space	Revenue per bed	Numbers of days in the garden	Rank (sales)	Rank (reve-nue/ bed)	Profit-ability
Greenhouse tomato	$35,200	$2.75/ lb.	4	3%	$8,800	180	1	1	High
Mesclun mix	$15,750	$6.00/ lb.	35	18%	$450	45	2	19	High
Lettuce	$9,000	$2.00/ unit	18	9%	$500	50	3	15	High
Greenhouse cucumber	$8,280	$2.00/ unit	6	2%	$1,380	90	4	2	High
Garlic	$6,600	$1.50/ lb.	8	4%	$825	90	5	5	High
Carrots (bunch)	$6,515	$2.50/ unit	14	7%	$465	85	6	18	Medium
Onion	$6,075	$1.50/ lb.	9	4%	$675	110	7	10	Medium
Pepper	$4,400	$4.00/ lb.	8	4%	$550	120	8	13	Medium
Broccoli	$3,900	$2.50/ unit	13	7%	$300	65	9	28	Low
Snow/snap peas	$3,840	$6.00/ lb.	8	4%	$480	85	10	16	Medium
Summer squash	$3,690	$1.50/ lb.	6	3%	$615	70	11	11	Medium

Green onions	$3,360	$2.00/ unit	4	2%	$840	50	12	4	High
Beans	$3,280	$3.75/ lb.	8	4%	$410	70	13	24	Low
Spinach	$3,000	$6.00/ lb.	5	3%	$600	50	14	12	Medium
Beets (bunch)	$2,900	$2.50/ unit	7	4%	$415	70	15	23	Medium
Turnip	$2,100	$2.50/ unit	4	2%	$525	50	16	14	Medium
Radish	$2,000	$1.50/ unit	5	3%	$450	45	17	20	Medium
Cherry tomato	$1,930	$5.00/ lb.	2	1%	$965	120	18	3	High
Ground cherry	$1,650	$6.00/ lb.	2	1%	$825	120	19	6	Medium
Swiss chard	$1,600	$2.00/ unit	2	1%	$800	90	20	7	Medium
Kale	$1,600	$2.00/ unit	2	1%	$800	90	22	8	Medium
Cauliflower	$1,600	$3.00/ unit	4	2%	$400	80	21	25	Low
Basil	$1,400	$20.00/ lb.	2	1%	$700	120	23	9	Medium
Eggplant	$1,350	$3.00/ unit	3	2%	$450	120	24	21	Low
Melon	$1,225	$4.00/ lb.	5	3%	$245	85	25	29	Low
Leek	$1,200	$4.00/ unit	3	2%	$400	150	26	26	Low
Kohlrabi	$940	$1.25/ unit	2	1%	$470	55	27	17	Medium
Wild leek	$840	$3.00/ unit	2	1%	$420	135	28	22	Medium
Arugula (bunch)	$800	$2.00/ unit	2	1%	$400	45	29	27	Medium
Total	**$136,025**		193	100%					

SOIL

There are four parts of soil. Humus is organic matter in its final stages of decomposition. It is unrecognizable as plant material. Loam is the ideal soil and is made of sand, silt, and clay. Subsoil is the deeper layer of soil that stores water. It is usually a lighter color. Topsoil is the top 1-2 ft of soil, where most of the nutrients exist. It is darker and crumblier.

To determine what type of subsoil is present, check for specific indicators by digging down 2-3 ft and examining the soil characteristics.

Red-yellow subsoil indicates high amounts of iron oxides, good drainage, and higher acidity, which is common in warm climates.

Blue-grey subsoil indicates a lack of oxygen and poor drainage, which is common in thick layers of clay.

White to ash-grey subsoil indicates that nutrients and humus have leached away. It is acidic and/or sandy, and is common under pine trees.

An even, medium-brown subsoil indicates good drainage. Pale subsoil that looks similar to topsoil indicates poorly developed soil, often found in areas where the topsoil has been removed.

Dark brown subsoil indicates an abundance of decomposed organic matter, which is usually found where wetlands have been previously.

Subsoil with patches or streaks of color indicates pockets or poor drainage. Plants will often have difficulty in this soil type because of the varying soil content. When plant roots all end at the same depth, this indicates a cemented layer and poor drainage.

The best possible soil makeup is to have 5% of the soil be made up of added materials such as soybean meal, garbage, cottonseed meal, plant residue, sludge manure, and compost. The mineral content should be 45% of added materials such as lime, green sand, granite, dust, and nitrates in organic matter. Water should make up 25% of the soil. Water can be added through sprinklers or irrigation, but it is preferred to use the natural water table when possible. Lastly, air should make up 25% of soil. To add air, make the soil loose with organic material and cultivation.

SOIL CARE

Care of soil requires adding nutrients back into the soil that growing takes away. This can be accomplished by replacing matter and organisms with green manure. Green manure is an easy way to fertilize the soil, but most practical for big fields. To fertilize with green manure, plant a suitable crop then cover it with dirt and wait for it to decay.

Common types of green manure include, legumes sown in the fall so the flowers will attract beneficial insects, alfalfa (*Medicago sativa*) sown in the spring or the summer, and bell or fava beans (*Viciafaba*) sown in fall or very early spring since they can tolerate temperatures as low as 15 degrees Fahrenheit.

Clovers are commonly used types of green manure. Berseem clover (*Trifolium alexandrinium*) is a summer or winter annual. Crimson clover (*Trifolium incarnatum*) is winter-hardy and easily tilled. Dutch white clover (*Trifolium repens*) is easily cultivated. Red clover (*Trifolium pratense*) is a quick-growing biennial that can be planted from spring through fall. Subterranean clover (*Trifolium subterranean*) is a cool-season, reseeding annual that is best for sowing under taller crops. New Zealand white clover (*Trifolium repens*) is a hardy, long-lived, heat-resistant perennial.

Peas are another common green manure crop. Field peas (*Pisum sativum*) are sown in the fall or spring. Austrian field peas (*Lathyrus hirsutus*) are sown in fall or spring. Cowpeas/southern peas (*Vigna sinensis*) are grown as a summer annual.

Vetch is also a commonly grown green manure crop. Common vetch (*Vicia sativa*) grows in most soils. Hairy vetch (*Vicia villosa*) is tolerant of extreme cold. Purple vetch (*Vicia atropurpurea*) is less cold-tolerant and is used as a winter-kill mulch.

Implications of Soil Textures on Market Gardening

Clay Soil

Clay soil is sticky and forms a malleable ball when handled. It is hard, crusty, cracked, and generally difficult to fork. This soil type is the hardest to work with, especially in springtime, as it is slow to drain and dry out.

While clay soil is rich in nutrients, it compacts easily and is susceptible to poor aeration. To improve aeration and drainage, it may be necessary to add perlite, coarse sand, or fine gravel to transplant holes to avoid problems. It may also help to raise beds extra high to encourage proper drainage. Always use a broadfork before seeding or transplanting in order to improve aeration.

Work up the beds in the fall to prepare for the first spring seeding, but take care not to leave the soil bare over the winter. The structure of clay soil can be improved by repeatedly incorporating very large quantities of organic and mineral matter such as compost, peat moss, and coarse sand. It may take several years and require a financial investment to improve clay soil, but is often worthwhile.

Sandy Soil

Sandy soil is granular and crumbly, does not stay in a ball when wet, breaks up easily, and contains many stones or gravel. This type of soil is difficult to compact, but it is generally very permeable and offers greater aeration for crops. It also tends to be dry, leaches water easily, and generally lacks fertility.

It is often necessary to set up irrigation for the whole

site quickly, as very young plants in this type of soil will die after a few days without rain. To avoid leaching, make sure fertilizer is added in small doses over the course of the season. Develop a green manure program in which crop residues and compost are mixed in to increase the organic matter in the soil.

LOAM SOIL

Loam soil is fluffy and forms a ball that breaks apart easily. Loam contains roughly equal proportions of sand, silt, and clay, bringing together ideal soil qualities of good water, nutrient retention, and proper drainage and aeration. Sandy loam is considered the best soil for vegetable growing, but it is important to maintain soil fertility with an appropriate fertilizing plan and conserve proper soil structure with minimal tillage.

WEED INDICATORS OF SOIL TYPE

The types of weeds growing on a piece of land can also indicate the soil type and how well the soil drains.

The type of weeds present in alkali soil include saltgrass (*Distichlis spicata*) in coastal areas, chickweed (*Stellaria media*) in deserts, Shepherd's purse (*Capsella bursa pastoris*), blueweed (*Echium vulgare*), gromwell/ puccoon (*Lithospermum*), field peppergrass (*Lepidium campestre*), true chamomile (*Chamomilla matricaria*), bellflower (*Campanula*), salad burnet (*Poterium sanguisorba*), scarlet pimpernel (*Anagallis arvensis*), and bladder campion (*Silene latifolia*).

The types of weeds present in slightly acidic soil include bracken fern (*Pteridium aquilinum*), spurrey (*Spergula arvensis*), corn marigold (*Chrysanthemum segetum*), sow thistle (*Sonchus arvensis*), plantain

(*Plantago*), Lady's Thumb (*Polygonum persicaria*), goose tansy or rough cinquefoil (*Potentilla monspeliensis*), wild strawberry (*Fragaria*), rabbit foot clover (*Trifolium arvense*), horsetail (*Equisetum*), dock and sorel (*Rumex*), English daisy (*Bell's perennis*), and prostrate knotweed (*Polygonum aviculare*).

The types of weeds present in very acidic soil include knapweed (*Centaurea nigra*), hawkweed (*Hieracium*), silvery cinquefoil (*Potentilla argentea*), and horsetail (*Equisetum*), if the land is swampy.

The types of weeds present in salty soil include Russian thistle (*Salsola kali*), sea aster (*Aster tripolium*), asparagus (*Asparagus officinalis*), beet (*Beta*), Shepherd's purse (*Capsella bursa pastoris*), and mustards.

The types of weeds present in soil with poor drainage include dwarf St. John's Wort (*Hypericum*), horsetail (*Equisetum*), Silverwood (*Potentilla anserina*), creeping buttercup (*Ranunculus repens*), mosses, sumac (*Rhus integrifolia*), curly dock (*Rumex acetosella*), sorrel (*Rumex acetosella*), hedge nettle (*Stachys palustris*), May apple (*Podophyllum peltatum*), thyme-leaved speedwell (*Veronica serpyllifolia*), America hellebore (*Veratrum viride*), and white avens (*Geum album*).

The types of weeds present in heavy soil include coltsfoot (*Tussilago farfara*), creeping buttercup (*Ranunculus repens*), dandelion (*Taraxacum officinale*), plantain (*Plantago*), English daisy (*Bellis perennis*), and broadleaf dock (*Rumex obtusifolius*).

The types of weeds present in light or sandy soil include spurrey (*Spergula arvensis*), corn marigold (*Chrysanthemum segetum*), sheep's sorrel (*Rumex*), cornflower (*Centaurea cyanus*) – especially when flowers are pink, small nettle (*Urtica urens*), Shepherd's purse (*Capsella bursa pastoris*), white campion (*Lychnis alba*), Maltese thistle (*Centaurea melitensis*), and St. Barnaby's thistle (*Centaurea solstitialis*).

The types of weeds present in hard or crusted soil include all chamomile varieties, mustards, morning glory, quack grass (*Agropyron repens*), and goosefoot (*Chenopodium*), no matter how bad soil is.

Elements of a Proper Fertilization Strategy

Lab testing of soil can help determine how to correct nutrient deficiencies or imbalances in the soil. An agronomist can offer recommendations on corrections to make.

Liming soil involves applying calcium and magnesium to balance the soil's acidity and alkalinity. Proper liming will ensure the correct pH on all plots.

Develop a crop rotation plan that includes cover crops.

Fertilizer amendments should be calculated on the basis of existing soil fertility and the nutrient requirements of each vegetable crop.

Establish observation procedures to measure how fertilizer application influences crops and soil over time.

Soil Solarization

Use the sun to help eliminate weeds by leaving clear plastic in place for six weeks during the summer. This is an effective strategy for depleting the seed bank and is a solution for weed management in hoop houses, or during early spring planting when stale seedbed techniques are not possible.

Aside from requiring beds to be free during the growing season, the main drawback of this technique is that not only weed seeds are destroyed. Soil organisms and microbial life in the garden are destroyed as well. Under certain circumstances, however, such an effective strategy is worthwhile.

Organic Crop Fertilization:

Stimulating biological activity in the soil should be a priority in organic farming. It is important to constantly work to encourage soil that is well structured, well aerated, moist, and warm.

Biological activity is greatest at pH levels between 6.2 and 6.8. Liming soil can help achieve the ideal pH. Aim for a pH level of 6.5.

Organic matter is both food and habitat for soil micro-organisms. In the beginning, focus on building the soil and aim to achieve a high level of organic matter as quickly as possible. Later, focus on replacing the nutrients taken up by crops by adding organic amendments, including compost, animal manure, and perhaps green manure.

Feed the soil, but also feed the plant. This involves addressing the different crop requirements, the nutritional value of the inputs, and the role of each nutrient, especially nitrogen, in the early stages of crop development.

Soil testing is an important tool. It can detect potential mineral imbalances, determine the natural fertility of the soil, and help determine any fertilizer supplements that may be needed.

Since compost is the principal source of fertility, it must be of high quality. If the quality of compost made on the farm cannot be guaranteed, or it cannot be made efficiently and knowledgeably, it is best to purchase compost. Make sure purchased compost is made from as many sources as possible and amended with a rich source of micro-nutrients. Compost piles should always be well covered to keep nutrients from leaching.

Healthy crop rotation helps avoid many crop problems and will ultimately be what makes a system sustainable. New farmers should allow several seasons to develop a good knowledge of vegetable production before implementing a complex crop rotation.

Organic crop fertilization involves integrating a plethora of different agricultural practices. To manage this complexity, work on developing a coherent fertilization program. A systematic approach will, in the end, make day-to-day operations much easier.

Transplanting

Transplanting involves moving a plant's location, either from an indoor seed starting location or from one plot to another. Starting seeds indoors prior to the beginning of the outdoor growing season and moving them to outdoor plots when temperatures allow is the most common reason for transplanting.

There are several advantages to transplanting. Seeding begins before the start of the frost-free period, thereby extending the growing season considerably. Germination and growing conditions are controlled in the early stages, when plants are the most vulnerable.

The chances of crop success are improved because seeding density is perfect, and crops have a head start over weeds. It is also possible to engage in succession planting by starting crops in a greenhouse even before garden space is available.

Succession planting is a practice that involves seeding crops at intervals of one to three weeks in order to maintain a consistent supply of harvestable produce throughout a growing season.

Transplant Table

Based on a 30 in. by 100 ft bed with a 30% increase to cover any spoilage.

Vegetable	Number of Cell Flats	Number of Flats per Bed	Number of Days in Flat	Spacing in 30" bed	
				Rows	Plant Spacing
Asian greens	72	4	21	3	12 in.
Basil	128	3	25	3	12 in.
Beet	128	11	25	3	3.5 in.
Broccoli	72	3	30	2	18 in.
Brussels sprout	72	3	30	2	18 in.
Cauliflower	72	3	30	2	18 in.
Celery	72	10	60	3	6 in.
Celery root	72	5	60	3	12 in.
Chard and kale	72	5	30	3	12 in.
Corn	128	4	15	2	6 in.
Cucumber	72	1.5	15	1	18 in.
Eggplant	4 in. x 4 in.	85	50	1	18 in.
Fennel	72	7	30	2	6 in.
Green onion	500/tray	13	45	5	6 in./ clumps 5
Ground cherry	72	1	40	1	24 in.
Kohlrabi	72	9	30	3	7 in.
Leek	300/tray	2	65	3	6 in.
Lettuce	128	3	30	3	12 in.

Melon	72	2	15	1	18 in.
Onion	500/tray	3	50	3	10 in.
Parsley	128	8	40	4	6 in.
Pepper	4 in. x 4 in.	170	60	1	9 in.
Rutabaga	72	7	30	2	6 in.
Spinach	128	11	21	4	6 in.
Summer cabbage	72	3	30	2	18 in.
Summer squash	72	1	15	1	24 in.
Tomato	6 in. x 6 in.	170	60	1	9 in.
Chinese cabbage	72	3	30	2	18 in.

Rotation Crops

Examples of crop rotation plans. 1) First harvest. 2) Second harvest. 3) Do not plant.

1) Beans 2) Cauliflower, carrots, broccoli, cabbage, or corn 3) Onions and garlic
1) Beets 2) Spinach
1) Carrots 2) Lettuce or tomatoes 3) Dill
1) Cucumbers. 2) Peas or radishes 3) Potatoes
1) Kale   2) Beans or peas
1) Lettuce 2) Carrots, cucumbers, or radishes
1) Onions 2) Radishes or lettuce 3) Beans
1) Peas 2) Carrots, beans, or corn
1) Potatoes 2) Beans, cabbage, corn, or turnips 3) Tomatoes, squash, or pumpkin
1) Radish 2) Beans
1) Tomatoes 2) Carrots or onions

Harvesting and Storing Produce

The basic process for harvesting produce is to first collect the produce from the gardens. It should then be taken to a temporary storage area for washing. Once clean, it should be put into refrigeration or dry storage. Most fruits and vegetables should be sold within 24-48 hours of harvest.

The specific process of harvesting depends on the type of vegetable.

Leaf vegetables, including lettuce, are always the first to harvest and are brought to storage immediately in harvest bins. Upon arrival, the leaves should be sprayed with cold water to keep them cool until the washing step. The washing step involves carefully removing damaged leaves, submerging them in a cold-water bath, and then drip drying. Lastly, gently place it in a storage bin then close the bin and store it in the refrigerator.

Root vegetables sold in bunches should be sorted and bunched in the garden, or on hot days, brought to a cool, dry storage area in bulk and then bunched. Remove damaged leaves during assembly then calibrate bunches for uniformity and place them back in harvest bins. Spray with cool water for freshness. At the washing station, spray with a pressure hose to rinse off dirt. Stagger each bunch in the harvest bin and place them in the refrigerator.

Broccoli and cauliflower stay crisp longer when cooled immediately after harvest. Once in the storage area, immerse the heads in a cold-water bath then drain and place them in the refrigerator as soon as possible. They should be harvested as maturity is reached, not all at once. Mark each batch with the harvest date for first-in, first-out freshness.

Beans and peas do not need to be washed, but if it is midday when harvested, spray them with cool water for freshness, then place them in the refrigerator. Storage containers must allow for water drainage to prevent rust.

Cucumbers are crunchiest if cooled immediately after harvest. After harvesting, take them straight to the washroom. Refrigerate them immediately after washing and mark each batch with the harvest date.

Tomatoes can be harvested at any time of day, but should be done with extra gentle care. Damaged tomatoes have a shorter shelf life. Avoid handling them twice. Store in a harvest bin in dry/root storage.

Mesclun mix should be harvested separate from other harvesting activities so the entire cutting can be done during early morning. Harvest, then rinse in a cold-water bath in the washroom. Remove any weeds, insects, or damaged leaves then mix together different sizes and colors. Spin the greens in an electric spinner to remove excess water and prevent rot, then place the mix in plastic bags and refrigerate while stored.

Melons, like tomatoes, can be harvested at any time. Do not wash melons. It is better if they are stored in dry/ root storage where they can finish ripening if necessary. If harvested too late, when they are overripe, store in the refrigerator.

Basil can be harvested at any time, but must never be harvested wet or kept in a sealed bag. Moisture turns the leaves black. Store in the refrigerator in a half-open bin to prevent condensation.

Summer squash should be harvested every two to three days when the fruit is still small. Refrigerate for storage and mark each one with its harvest date.

Summer onions can be harvested at any time and are normally saved until most of the harvest is completed. They should be bunched in the garden, hosed down to remove any soil, then refrigerated.

For storing produce in dry storage or a root cellar, the optimal temperature is 60 degrees Fahrenheit (15 degrees

Celsius). The optimal temperature for a refrigerator or cold room is 36-39 degrees Fahrenheit (2-4 degrees Celsius).

Ways to Process Grain

Cracking is breaking the kernel into two or more pieces. Cracking is mainly used for corn.

Crimping flattens the kernel slightly. It is used for oats especially.

Flaking is treating with heat and/or moisture, then flattening.

Grinding is forcing the grain through rollers and screens.

Rolling is smashing between rollers at different speeds with or without steaming.

Saving is storing the wheat to grow as seed for the next year.

Ecological Pest Control

Ecological pest control means more than simply relying on biopesticides, which may or may not disrupt the spread of insect pests and diseases. This method requires forethought and planning prior to the growing season.

For every pest common to the growing area, it is important to know in advance an appropriate, natural method of control and knowledge of when to intervene to disrupt the spread of the problem. Writing down the various management practices for dealing with pests is important. For example: if carrot rust flies usually emerge in August, make a note in the crop planning calendar to cover carrots with a net around that time.

Conducting a Morning Walk

Making a morning walk part of a daily routine is strongly recommended. This allows for monitoring of crops for any signs of damage from pests or disease and for assessing all the maintenance work needing to be done in the garden. An ideal complement to this daily practice is to also make a list of things to do every day. Writing an action plan on a daily basis is the first step to keeping the site(s) under control.

Cover Crops

Cover crops help improve soil health over time. They also help prevent erosion, enhance water availability, reduce weeds, help control pests and disease, increase biodiversity, and may attract pollinators, depending on the type used. Common cover crops include clover, oats, legumes, wheat, and rye.

White clover is cheaper than red clover and also less vigorous. It is slow to establish itself, but very hardy. It is, however, hard to get rid of once established. Plant it around the edges of gardens, where it will add nitrogen to the soil. It survives winters well and does not require regular mowing. Seeds are very fine, so they should be mixed 50/50 with sand before broadcasting to ensure seeding is not too dense. The recommended seeding rate is 2.2 lbs per 100 ft bed, including 50% sand.

With oats and legumes, the ideal catch crop is an oat-pea mix. It can be seeded very early in spring, often as soon as the snow is gone. This mix adds a lot of nitrogen and biomass to the soil and is a great weed smotherer. In fall, replace the peas with common vetch. Either mix (oats and peas or oats and common vetch) requires eight weeks to grow before being turned under. Aim to seed this cover crop by September 1st. The seeding rate is 3.3 lbs per 100 ft bed. Use a mix of 60% peas to 40% vetch or oats.

Buckwheat, as a cover crop, is useful for rapidly covering soil and crowding out weeds. Because it goes to seed 8-10 weeks after being seeded, it should be mowed before then. It is highly sensitive to frost, so late August is the latest seeding date. The seeding rate is 3.3 lbs per 100 ft bed.

Fall rye is very useful in providing plant cover for beds where late harvests have to take place. This species requires 4-6 weeks to fully develop and grows even in cold conditions. It is very hard to eliminate. Even after shredding, a simple pass with the rotary tiller is generally not enough to kill it. Aim to seed by the first week of October. Plants will come up again in the spring and produce plenty of biomass by the end of May. The seeding rate is 3.3 lbs per 100 ft bed.

Estimated Average Equipment Startup Costs

Harvest baskets, scales, misc. equipment: $300
1 Greenhouse (25' x 100'): $11,000
2-wheeled tractor and accessories: $8,500
2 hoop houses (15' x 100'): $7,000
Cold room: $4,000
Irrigation system: $3,000
Furnace: $1,150
Flame weeder: $600
Indoor seeding equipment: $600
Hoes and wheel hoe: $600
Broadfork: $200
Harvest cart: $350
Floating row, cover, hoops, anti-insect netting: $200
Sprayers: $100
Electric fence: $500
Total: $39K

Market Farming Booklist

Eat Local for Less by Julie Castillo
The Occidental Arts and Ecology Center Cookbook by Olivia Rathbone
Super Foods Collection (Snacks, Juices, Smoothies, Kitchen) by Julie Morris
Edible Landscaping by Rosalind Creasy
**The Market Gardener* by Jean-Martin Fortier
**The New Organic Grower* by Eliot Coleman
Growing for Market Magazine
Market Farming Success by Lynn Byczynski
**Crop Planning for Organic Vegetable Growers* by Dan Brisebois and Fred Theriault
Earth Ponds by Tim Matson
The Winter Harvest Handbook by Eliot Coleman
Building Soils for Better Crops by Fred Magdoff and Harold Van Es
The Soul of Soil by Joseph Smillie and Grace Gershuny
Living the Good Life by Scott and Helen Nearing

*Must have books

COMPOST, MANURE, ORGANIC FERTILIZER, AND MULCH

COMPOST

Composting has many benefits, including environmental, financial, and waste reduction. There are various methods of composting, which this guide will not cover, but it will discuss composting from manure and the equipment needed to develop compost. Bins or piles should be located out of the way and downwind, but close enough to be convenient.

Composting Tools and Equipment

1, 5, and 10 lbs bags/containers
Composting pots
Compost tea
Shovels: spade, square, scoop
Hoe
Pruner
Shears
Garden fork/pitchfork
Metal and lawn rakes
Potato rakes
Broadfork

Additional Farm/Ranch Tools

Sledgehammer
Baby sledgehammer
Functional mini tools
Hand and power tools
Rope
Chainsaw with chains at 3/8 in., ¼ in., and 7/8 in. links
Come along tool
Grinder
Bow saw

Manure

Livestock manure can be collected and used in producing high-quality compost for use on the farm for gardening and for generating compost for sale. Compost and manures should age an average of 90 days before use. They are "finished" once the material no longer heats up after being turned and most materials are broken down. On average, chickens will produce 95 lbs of manure per chicken per year. A 100 lb goat will produce about 4 lbs of manure per day or 1,460 lbs per year. A 500 lb pig will produce about 32.5 lbs of manure per day or 11,860 lbs per yr.

Organic Fertilizer

Organic fertilizer typically offers better nutrients to plants and is gentler than chemical fertilizers. It is also less likely to overfeed plants, when compared to chemical fertilizers, because nutrients are not immediately absorbed by the plants. Organic fertilizers are usually more resistant to being washed away by rain as well.

Below is a list of organic fertilizer components and their uses.

Bonemeal contributes 20-35% phosphorous. It is very slow acting, which helps avoid burning the roots of plants.

Compost contributes organic matter with nutrients in varying proportions. It is the best all-around organic fertilizer. It can be used in combination with chemical fertilizers.

Cottonseed contributes 69% nitrogen, 2-3% phosphorus, and 1.5-2% potassium. It has a low pH, which is good for acid-loving crops.

Dried blood and tankage contribute 5-12% nitrogen and 3-13% phosphorus. It is one of best organic nitrogen sources. It is quick-acting, and it aids the growth of soil organisms.

Fishmeal and fish emulsion contribute 6-8% nitrogen, 13% phosphorus, 3-4% potassium, and trace elements. It is quick-acting.

Horn- and hoof-meal contribute 7-15% nitrogen. It is quick-acting.

Fresh cow manure contributes 6% nitrogen, 15% phosphorus, 1.5% potassium, and organic matter. It is relatively low in nitrogen. It can be used without drying and can go straight to the garden.

Dried goat and sheep manure contribute 2.5% nitrogen, 1.5% phosphorus, 1.5% potassium, and organic matter. It is relatively high in nitrogen and should be aged or composted at least 90 days before use in gardens.

Fresh horse manure contributes 7% nitrogen, 0.25% phosphorus, 0.55% potassium, and organic matter. It is relatively high in nitrogen and should be aged or composted at least 90 days before use in the garden.

Dried poultry manure contributes 4.5% nitrogen, 3.2% phosphorus, and 1.3% potassium 1.3%. It is low in organic matter, but it is very high in nitrogen. It should not be used on plants directly because it may burn through.

Dried rabbit manure contributes 2.4% nitrogen, 1.4% phosphorus, 6% potassium, and organic matter. It is relatively high in nitrogen and should be aged or composted at least 90 days before use in the garden.

Rock phosphate contributes 24-30% phosphorus and 1-2% nitrogen. It is slow-acting, non-burning, and a good soil conditioner because the colloids retain nutrients.

Dried seaweed contributes 0.75% phosphorus, 5% potassium, and some organic matter. It is slow-acting, non-burning, and a good soil conditioner because the colloids retain nutrients.

Sterilized sewage sludge contributes 4-6% nitrogen, 3-4% phosphorus, some potassium and trace elements, and organic matter. It may contain heavy metals which build up over years.

Wood ashes contribute 1-2% phosphorus and 3-7% potassium. It has an alkaline effect on soil and is considered an old standard.

Mulch

Mulch helps to slow moisture evaporation, helps to prevent weeds, enriches the soil with nutrients, and helps regulate soil temperature. There are a variety of mulch types, both commercial and organic. Using organic mulch helps repurpose materials and is more cost-efficient.

Sawdust can be used as mulch by applying it 1.5-2 in. thick. Let the dust rot until it is dark before use. Sawdust can be obtained from sawmills and lumberyards, or from the homestead's wood pile.

Leaves make an effective mulch when applied 4-6 in. thick. Leaves are easy to come by in most regions of the country.

Pine needles are very effective as mulch because their resin content makes them long-lasting and neat in appearance. They should be applied 4-6 in. thick.

Hay and straw require a depth of 6-8 in. to be effective as mulch. They can be obtained from local farmers, garden-supply centers, or as a grown crop. Spoiled hay, which is unfit for animals, and salt hay, from tidal flats, make excellent mulches.

Black plastic film is sold by most garden-supply and hardware stores in 25 ft, 50 ft, and 100 ft rolls with a standard 3 ft width. Do not walk on it, due to the thinness of the material. Holes can be cut as needed for plants. Cut x-shaped slits at even intervals to allow for watering.

Cocoa bean hulls can be used as mulch and should be applied at a depth of 3-6 in. The hulls are alkaline and help to sweeten the soil. They should not be used on acid-loving vegetables. These are typically the most expensive option.

Old newspapers can also be used as biodegradable mulch. They should be applied in layers at least 6 sheets thick and should be weighted down to keep them from blowing away. Avoid colored newsprint.

Wood chips should be applied 3-6 in deep to be effective as mulch. They are durable and slow decaying, and can be obtained (usually for free) from power or telephone companies who chip old or damaged poles.

Lawn clippings can be used as mulch and should be applied at a depth of 3-6 in. Allow the clippings to dry before use.

Compost can also be used as mulch when applied 3-6 in. deep. Compost is one of the best garden mulches because it supplies nutrients in addition to performing natural mulch functions. Compost should only be partially broken down when used as mulch so as not to encourage weed growth.

MARKET GARDENING GLOSSARY

Alternaria: A fungal disease that infects leaves and can cause dieback in the plant. It is common in tomatoes and appears as brown spots in concentric circles.

Amend: To incorporate substances (e.g., organic matter, clay, lime) into the soil to improve its physical and biological fertility, unlike fertilizers, which improve chemical fertility.

Basalt: Black volcanic rock used as a fertilizer in powder form.

Bed: The technique of organizing the garden into rows, separated by pathways. Bed width is determined in advance and measured from the middle of one pathway to the middle of the next.

Bio-activators: Different preparations of micro-organisms (mycorrhizae, bacteria, etc.) that improve soil fertility by increasing the availability of nutrients already present in the soil. Bio-stimulant is an equivalent term.

Biocontrol agents: Living organisms, generally insects, used to control crop pests. Example: Trichogramma are tiny wasps that parasitize the European corn borer at the larval (caterpillar) stage.

Biodynamics: An approach to agriculture proposed in 1924 by the anthroposophist Rudolph Steiner (1861-1925). The main agricultural practices that characterize biodynamics are the application of biodynamic preparations (e.g., cow horn manure) to compost and plants to stimulate beneficial interactions (e.g., those involving micro-organisms), the use of a calendar to plan operations based on lunar phases and constellations, and having a complete life cycle on the farm that includes growing plants and raising animals.

Biointensive farming: Broadly refers to a horticultural method in which growers maximize crop yields from a minimum area of land, while seeking to preserve or even improve the quality of the soil.

Biopesticides: Plant protection products made of plant extract (e.g., pyrethrum) or micro-organisms or their derivative (e.g., Bacillus thuringiensis/Bt). They are generally available in liquid or wettable powder form.

Blossom-end rot: A physiological disease that is common in peppers and tomatoes. It generally occurs when the weather changes from dry to wet and is caused by a lack of calcium in the soil or irregular watering, which limits the availability of calcium to the plant. It appears as a circular black spot that develops at the base of the fruit. It is common to see opportunistic fungi colonizing this fragile zone.

Bolting: Process during which a plant goes to seed. Harvest may be lost if the plants bolt prematurely, which is usually caused by extreme climate conditions.

***Brassicaceae*:** Botanical family that includes many vegetables such as broccoli, cabbage, turnips, and radish. The plants, crucifers, are recognized by their cross-shaped flower, from which the name "crucifer" is derived.

Broadfork: A long u-shaped fork with several teeth that drive into the soil vertically. This ergonomic gardening tool makes it possible to use leverage to work the soil deep down to aerate without turning it. The purpose of this cultivation is to create loose, fertile soil, which encourages the crop roots to spread downward rather than side-ways. This makes it possible to plant crops close together without them running into each other at the root level.

***Bacillus thuringiensis var. Kurstaki* (Btk):** Btk is a species of bacteria that is naturally present in the soil. It is used as a biopesticide to suppress the population of many insect pests in agriculture and forestry. In market gardening, it is mainly used to control *lepidopterans* (butterflies and moths).

Canopy: In horticulture, this term refers to the upper level of the plants where the leaves are found. If the crops are planted closely together, the canopy "umbrella" creates a micro-climate and limits weed growth.

Capillary action: The process by which liquid is pulled up thru the soil. Water climbs through capillary action in micro-pores that are created by compaction of the soil surface. This process is what allows moisture deep in the soil to reach the plant growth zone near the surface.

Channel: A small, sloped ditch for water drainage.

Chisel plow: A deep tillage tool pulled by a tractor. The tool is equipped with fixed teeth that tear up and loosen the soil without turning it. It was invented to replace the plow. It helps to preserve a cover of crop residues on the soil surface to prevent erosion. The tool dates from the Dust Bowl period, when a series of dust storms struck the U.S. in the 1930s.

Compaction: An increase in soil density caused by packing of the upper layer. In market gardening, the main causes of compaction are the weight of the tools and the number of trips they make over the soil, as well as excessive tillage.

Cotyledon: The first leaves which appear on seedlings that have just germinated from the seed. Dicotyledonous plants (e.g., legumes) have two cotyledons, while monocotyledonous plants (e.g., grasses) have only one.

Couch grass: A perennial weed in the *Poaceae* family. It is difficult to control in crops because of its vigorous rhizomes, which propagate quickly and multiply when cut by the action of a hoe or rotary tilling machine.

Crop rotation: A technique of growing different groups of crops in succession on the same plot.

Crop system: A set of procedures adopted by a vegetable grower for production. A variety of practices make up the cropping system, such as permanent beds, crop rotation, succession, etc.

Cultivar: A variety of vegetable species developed by humans through genetic selection with the goal of encouraging certain characteristics, such as beauty, productivity, growth rate, and resistance to certain diseases. The terms "variety" and "cultivar" are often used interchangeably.

Cultivating: Scraping the soil superficially, with a hoe or other tool, to eliminate weeds. The terms "hoeing" and "cultivating" are often used interchangeably, as the same tools can be used to do both. However, the objective to hoeing is to aerate the soil, not to weed it.

Cucurbitaceae: A family of plants with creeping, often thick vines and large fruits (e.g., pumpkins, squash, cucumbers, and melons).

Damping off: A disease that appears as the base of a plant's stem, becoming shriveled and lanky. It leads to weakness and subsequent death of the plant. It is common in plant nurseries, but there are few ways to fight it. Preventative measures are important.

Deficiency: A condition that results when a plant lacks a substance which is essential to its growth. It may be caused by lack of nutrients in the soil or the unavailability of these nutrients. It can cause any number of symptoms, notably discoloration in the leaves. This is not to be confused with phytosanitary problems (e.g., pathogenic fungi and bacteria, insect pests, or viruses).

Drip irrigation: A technique that uses a polyethylene pipe, in which emitters (aka drippers) distribute water to the base of the plants in a slow and controlled fashion. It is much more precise and economical (in terms of water usage) than sprinkler systems. It is also called "trickle irrigation" or "micro-irrigation."

Dumping: A commercial practice that consists of selling a product for less than it costs to produce (i.e., at a loss) with the goal of selling the merchandise quickly or beating the competition. It is generally considered an underhanded practice.

Early crops: The first vegetables of a crop harvested outside their normal season. Producing early crops can give farmers a major competitive advantage at market. There are different techniques to produce early crops, such as row cover, tunnels, greenhouses, etc.

Energy efficiency: A strategy to save energy through various means. In the case of a green housing, energy efficiency is mostly a question of insulating the building, eliminating drafts, and using thermal screens and heat mats.

Erosion: Degradation of the soil by atmospheric elements, chiefly wind and water, leading to the loss of topsoil, which is the most productive soil in vegetable production. Erosion is a horizontal motion, while leaching is a vertical motion.

Etiolated: Describes a plant that lacks light and grows

taller to compensate. Etiolated plants are leggy, discolored, and less vigorous.

Fertigation: A technique of applying water-soluble fertilizers via an irrigation system. It is a combination of "fertilization" and "irrigation."

Fertilizer: An organic or mineral substance incorporated into the soil to maintain or increase fertility.

Fertilizing waster substances: The name given to all organic or mineral substances from human activity that have fertilizing potential. They include sludge (aka "biosolids") and compost management (e.g., storage and spreading). Production of fertilizing waste substances is governed by government standards.

Flame weeder: Device that produces flames used to eliminate weeds by thermal shock rather than calcination.

Flea beetle: A member of a group of small beetles with shiny black shells that jump when disturbed. Their damage is easy to spot. Adults leave small, roundish holes in leaves.

Forcing: The use of different horticultural techniques to bring a crop to harvest before the end of its normal growth duration.

Fruiting period: Period during which a plant forms fruit.

Genetically modified: An organism whose genomes has been modified by genetic engineering to give it unnatural properties.

Greenhouse grower: A vegetable grower specializing in greenhouse production.

Green manure: A crop intended to amend the soil, to prevent erosion and leaching of nutrients, and/or to fight weeds (e.g., by smothering or allelopathy). Green manures are not intended for sale.

Green Revolution: The name for the technological leap in agriculture between 1960 and 1990, characterized by increased specialization in crops, which, in conjunction with the use of synthetic chemicals and pesticides, resulted in a spectacular increase in agricultural productivity.

Hardening off: Exposing transplants to harsh weather conditions in order to increase their resistance once they are planted in the garden. The term "acclimatized" is also used.

Hardiness zones: The hardiness scale is a series of codes attributed to ornamental plants based on their capacity to resist frost. Geographic zones are defined based on a formula which takes account several climatic factors influencing plant hardiness in a given area. Minimum winter temperature is the most important factor with respect to plant survival.

Hilling: Forming a mound or hill at the base of a plant.

Hoeing: The action of loosening and aerating the upper layer of soil around the crops.

Horticultural techniques: Methods used in vegetable production. Examples include false seed bed technique, flame weeding, pruning, etc.

Inflorescence: A plant organ with a cluster of flowers, such as that found in the center of a broccoli or cauliflower plant.

Leaf spot: A fungal disease affecting plant leaves. It is frequently found in carrots and beets. The pathogenic fungus makes a dark brown spot that eventually transforms into localized necrosis, or dead, dry tissue. In serious cases, spots may multiply and kill the leaves of a crop.

Liming: Amending the soil with lime or other calcic substance. The practice is often necessary in soil that is overly acidic or deficient in calcium.

Loam: A type of soil made up of a relatively even mix of sand, silt and clay particles. Depending on the exact proportions of these particles, the loam maybe further described as sandy, silty or clayey.

Market gardener: An artisan of the soil who does his/her work on a small cultivated area in greenhouses and open fields. He/she produces a wide variety of vegetables and sells them directly to consumers.

Member: The name given to a "customer" of a community supported agriculture (CSA) farm service. Unlike normal customers, members purchase part of a harvest in advance, thus sharing with the farmer the risk involved in farming.

Microclimate: Special climatic conditions in a localized area (e.g., a valley, a site, a farm) which differ from the rest of the area. It may be favorable to specific crops due to factors such as humidity, temperature, and sun.

Microgreens: Young leaves of a crop of greens.

Mineralization: The release of mineral elements (e.g., nitrogen potassium, phosphorus) contained in organic matter via the action of biological activity in the soil. Mineralization makes available the nutrients needed for plant growth.

Mite: A tiny insect predator used to biocontrol, mainly in greenhouse production.

Node: The part of the plant where a new leaf develops from the main stem.

Organic matter: All living or dead material of animal or plant origin found in the soil. It is in most soil in varying proportions (usually between 0.5% and 10%). Fresh organic matter is made of leaves, twigs, crop residues, roots, micro-organisms, etc. Decomposed organic matter forms the humus in the soil.

Peatmoss: A spongy, organic material resulting from the slow decomposition of plants (sphagnum moss) in the wet, acidic, oxygen-poor conditions of bogs.

Peduncle: Points of attachment between the fruit and the stem of the plant.

Permaculture: A farm system design developed in the 70s by Australian Bill Mollison and David Holmgren. It was founded on principles of ecology and design. It endeavors to create self- managed, productive, and energetically efficient agricultural systems. Today, it applies to all spheres of human activity through initiatives, such as Cites in Transition.

Pests: Insects and other organisms (e.g., mammals, birds) which harm crops.

Phenology: The study of the influence of climate on the development of plants (e.g., foliation, flowering, fruiting) and animals.

Plant nursery: A place where young plants are grown for the purpose of transplanting, usually a greenhouse.

Plant protection: A set of preventative and curative strategies designed to protect crops from pests in light of their break-even point.

Potassium sulfate: Ground rock used as a natural fertilizer in organic agriculture.

Potting up: The action of transplanting seedlings grown

in containers into larger containers in order to give them more space to grow.

Powdery mildew: A disease that is caused by microscopic fungi. It appears as fluffy white spots and especially affects the leaves of *Cucurbitaceae* crops, generally at the end of the season. It should not be confused with "real" mildew, which affects potatoes, tomatoes, and other crops

Pyrethrum: An insecticidal powder extracted from dried chrysanthemum flowers. It is slightly toxic to humans.

Ramial chipped wood (RCW): An uncomposed mix of chipped wood branches. By extension, the term also refers to a growing technique designed to restore humus-rich soil that imitates soil found in forests. It consists of introducing freshly cut branches, up to 2¾ in. in diameter, and shredded wood.

Rotary harrow: A tool for shallow tillage, with teeth that turn on a vertical axis, unlike the rototiller, whose teeth are on a horizontal axis. This machinery is mainly used to prepare seedbeds.

Rotenone: An insecticide derived from the roots of plants in the *Fabaceae* family. It has been used in agriculture for a long time. However, its harmlessness is now being questioned.

Rototiller: A tilling machine that turns and mixes the soil by the action of bent teeth mounted on a horizontal axis.

Runoff: Drainage of any rainwater that does not soak into the soil or evaporate in the air. One cause of erosion is water that carries away soil particles as it drains. The particle size depends upon flow rate and slope.

Seeding: A group of plants grown from seed on a given date. They can be started directly in the garden (direct seeding) or indoors to be transplanted at a later time (indoor seeding).

Seedling: A young plant with only a few leaves.

Shade cloth: A tarp or net with fairly tight mesh that is used to cover a crop to protect it from the sun, and by extension, from overheating. The material makes it possible to maintain the right conditions for cool-climate crops when temperatures are high.

Share: In CSA, the share is part of the harvest distributed each week to members. It is generally made up of 8-12 different vegetables and herbs.

Soil mix: The substrate for crops seeded indoors. It is made of soil mixed with minerals or decomposed plant or animal matter (e.g., peat moss, perlite, vermiculite, and compost).

***Solanaceae*:** A botanical family which includes potatoes, tomatoes, peppers, eggplants, and ground cherries.

Straw mulch: The remnants of cereal and grain crops used as mulch material. It can be problematic, because most grain farmers who sell straw use herbicides to control weeds. Herbicidal residues can be carried into a garden. Organic straw is hard to find, and may still contain large amounts of weed seeds, which will be brought into the garden. Straw made from first-cut fall rye is best to use because it is harvested at the beginning of the summer when few weeds have gone to flower. This makes it more likely to be clean and free of herbicides, even if produced by a conventional farmer.

Striped cucumber beetle: The main insect pest affecting the *Cucurbitaceae* family. In the adult stage, it has a black head and a yellow/orange body with three black stripes.

Thinning: Removing certain plants to allow the remaining ones to develop better. The goal is to achieve the optimal density for a direct-seed crop. It is also called pricking out.

It is generally done by hand.

Topping: Cutting off the main ends of a plant so that is stops putting out leaves and instead concentrates its energy on fruiting. This allows fruit crops (tomato, pepper, cucumber, brussels sprouts, etc.) to reach maturity sooner than expected.

Tops: The name for the leaves of certain vegetables, most notably carrots.

Transplanting: A horticultural technique in which plants are started indoors in soil mix and later planted in gardens.

Vegetable grower: A farmer who grows vegetables commercially, in greenhouses or fields.

Vetch: A plant in the *Fabaceae* family grown as a green manure. Common vetch is an annual species, while hairy vetch can be grown as a biennial. It should not be confused with tufted vetch, which is a weed.

Water budget: The relationship between amount of water that accumulates in the soil from precipitation and the amount that is lost by evapotranspiration, over a defined period. The water budget makes it possible to estimate the amount of water available in the soil to meet plant needs.

Yurt: A round tent traditionally used as a house by the nomad people of central Asia (e.g., Mongolia). It is made out of canvas or acrylic. It makes an excellent temporary shelter in a temperate climate.

Homesteading Vocabulary

Above the bit: When a horse raises his head above the level of the rider's hands in order to ignore the rider's commands, therefore reducing the control the rider has over the horse.

Abscess: A pocket of pus-surrounding inflamed tissue.

AC: Alternating current, an electric current provided by electric company.

Achilles tendon: Leg tendon that connects the heel bone to the calf muscle on the leg.

Action: In horse terms, movement of the horse's legs.

Adze: A cutting tool with a curved blade at a right angle from the handle. It is used to hollow out, hew, scrape, and roughly shape leg pieces of wood, especially logs.

Aerial roots: Roots that come out of the ground as additional support for the plant, to enable climbing or to increase the amount of nutrients and gases the plant is absorbing.

Aerobic: A process which depends on free oxygen air, especially for fermentation or decomposition, such as for human waste.

Afterbirth: Placenta and blood delivered from the uterus after giving birth to offspring.

Agalactia: When a lactating mother does not produce milk right after giving birth.

Aids: In horse terms, signals or cues that a rider gives to the horse to tell it what to do. Natural aides are voice, legs, hands, and weight. Artificial aids are whips and spurs.

Air compressor: A device which takes air and compresses it, then delivers it at a high pressure.

Air above the ground: When a highly-trained horse performs complicated moves, such as high school movements, where either the front legs or all four legs are off the ground.

Albino: Lacking pigment in the skin. A true albino has very white or pink skin, white hair/fur, and pink eyes.

Alkali: Any water-soluble salts found in soils that turn litmus paper blue. In too large of quantities, it can be harmful to agriculture.

Amble: In horse terms, a slower gait than pacing.

Amperage: The strength of a current of electricity.

Anaerobic: The process of being alive or active without free oxygen, such as for anaerobic bacteria that breaks down human waste. It is the opposite of aerobic activity.

Anesthetic: Partial or total loss of sensation, induced by injecting a drug or with an oral medication.

Anhidrosis: Limited or complete inability to sweat.

Annual: A plant which completes its life cycle within a year.

Anther: The primary male reproductive structure at the tip of a flower's stamen. The anther produces pollen which fertilizes the ovules to make seeds.

Anthropomorphize: To ascribe human characteristics to something that is not human, such as an animal or object.

Antifreeze: Liquid added to water in a cooling system in order to lower the temperature at which it freezes.

Anvil: A heavy iron table used by blacksmiths to hammer metal. It has various parts for different kinds of work including a face, pritchel hold, table, and horn.

Areola: A small ring of pigment around the nipple of the breast.

Array: A single solar module is a glass sheet enclosing either a single crystal or poly-crystal solar cells on top of a waterproof backing material and edged with an aluminum mounting frame. Several modules make a solar array.

Artery: Any tube in the body that carries blood from the heart to cells, tissues, and organs.

Artesian: A type of well in which water fills it through internal hydrostatic pressure, or simply the pressure water has when sitting still. When digging such a well, it will fill with water quickly without further effort.

Artificial aids: Tools used to help command the horse, such as spurs or whips.

Ascarids: Internal parasites that plague animals, such as round worms.

At grass: A horse who has been turned out to pasture, paddock, or field.

Auger: A metal hand tool for drilling holes, especially in wood.

Awl: A tool with handle and a sharp, straight metal end used to poke holes in tough material, such as canvas or leather.

Ax: A tool with a wooden handle called a helve and a heavy metal head with sharp edge. It is used in a chopping motion to cut wood.

Azoturia: A technical term for tying up or Monday morning sickness, when horse has prolonged muscle contractions during exercise.

Back at the knee: A conformational fault in a horse where the upper leg is set back further than lower leg. It is more serious than over at the knee because it puts more strain on tendons.

Back breeding: In horse terms, breeding back to a certain stallion to preserve a certain genetic trait.

Back cut: The second cut that causes tree to fall. Also known as the felling cut.

Bacteria: A single-celled organism, some which are good for humans, breaking down waste material, and some which are bad, causing infections and disease. A single bacteria is called a bacterium.

Bail: The handle of a bucket, a half-circle made of wire or wood.

Balustrade: The railing used on the edge of balconies and stairs.

Bandy-legged: When a horse's hock turns outward, also known as bow-hocks. It is the opposite of cow-hocks.

Banged tail: A horse's tail that has been trimmed flat at the bottom. It is only seen on dressage and hunter horses.

Barn sour: A horse who does not like being ridden away from the barn or leaving their pasture mates.

Barrel: The area of the horse's body between forelegs and loins.

Barren tillers: Secondary stalks which grow from the base of a wheat plant that do not grow grain seeds.

Bars: In horse terms, the fleshly area between the front and back teeth where the bit rests.

Bascule: In horse terms, the arc a horse makes when jumping a fence.

Bast: Fibers in hemp plants that are used in making hemp paper.

Bat: Also known as a whip or crop. An artificial aid used to encourage a reluctant or lazy horse to move forward. It is also used to punish. In making pottery, a wooden or plastic circular board which is put on the wheel so that the pot can be removed easily once formed.

Bay: In horse terms, a deep reddish-brown coat color with a black main and tail.

Bay window: Any window space that projects outward from the walls of a building.

Beam: A structural member of a building made of wood or metal that transversely supports a load.

Bedding: Absorbent material put on the ground in animal housing to soak up urine and make cleanup easier. It also provides softness for the hooves and feet.

Beetle: A wooden mallet or hammer made of ironwood and a band, with metal bands on the head to strengthen it. It is used to drive in gluts or make mortise and tenon joints.

Bellows: Two triangular pieces of wood hinged together. The top piece has a handle and a hole in the middle of the board. Between the boards is a folding frame covered in airtight material. On the end of the bellows is a round hole or spout to let air out. The top board is pushed up and down, forging air out of the spout. Bellows are used to heat a forge fire.

Behind the pit: When a horse holds its head close in order to ignore the rider's commands. It is also known as over-bent.

Bent: A section of a timber frame house, or one "frame," which consists of two vertical sides and a peak which supports the roof of the house.

Biennial: A plant that takes two seasons to complete its life cycle.

Billets/Billets straps: Straps used to attach the girth to saddle.

Billy: A male goat.

Bind: When cutting down tree, when the saw gets caught or stuck in the tree during cutting.

Binder's knot: A knot tied with wheat stalks around a handful of stalks to make a sheave.

Biodiesel: A mix of ethanol, vegetable oil, and lye, processed through transesterification to produce a substitute for regular diesel.

Biodynamics: A method of agriculture created by Rudolf Steiner which seeks to work with the health-giving forces of nature. It attempts to follow the rhythms of the earth and cosmos. It has special formulas of compost for the soil.

Biofilter: Biological filtration. The process of filtration and purification using natural biomass. It can be used to remove odors, purify water, clean fish tanks, or treat home waste.

Biointensive: A method of agriculture which utilizes small spaces to create a sustainable garden that can grow enough calories to feed people. It uses compost, intensive planting, companion planting, and open pollination seeds.

Biomass: The total mass of plant material and animal waste in a given area that is being converted into a fuel. The usual result of this process is heat.

Bit: A mouthpiece made of metal, rubber, or some other material which is held on by the bridle. It is used to convey instructions to a horse.

Bitumastic: A protective coating over metal structures that are exposed to weathering, usually made partly of asphalt.

Blade: A metal or wooden part of plow that turns over soil without cutting the soil.

Blanch: To cook briefly, especially for vegetables.

Block plane: A tool that has a shallow-pitched blade. It is used to shrink a stick that fits too tightly.

Bog spavin: A soft, liquid-filled swelling on the inside of a horse's hock that does not usually cause lameness, unlike regular spavin.

Boll: A ball formed of leaves on a cotton plant that forms after the flower falls off. The boll holds the ball of cotton that holds the seeds, similar to a seed pod.

Bone: In horse terms, the measurement around the leg just below the knee or hock. This measurement determines a horses' ability to carry weight. Light-boned means a limited weight capacity.

Bosal: A braided nose band used in western riding that is the equivalent of a bitless bridle.

Bot: A parasite that bothers horses. Also known as botflies.

Bottom: The blade of a plow that turns over soil.

Bovine: A family of mammals which include bulls, cows, steer, and oxen.

Bowed hocks: In horse terms, when the hock turns outward. Also known as bandy-legged. It is the opposite of cow-hocks.

Bowed tendon: An injury to a tendon that runs down the back of a horse's lower leg.

Boxy hooves: In horse terms, it describes a narrow, upright hoof with a small frog and a closed heel. Also known as a clubbed foot.

Breaking/breaking in: When a young horse is taught basic skills prior to learning riding and driving.

Breaking loose: When removing a tire, loosening all of the lug nuts before removing them.

Breed: A certain type of animal that is bred for certain characteristics over a long period of time. It is also a word describing the act of mating two animals together.

Bridle: A piece of equipment worn on the horse's head, which bits and reins can be attached to in order to communicate with the horse.

Bridging: A network of boards that connect floor joists together to help support the floor.

Bridoon: A snaffle bit used with a curb bit in a double bridle.

Broadax: An ax with a 12-14 in. blade. The eye, the hole where the blade fits into the handle, is at an angle so it will swing out of the way for the knuckles.

Broadcasting: A method of planting seeds in which they are scattered randomly rather than planted in rows, sometimes utilizing the wind to sow them further.

Brood: A group of young animals hatched at one time, especially for birds, but also applicable to bees. To brood is to sit on or hatch eggs, or the mothering protection of hovering near and defending one's young.

Brood cell: Cells in honeycomb that hold growing baby bees.

Brood mare: In horse terms, a mare used for breeding.

Broken winded: A horse with abnormal breathing patterns caused by chronic obstructive pulmonary disease, also known as heaves.

Brushing: In horse terms, when the hoof or the shoe hits the inside of the leg near the fetlock, usually due to poor conformation or action.

Brushing boots: Boots made especially for horses who have problems with brushing to avoid injury.

Buck: In horse terms, when the horse leaps into the air with the head lowered and the back arched.

Bucking: Cutting a log into the lengths of wood needed for building.

Bucksaw: The best tool for sawing wood. It has a wood frame and wire that tightens.

Bull: A male bovine animal.

Bungee: An elastic cord with J or S hooks on each end. They are used for anything from tying down things to holding a clutch on a truck together.

Burr mill: Two millstones set a distance apart of 1/16 in. so it can scrape the hulls of oats off without crumbling the groats, the grain, inside.

Butcher: To kill and prepare animals for food, or a person with the knowledge to do so.

Butter mold: A round dish with sides, and sometimes a lid that has a carved picture on the inside. It is greased then butter is pressed into it to make a picture in the butter.

Butt-up: The type of roof ridge made in thatching, which forces the straw together from both sides of the roof to form a peak.

Cable hoist puller: Also known as a come along. A tool attached to a log chain that ratchets the chains tight and helps to control a tree's fall as it is being cut down.

Calf: Young cattle usually under 1.5 years old.

Calorie: A unit of how much energy a food has or has the potential to make when it is oxidized in the body. Energy is created by heat.

Calve: When a cow gives birth to a calf.

Calyx: The outer ring of sepals that protect the unopened forming flower bud.

Cannon bone: In horses, the bone in the lower foreleg between the knee and the fetlock. Also known as the shinbone.

Canter: A horse's gait with three beats where the leading hind leg strikes first followed by the opposite diagonal pair. In western riding it is called a lope.

Cantle: The back ridge of an English saddle.

Capped hocks: In horse terms, swelling on the point of the hock caused by an injury or lying down without enough bedding.

Capstone: A flat stone set on top of a rock wall to finish it off.

Carburetor: Part of an engine that mixes gasoline vapor with air before it is ignited.

Cast: A horse that rolls and gets stuck against some wall or fence.

Castings: Worm manure. It is the best manure for soil.

Castrate: To remove reproductive organs, either the testicles or ovaries. It is most often done to male mammals.

Catgut: Thin strips of sheep intestine sterilized and used as thread to suture or stitch up a wound.

Caulking: Material used to top up joints and seams to make them waterproof. To caulk is to install this material.

Cavalletti: A low wooden jump used to teach a horse and rider how to jump.

Cavesson: A noseband that fits onto a bridle; a leather or nylon headgear with attachments for side rains, and a lunge line for lunging.

Cold Cranking Amps (CCA): A rating for how well an engine battery starts in cold temperatures. The higher the CCA number the better.

Cellar: A dark, cold room usually dug underground and used to store food. A storm cellar is used to protect people from tornadoes and hurricanes.

Cellular respiration: The process plants use to extract energy through a chemical breakdown of stored food molecules.

Cetane: The cetane number is a measure of how well a fuel ignites when it is compressed. The higher the cetane number, the cooler it burns and better the fuel it is.

Chaff: The dry outer parts over the husk of mature wheat and other grains that can be remove by threshing or flailing.

Chainsaw: A cutting tool with a gas engine that turns a chain at high speeds. It is used to cut long pieces of wood and logs.

Chainsaw file: A special round file for sharpening the hook in the chain of a chainsaw.

Charkha: A tiny spinning wheel designed by Gandhi to spin cotton. The spindle unfolds from a small box and sits on the floor.

Checking: When a board that is drying shrinks unevenly, causing it to warp and crack.

Chestnut: In horse terms, a small rubbery bump on the inside of the legs.

Chicken wire: A type of fencing made of thin wire woven into small hexagons, which chickens cannot get through.

Chinking: Waterproof material such as clay or mortar that is stuffed into spaces between the logs in a cabin. To chink is to perform this task.

Chip/chip in: When a horse adds a small step right in front of a fence before jumping.

Churn: A container that uses either paddles run by a handle and crank mechanism or a pole that is dashed up and down into milk in the container. It is used to make cream into butter.

Cider press: A mill and press that crushes apples for juice. It is turned by a hand crank.

Cinch: In horse terms, a strap attaching the saddle to the horse. It is called the girth in English riding.

Cistern: Any kind of underground tank used to store water, but especially for storing rainwater.

Class: In Latin classification, it is a category within the phyla of a plant kingdom. For example, *Monocot* class in the *Angiosperm* phyla in the plant kingdom.

Clean-legged: A horse that does not have feathering on the lower legs.

Clevis/clevy: On a plow, where the draught is attached.

Cloaca: A cavity in birds and fish that contains intestinal, genital, and urinary tracts.

Cloche: Like a miniature green house, it is a small flexible frame with a plastic cover in a dome shape that sits over plants to protect them from frost.

Clod crusher: A machine drawn by horses that breaks up tough clods left after plowing. There are 24 cast iron discs with teeth that revolve separately. The wheels alternatively rise and fall to prevent clogging.

Cob: A horse that is stocky and well-built for carrying heavy riders. It can also refer to a form of natural building material based on mud.

Coffin bone: In horse terms, a small bone within the hoof.

Cohousing: Usually built in a city, it is housing that is created to help build community. The goal is usually to lower housing costs, however, most cohousing is now more expensive because of community benefits.

Cold blood: Any heavy European breed of horses descended from the forest horse.

Cold frame: A wooden box with a glass lid on a hinge so it can be opened and closed. Plants are grown in the frame so it can act like a small greenhouse, protecting plants from cold weather.

Collection: In horse terms, when the rider causes the horses' frame to be compacted. The horse is light and supple, the baseline shortened, the croup lowered, the shoulder raised, and the head vertical.

Colic: Severe abdominal pain. It can happen in any animal or human.

Colostrum: The first milk produced by a mammal which is essential for the survival of the creature. It protects infants from disease and builds immunity.

Colt: An uncastrated male horse up to 4 years old. A male foal is a colt foal.

Come along: See cable hoist puller.

Coming: In horse terms, when a horse is approaching a certain age, he is said to be coming to it (i.e., coming to).

Commune: A community in which all the members have given up personal property rights. Instead, the community as a whole owns the property. Members often share a common interest, work, and income.

Companion planting: Growing a plant next to another plant because they complement and benefit each other.

Compost: The act of converting organic material into its basic state, rich dirt and soil. Any mixture of decaying plant waste and manure is compost.

Condensation: With liquids, the process of changing from a gas to a liquid or solids, such as turning steam back into water.

Conformation: The overall way in which a horse is put to gather, the proportions of its anatomy.

Coolant: A liquid which produces a cooling effect, especially if it is used to transfer heat away from one part to another.

Chronic Obstructive Pulmonary Disease (COPD): See broken winded.

Cord: A stack of wood 4 ft high, 4 ft wide, and 8 ft long.

Corn cultivator: A cultivator made specifically to cultivate corn.

Corn knife: A knife with a straight blade that is about 1.5 ft (18 in) long and is used to cut corn stalks. It is kept very sharp. The older type is strapped to the leg so bending over is not necessary.

Corolla: The part of the plant known as the flower. Layers of petals ring the receptacle and are pretty to attract bees and birds.

Corrosion: Any kind of decay or erosion caused by a chemical reaction.

Cotton cultivator: A cultivator made especially for cotton.

Cotyledon: Part of the seed where the seedling gets food. In some cases, it is a storage area, and in other seeds it absorbs the food from the endosperm.

Coulter: Part of a plow that cuts the furrow slice in front of the share.

Counter canters: The horse canters in a circle with the outside leg leading instead of the common inside leg.

Cow: Any bovine female animal.

Cow-hocked: In horse terms, the hocks are turned in like a cow. It is the opposite of bow-hocked.

Cardiopulmonary Resuscitation (CPR): The process of restoring a person's heartbeat and respiration when they have lost consciousness.

Cracked heels: In horse terms, when the heels become inflamed and the skin cracks and pus releases.

Cracking: Breaking the kernel of a grain into two or more pieces.

Cradle: A rack connected to a snath for catching the grain as it is cut.

Crawl space: A low space beneath the floor that gives people access to a building's plumbing and wiring.

Cream separator: A device that uses centrifugal force to remove cream from milk. It has a maximum of 18 discs that milk is forced through. When used with goat's milk, either adjust the separator or buy one especially for goat's milk.

Crib-biting/cribbing: When a horse hooks his teeth into something solid and sucks air in through the mouth. If done without latching onto something it is called "wind sucking."

Crimping: Flattening the kernel of a grain slightly, especially oats.

Crop: A whip or bat. An artificial aid used to encourage reluctant/lazy horses, or used to punish. It is also a group of a specific agriculture produce grown in a year. In bird anatomy, it is the pouch in the gullet where food is partially digested so it can be regurgitated for its young.

Crossbreeding: Mating two horses of different breeds or types.

Crosscut saw: A saw used for cutting across the grain of wood. It can have one handle or two handles for two people to use at the same time.

Cross pein: A blacksmith's hammer, shaped with a ball instead of a flat circle, similar to a claw hammer.

Cross-pollinator: A plant that has to have help from wind or insects to pollinate

Crossties: Using two ropes or ties to tether a horse by putting one on each side and connecting them to a post or wall.

Croup: In horse terms, the top of the hindquarters from the point of the hip to the tail.

Crow hopping: When a horse leaps in the air with all four feet off the ground at the same time.

Cues: Also known as aids. They are signals used by a rider to communicate to a horse.

Cultivator: The name properly means any implement that is used to cultivate plants after they have started growing, but it has been improperly used for tools that prepare the ground, such as the harrow. It is mostly used to destroy weeds that have grown between plants that have been planted in rows only. Most can be adjusted for the width of the rows using screws or iron keys. It is usually shaped with several bars with curved teeth coming out of them, but some are shaped like plows, which throws dirt on either side.

Curb: When the tendon or ligament below the point of the hock thickens from strain.

Curb bit: A bit that has cheeks and a curb chain, which lies in a chin groove. In double-bridle, it is used with a bridoon or snaffle bit.

Curb chain: A chain used with a curb bit.

Curriculum: All the courses of study offered by an educational institution or a group of related courses in a field of study.

Cutting down ax: An ax that has a handle the perfect length for the user. It is used for cutting down trees.

Cutting up ax: An ax with a good length helve, or handle, for the user. It is used to cut up cordwood.

Cyst: A pouch or sac without an opening that contains fluid and develops abnormally in a body.

Daisy clipper: A horse that seems to be hugging the ground when it moves.

Dam: A horse's or calf's biological mother. It is also an obstruction to running water, such as a stream or river, which slows the flow of water to create a pond or lake.

Dumping off: Death of seedlings by fungal disease before or after they emerge from the pod.

Debeak: Clipping the tip off of a chicken's beak so it cannot hurt itself or others.

Decant: To pour off a liquid without disturbing the sediment at bottom.

Deckle: A frame with a screen used in making paper.

Deadhead: To remove dead flowers from a plant by pinching off the flower and ovary from the stem in order to encourage more blooming.

Depth of girth: The measurement from the top of the withers to the elbow. Large measurements are good depth of girth.

Detangler: A solution put into the hair or fur which prevents it from tangling, usually a type of conditioner.

Dewormer: Medication for curing an animal of worms.

Diagonals: In horse terms, when the legs move in pairs. A left diagonal is when the left foreleg and right hindleg move together. A right diagonal is when the right foreleg and left hindleg move together.

Dibber: A tool used to make holes in the soil to plant bulbs or seedlings.

Dicot: A plant that has two seed leaves or cotyledons.

Dimension lumber: Wood cut into pieces of specific size.

Dipped back: Also called swayback; when horse's back is unusually hollow or dipped in.

Dipstick: A metal rod that is dipped into a container in order to find out the fluid level.

Disc: Also known as a wheel harrow. It is used for land

with many roots or stiff clay. Instead of teeth, there is a shaft that the discs are fixed to, called the wheel gang. It is attached to the pole and draft bars by a ball joint. It cuts and separates rather than scratches.

Dished face: In horse terms, when the nose is concave instead of straight.

Dishing: An undesirable action, where the toe of a horse's foreleg is moved outward in a circular motion with each step.

Distemper: In horse terms, a highly contagious disease also called strangles.

Distillation: A process of purifying a liquid by boiling it and condensing the vapors using a still.

Disunited: In horse terms, when the horse's legs are out of sequence during a canter.

Dock: The bony part of a horse's tail from where the hair grows.

Docking tool: A bloody, dangerous way of removing an animal's testicles. It used to be used to remove an animal's tail, which is now considered inhumane.

Dormant: A state of suspended activity in which plants stop growing to protect themselves against extreme cold or heat.

Dormer: Rooms located in the attic of a house or the windows which are put into the roof. Windows are usually perpendicular to the wall and have their own roofs.

Double bridle: A traditional English bridle has two bits, a snaffle and a curb, which gives rider greater control.

Double cultivator: A cultivator capable of cultivating three rows at a time.

Double dug: A type of raised bed garden in which the soil is double dug, or dug twice to make it fluffy and light. This method is also called French intensive gardening.

Double Michigan plow: Also called a sod and subsoil plow. It has two blades, which creates two furrows that are twisted into one. It completely breaks up the soil and plows a deep furrow, but takes more work.

Dovetail: A type of joint in woodworking that looks somewhat like the tail of a bird, with a flared shaped and fits into a notch.

Dowsing: To find water using the mysterious skill of using sticks or wire to locate underground pipes or ground water. A person with this skill is a dowser.

Draft horse: Any horse used for hauling heavy loads, but usually used for large breed horses.

Draught: Another term for a harness for an animal team, or an animal team that is especially bred for pulling.

Draw rein: A rein that attaches to the firth at one end, goes through the rings of the bit, and then back to the rider's hands. It gives the rider more control but is easily used incorrectly.

Dressage: The art of training a horse so that it is completely obedient, or the competitive sport in which a horse's dressage is judged.

Drone: A bee whose only purpose is to compete to mate with the queen bee. They have no stingers and are very fat.

Drop spindle: A wooden disc usually rounded on the bottom with a small dowel going through it. The end of the dowel protrudes down through the disc so that when it hits the floor it can spin. The end of unspun wool is attached to the dowel and then it is spun down to the floor, making thread.

Dryland distemper: Also called pigeon fever. It causes abscesses in the chest and belly.

Dutch oven: A cast iron pot with legs and a lid used directly in the fire like an oven.

Easement: A legal right-of-way on another person's property, such as road access.

Eaves: The lower border of a roof that overhangs a wall.

Equine Infectious Anemia (EIA): A virus without a cure. It is also called swamp fever.

Elastrator: A tool used to castrate an animal with the use of an elastic band. It is also called an emasculator.

Electrolyte: In the human body, ionized salts in body fluids which the body needs to live. The mixture of electrolytes conducts electricity.

Elizabethan collar: A special collar made for goats that prevent a female goat from sucking on her own udder.

Emasculator: See elastrator.

Embryo: An organism that is in the process of growing before it is born or hatched. An egg becomes an embryo when fertilized. A plant has an embryo inside the seed.

Embankment: A mound of earth or stone built to hold back water or support a road.

Enamel: Paint that dries to a hard glossy finish, or a colored glassy compound that is fused to metal, glass, or pottery for decoration or protection.

Encumbrances: On a property, when the former owner sold or reserved the right to mine, cut trees, or take water, even though the land belongs to the new owner. For example, if the new owner cuts a tree and there was an encumbrance, the new owner would be stealing the former owners' trees.

Endemic: A species that is only found in a certain location and nowhere else.

Endosperm: Food storage that surrounds the plant embryo inside the seed. The endosperm nourishes the seedling during germination.

Engagement: In horse terms, when the hind legs are well under the body.

Entire: An uncastrated male horse.

Epiphyte: Plants that grow on other plants, but are not parasites because they get their nutrients from the air, such as orchids, mosses, lichens, and some cacti.

Equine Protozoal Myeloencephalitis (EPM): A neurological disorder.

Equine Polysaccharide Storage Myopathy (EPSM): When the muscles waste away, usually in draft horses.

Equitation: The art of riding a horse.

Ergot: A horny growth on the back of a horse's fetlock joint.

Erosion: When something is worn away over time, but especially for soil. It can be caused by wind and water.

Ethanol: Another term for ethyl alcohol. It is pure alcohol which is used as a fuel, in perfumes and medicines, and as a solvent.

Euthanization: A method of purposely killing an animal in the least painful way possible, usually with gas or injection, in order to prevent further suffering.

Ewe: A female sheep.

Ewe-neck: In horse terms, a conformation fault in which the neck is concave along the top edge, instead of straight or curved outward.

Evaporator tray: A tray measuring 5 ft wide and 16 ft long that is used to evaporate sweet sorghum green juice to make syrup. It has 3-10 compartments with small openings and a spigot at the end to pour the syrup out. It should be made of black iron or stainless steel.

Eventing: An equestrian competition where riders demonstrate dressage, cross-country, and show jumping. It is also called combined training.

Extension: In horse terms, the lengthening of the horse's frame and step. It is the opposite of collection.

Extravagant action: Hackneys and saddlebred horses are often trained to have high knee and hock action called "extravagant."

Eye ring: The edges of a bird's eyelids.

Face: The top of an anvil.

Farrier: A person who shoes horses and has knowledge of hoof care.

Farrier's anvil: A smaller anvil used by a farrier to create horseshoes. It weighs between 50 and 150 lbs.

Fault: A crack in the surface of the earth. The space between two plates of the earth's crust, which often shift, causing earthquakes.

Feathering: In horse terms, long hair on the lower legs and fetlocks; usually seen on heavy breeds.

Feed cutter: A grinder especially made for cutting straw, corn, and corncobs into feed for cattle and horses. A straw cutter has self-feeding spiked rollers turned by a hand crank. It turns it into a revolving knife grinding against a fixed knife and through a chute.

Felling: When cutting down a tree, a second cut above the first cut that causes the tree to fall. Also, the act of cutting a tree.

Fermenter: A device used to ferment alcohol, usually with an airlock and a gauge.

Fertile: Anything that is capable of starting or supporting reproduction.

Fertilization: To add fertilizer to the soil; or the act of starting reproduction either through insemination or pollination.

Fertilizer: A large number of materials that, when mixed together and worked into the soil, increase its nutrient value for growing plants.

Fetlock: The lowest joint on an animal's leg.

Figure-eight noseband: Also called a Grackle noseband. In horse terms, a noseband with thin leather straps cross over at the front and buckle above and below the bit.

File: Metal tools with rough sides used to sharpen and grind by hand. There are wood files, metal files, chainsaw files, and many other files in a variety of shapes.

Filly: A female horse under 4 years old. A female foal is called a filly foal.

Firing: In horse terms, when the skin over a leg injury is burned with a hot iron to make scar tissue.

Fistulous withers: Inflammation and infection at the top of a horse's withers.

Five-gaited: A horse shown at a walk, trot, canter, slow gait, and rack instead of just the first three.

Flail: A tool for threshing, or beating, grain to remove hulls and other unwanted material called chaff. The handle is called a stave and the swinging part is the swingle. The swingle is about 2 ft long and all made of wood. The swingle is attached to the stave with wire or another material so it swings right and left.

Flashing: Sheet metal put around the chimney and dormers of a house where they connect to the roof in order to keep moisture out.

Flax breaker: A machine with two big timbers fastened together that are hinged on one end so that they move up and down. They are shaped into triangular blades and drop down into triangular slots on a special table. It looks similar to a mouth with two teeth on the top and two dents on the bottom to fit them into.

Flax card: Wooden paddles with wires poking out, similar to wool cards. It is used to comb out flax.

Flax wheel: A flax wheel it the smallest spinning wheel and runs with a foot treadle, unlike other wheels which run by hand. It is used for flax because it spins it tighter than a big wheel.

Flexion: When a horse bends his head to loosen the pressure of the bit on the lower jaw. It also describes the full bending of the hock joints. Veterinarians perform flexion tests when diagnosing lameness.

Flexor tendon: The tendon at the back of an animal's leg.

Flint: A hard stone that when struck can create a spark, which is useful for starting fires.

Floating: Rasping a horse's teeth as part of normal dental care.

Flush/flushing: Putting ewes on the richest feed or pasture in order to increase the chances of having twins or triplets.

Flying change : In horse terms, changing the canter lead to gain balance during turns.

Foal: Any horse up to 1 year old.

Foaling: The act of a horse giving birth. The dam is said to be foaling.

Fodder: Food for domestic animals.

Footing drain: A pipe placed underground around the basement which diverts flood water away or into a sewer. It is found mainly on older homes with a basement and no sump pumps.

Forage: Food for domestic animals that is usually found in the field or pasture. It is also the act of looking or searching for food, i.e., foraging for wild strawberries.

Force: To make a plant grow earlier than the normal season by tricking it into thinking it is warm outside. Bulb plants are often forced.

Forearm: In animals, the part of the foreleg above the knee.

Forehand: In horse terms, the head, neck, shoulder, withers, and forelegs. Horses with little training who pull forward on the bridle are on the forehand.

Forelock: In horse terms, the section of mane between the ear which lies on the forehead.

Forge: A forge is a building housing a large fireplace for heating metal. It contains a large bellows to heat the fire, a tub of water, an anvil, forging tools, and a woodpile. The apparatus or fire that heats the metal is also called a forge.

Forge hammer: A hammer with a large, rounded metal head, used to pound hot metal.

Forging anvil: A very heavy anvil used especially by a blacksmith, weighing between 75 and 500 lbs.

Foundation: The concrete or rock that is put into a hole the shape of the house which supports the entire house. In a beehive, a sheet of beeswax with a honeycomb imprint which encourages bees to build combs where desired.

Founder: In animals, when the coffin bone in the foot becomes detached and rotates during a severe case of laminitis. A horse with this problem is foundered.

Four-in-hand: A team of four harness horses.

Furrow: Long strips of earth which have been turned over by a plow.

Framing chisel: A thick chisel for making the holes in mortise squares.

French intensive: See double dug.

Friedman harrows: An angular harrow shaped like two wings, or a triangle. It is pulled from the peak of a triangle.

Frog: In horse terms, a triangular rubber pad on the sole of the foot that acts as a shock absorber.

Frying pan: An iron pan with an iron lid and a 3 ft iron handle.

Full mouth: A horse that has all its permanent teeth after 6 years old.

Fungus: A member of the fungal family, organisms which live as parasites. It includes mushrooms, mold, toadstools, mildew, and rust.

Fuse: A safety device that melts and interrupts an electrical circuit.

Gable: The vertical triangular end of a building from the level of the eaves to the ridge of roof.

Gad: A 4-5 ft long hardwood sapling with 2-3 ft of leather used as a whip for ox teams.

Gaggle: A group of geese.

Gait horse: A horse who moves at paces other than the regular walk, trot, and canter.

Gallop: The four-beat gait of the horse where each foot touches the ground separately.

Galvayne's Groove: A dark line appearing on the upper corner incisor of horses between the ages of 8 and 10. It is used to estimate age.

Gambrel: A large metal tool for hanging an animal during butchering. It is usually used with a hoist. It is actually two hooks that are inserted between the Achilles tendon and the ankles of the animal.

Gander: A male goose.

Gauge wheel: On a plow, it runs along the surface of the ground and determines the depth of a furrow.

Gaskin: In animals, the second thigh extending from above the hock upwards to the stifle.

Gelatin: A yellowish, transparent substance taken from boiling down animal parts, which is used in different foods.

Gelding: A castrated male horse.

Generator: An engine, either diesel or gasoline powered, which converts mechanical energy into electrical energy.

Gestation: The period of development from conception to birth inside the uterus. Also called pregnancy.

Girth: The circumference of the horse's body measured

around the barrel right behind the withers. Also, the strap on an English saddle that secures the saddle to the horse, which is also called a cinch in Western riding.

Glut: A round wedge with a thin, flat end made of ironwood that is used to wedge into logs to split boards.

Glycerin: A sweet, syrupy byproduct of a chemical reaction of fats and oils. In a homestead situation, a byproduct of biodiesel which is useful for texture in soaps and herbal remedies.

Going: In horse terms, the texture of the ground, deep going, good going, rough going, etc.

Good doer: An easy-to-keep horse that keeps healthy on a minimal amount of food.

Goose: A female goose.

Goose-pumped: A muscle developed by jumping horses on the croup. Also called a jumper's bump.

Gosling: A baby goose.

Grackle noseband: See figure-eight noseband.

Grade: A horse that is not registered by any breed association.

Grafting: To attach a branch of one variety of fruit to a tree of another variety.

Grain mill: A machine with two grinders which grains run between, grinding into smaller and smaller pieces. It can be hand cranked or electric.

Grey water: Wastewater that is not sewage or toilet waste, such as what goes down the sink or shower drain.

Grease: In horse terms, inflamed skin at the back of the fetlock and pasterns from being in the wet all the time.

Green: A horse still in the early stages of training, i.e., a green horse.

Green broke: A horse who is used to tack and rider and knows basic trainings, i.e., broken-in or broke to ride.

Greenhouse: A building made of panels which let in sunlight and is used to grow plants, especially if the plants require a warmer temperature than is currently available.

Green manure: A crop that is planted, grown to maturity, then plowed into the soil to provide fertilizer.

Grindstone: A flat, circular stone set so it can spin when it is turned with a crank or pedal. It has a small bucket hanging over the stone to be filled with water and a trough under the stone filled with water. When in use, it runs through the trough to stay wet.

Groats: Hulled buckwheat.

Grog: When making pottery, bits of dried clay particles in wet clay that gives it a grainy or sandy feel.

Grooming kit: A collection of brushes, combs, and equipment for cleaning an animal's coat, hair, and hooves.

Ground: To fasten electrical equipment to the earth to safely discharge an electrical flow.

Ground line: A pole put on the ground right in front of a fence so the horse and rider can judge the take off point for jumping.

Ground manners: The behavior of a horse while being handled during grooming, saddling, etc.

Grout: A thin mortar used to fill cracks in masonry or brickwork, but especially for laying tile. Also, the action of filling cracks with grout.

Gullet: The throat and the esophagus.

Gymnastic: Fences placed at certain distances from each other for training a jumping horse.

Habit: Riding clothes made for riding sidesaddle.

Hack: A type of horses that are elegant riding horses, or to hack or go for a ride.

Half halt: An exercise that tells the horse to pay attention before changing direction, gait, or some other movement.

Halter-broke: A young horse who only knows how to wear a halter and not much more.

Hames: In horse terms, metal arms fitted into the harness collar and linked to the traces.

Hand: In horse terms, a unit of measure to gauge height. 1 hand equals 4 in.

Hand ax: A small ax similar to a small broadax, with a handle about 1.5 ft long. It is used for hewing and cutting small things.

Hardwood: Some hardwoods maybe softer than some softwoods. The difference is in the way they produce seeds. Hardwoods make seeds with some covering, such as apples or acorns.

Hardy: A pointed tool used in blacksmithing used to make edges and cut off metal.

Harness: Horse equipment for driving a horse instead of riding.

Harness horse: A horse used for harness that has harness conformation, such as straight shoulders, etc.

Harrow: Also called spring-tooth. A tool used to break up dirt into finer pieces than a disc can accomplish and to cover up planted seeds which are drawn by a draft animal that works equipment like a large rake. A spike harrow consists of a lattice frame with teeth coming straight down which are pulled through the soil. A wheel harrow consists of a row of wheels. A shares harrow consists of sharp flat blades.

Hay: Grass or other plants such as clover or alfalfa that has been cut and dried for animal feed.

Hay rake: Equipment that gathers up the hay before it is removed from the field. A sulky hay rake has a seat to ride on. The spring-teeth gathers the hay until a lever that lifts the teeth is pulled. Hay passes under the rake and then the teeth are lowered to gather more.

Hay wagon: A wagon with tall, fence-like sides capable of holding a great amount of hay.

Header: A board at the top of the wall of a house to which the roof is attached.

Head: The measure of the pressure of falling water, such as in a stream.

Head loss: In calculating how much power is available from a stream, head loss is the amount the stream slows down from obstructions and bends.

Heart girth: On a horse, the girth of the barrel is just behind the withers, or where the heart is located.

Heart room: A horse's barrel or the space within it.

Heaves: See COPD and/or broken winded.

Heavyweight: A horse capable of carrying more than 196 lbs.

Heddle: The part of a loom that holds the warp. It may be stationary or movable with hand levers or foot pedals in order to move the warp up and down for easier weaving.

Heel: The back of an anvil.

Heifer: A female cow before she has had her first or second calf.

Heirloom: A strain of seeds which has been preserved for its unique traits, usually varieties that are very old. They are non-hybrid, organic, and open-pollinated.

Helve: An ax handle.

Hemorrhage: Too much bleeding, which begins rapidly.

Herniated disc: Also called a ruptured disc. When the cartilage between the vertebrae of the spine ruptures.

Hetchel: A wooden board with long, sharp, metal spikes sticking out of it. It is used to pip flax into shreds prior to weaving.

Hew: To wear away wood, usually by carving, whittling, or sanding, when shaping a tool or other object.

Hindquarter: On animals, the area from the rear of the flank to the top of the tail, down to the top of the gaskin. Also called the quarters.

Hinny: The child of a male horse and a female donkey.

Hives: An allergic reaction with bumps or red lesions on the skin. The technical term is urticaria.

Hock: On animals, the joint midway up the hindleg that provides most of the forward motion of the animal.

Hocks well let down: In horse terms, a horse with short cannon bones, or shanks, which is desirable because it gives strength. Long cannons are a conformational fault.

Hoe: A garden tool with a long wooden handle and a metal blade at right angles to the handle that is used to cut and dig up weeds.

Hogged mane: A horse's mane that has been shaved close.

Homeschool: Also called home education. A type of education where parents remove their children from an outside educational institution and educate them at home.

Homestead: A place where all the necessities of life are produced. In the 1800s, a homestead was free government land given to people to promote the expansion of the United States.

Horn: In horse terms, either the hard outer covering of the hoof, the toenail, or the prominent pommel on the front of a Western saddle, also called the saddle horn. On an anvil, the pointed cone on the back.

Horsemanship: The art of riding or equitation.

Horsepower: A old measurement of power based on how many horses it takes to pull a load. In modern terms, a unit of power equal to 746 watts.

Hot: In horse terms, a horse that is overly excited or a horse that becomes easily excited.

Hot blood: Any horse from Arabian or thoroughbred blood.

Huller: A grinder, not unlike a grain mill, which is especially made to remove hulls of grain. Barley requires a huller, either hand-cranked or electric.

Humanure: Human waste that is prepared to be used as manure for growing plants.

Humus: The part of dirt that comes from organic material, such as compost. It is in the final stage of decomposition and is unrecognizable as plant material.

Hunter: A type of horse suitable for being ridden with dogs for fox hunting, or any well-mannered, smooth-gaited jumping horse.

Hurd: The pulp made from a hemp plant that is used in

making hemp paper.

Husk: The tough outer cover of grain, such as corn or barley, which is not edible. To husk is to remove this outer cover.

Husking peg: A round pointed peg 3-4 ft long with a thong to attach it to the fingers. It is used to tear the corn husk loose with one quick motion.

Hybrid: A cross between a horse and any other horse-relation, such as an ass, donkey, or zebra. Also, a plant that is the result of crossbreeding two related species in very controlled conditions.

Hydrometer: A device used to determine the proof of alcohol.

Hydroponic: A method of growing plants indoors using water and special growing chemicals under UV lights.

Implement: Any farm equipment that is dragged behind a horse or tractor, such as a cultivator, harrow, plow, etc. It is used to work the ground and grow plants.

Impulsion: When a horse is moving forward in a controlled and strong fashion. It does not refer to speed.

Inbreeding: The mating of relatives and siblings. In horses, it is done to promote a certain family trait.

Incisor: The teeth located at the front of the mouth that are made for cutting and gnawing.

Incubate: To provide heat to eggs so they can complete their development in the embryo and then can hatch. Birds incubate eggs by sitting on them, and humans can do it with an incubator.

Indirect rein: Pressing the rein opposite the direction the horse is moving, against the horse's neck.

In front of the bit: When a horse pulls or hangs heavily on the rider's hand.

In hand: Controlling a horse from the ground instead of from its back.

Insemination: To put semen from a male into the reproductive tract of a female.

Inside leg: In horse terms, the legs of the horse and rider which are on the inside of the circle being traveled.

Insulation: Any material that insulates something. Material that stops the loss of heat or cold from a container or building.

Interplanting: With careful planning, some plants can be grown very close together so they can benefit each other.

Intramuscular: Within a muscle or into a muscle.

Irons: Also called stirrups. Metal pieces attached by leather stays to the saddle used for the rider's feet.

Jack: A male donkey. In automotive terms, a tool used to raise a vehicle off the ground in order to remove a tire or get under a vehicle.

Jennet/Jenny: A female donkey.

Jig: A flat piece of board with a roller on the bottom. It is used to sharpen chisels. The chisel is fastened to the board, so the blade hangs over the end. The roller is set on the grindstone, so it spins and supports the board while the chisel is sharpened. There is typically an adjuster attached to the board so different angles can be made for different chisels.

Jog: In western riding, the term for trot. In English riding, it describes a slower, shortened pace.

Joint III: A disease in foals caused by bacteria in the navel.

Jointer: A long plane with a block 2 ft long and a 2 in. wide blade that is used to level off joints and to smooth board edges. It is used prior to taking a long shaving all the way down the board.

Joist: Supports for the floor (floor joist) or ceiling (ceiling joist) in a building.

Jump and coulter plow: Equipment that is all wood with a square blade and a stick before the blade. The stick cuts a furrow, or small ditch for seeds, and the bottom makes it deeper.

Jumper: A horse bred for jumping who competes in jumping classes.

Junction box: A box that houses electrical circuits that are connected.

Kettle: An iron kettle that has legs to stand right in the fire and a handle to hang from kettle crane.

Kettle crane: A crane in the fireplace for hanging a kettle over a fire.

Kid: A young goat.

Kingdom: In Latin classification, all living things are categorized into five kingdoms.

Knob and tube: A type of electrical wiring used before 1940.

Knock-kneed: In horse terms, a conformation fault in which the knees point toward each other.

Lagoon: A septic system that is a large pool into which human waste is stirred. Air is mixed with the waste to create aerobic treatment.

Laminitis: In animals, a condition in which the laminae inside the hoof gets inflamed and painful. It can lead to founder.

Lampas: When the hard palate inside an animal's mouth swells.

Lampblack: A black substance made mostly of carbon, such as soot, that is used to make pigments and ink.

Lateral cartilages: In horse terms, the wings of cartilage attached to the coffin bone in the foot.

Lath: Thin strips of wood made in a lattice as a backing for plaster on a wall.

Laryngeal hemiplegia: Partial paralysis of the larynx causing a breathing difficulty called roaring.

Lead: In horse terms, the leading leg during a canter, e.g., right lead canter, left lead canter.

Leader: In horse terms, either the two leading horses in a team of four, or a horse harnessed in front of one or more horses. The near leader is on the left, the off leader is on the right. When spinning, any previously spun yarn that is used to start off a new bunch of wool or other fiber for spinning.

Legume: Any erect or climbing bean or pea plant of the *Leguminosae* family.

Leg up: Helping someone mount a horse by holding his or her leg, or some other assistance in climbing up something tall.

Level: A long board with a square cavity in the center. A half circle of wood, arching over the center of the board horizontally that has a notch in the top center of it. Tied onto the notch is a horsehair string with a metal weight on the end that hangs into the cavity. The weight stays inside the cavity by a small gate of wood. The board is set on the item to be measured. When the weight is off-center, the item is not level.

Lien: The right to take someone's property if they do not pay off a debt or loan. When buying property, it can have a lien or someone else can have the right to take it away if the person selling it does not repay a debt.

Light horse: Any horse other than a heavy horse or pony that is used for riding or carriages.

Light of bone: A conformation fault in which there is not enough bone below the knee to support the horse and rider without strain.

Limb: Any of the main branches coming from the trunk of a tree.

Limbing: Removing any of the main branches from the trunk of the tree, usually when preparing to cut up a tree that has been felled.

Line breeding: Mating horses with a common ancestor several generations back in order to promote a particular trait.

Loam: The ideal mixture of sand, silt, clay, and organic material in soil to make the best dirt for growing plants.

Loft: A floor in a building that is closer to the roof than a normal upstairs. It usually only covers a small portion of the house space.

Log chain: A chain used to anchor a tree as it is being chopped down, in order to control its fall.

Loins: An area on either side of the vertebrae just behind the middle of the back. In horses, this area is just behind the saddle and is the weakest part of a horse's back.

Longe/Lunge: Training a horse by working through paces in a circle with a lunge rein attached to a cavesson.

Longitudinal: When drying wood, shrinkage that causes the wood to shrink along its length.

Loom: An apparatus with several frames that are used to weave thread or yarn into fabric and rugs

Lope: In western riding, the same as a slow canter.

Lymphangitis: When the lymphatic system becomes swollen and painful, usually in the hind legs.

Mallet lever: A mallet-shaped wood tool made out of a section of a log with one branch sticking out. On the end of the "handle" is a metal loop for hitching an animal. It works like a lever to pull stumps out of the ground, by putting it next to the stump with the "handle" sticking up.

Malt: Grain that has been prepared through soaking and drying before using it to create mash for the process of brewing alcohol

Manure: Barnyard and stable dung, often mixed with animal bedding, that is gathered and used to fertilize the soil.

Mare: A female horse 4 years old or older.

Martingale: In horse terms, a neck strap that buckles around the horse's neck and another strap that attaches to the noseband or reins. The noseband attachment is a standing martingale. The reins attachment is a running martingale. It prevents the horse from raising its head.

Mash: A mixture of mashed malted grains and hot water used in brewing alcohol.

Maul: A wooden tool used to pound. It looks somewhat like a potato masher.

Meat grinder: A kitchen tool that either has a cutter blade on the outside of the grinder body or a blade or knife on the inside of the grinder body. A meat grinder can be used to grind anything, but is primarily used to grind meat.

Meconium: The dark brown or black feces passed by babies shortly after birth, and sometimes during birth. If the baby passes meconium before birth, it indicates that it is under stress. Meconium can cause severe brain damage.

Membrane: A thin, flexible layer of tissue covering a surface or separating regions or organs in an animal or plant. When a mammal gives birth, there may be a membrane around the face of the new offspring.

Menstruation: A woman's menstrual flow or menses. When a woman's uterus goes through a monthly cycle of releasing blood and debris.

Middleweight: A horse who is capable of carrying up to 196 lbs.

Mitbah: The angle of the neck of the Arabian horse that gives it the breed's characteristic arch.

Molt: Many birds lose their feathers once a year, usually after egg-laying season is over. A bird doing this is said to be molting.

Monday morning disease: Also called azoturia or tying up.

Monocot: A plant that has one seed leaf or cotyledon.

Mortar: A building material made of lime, cement, or plaster of Paris. It is used in laying bricks, tile, stone, etc.

Mortar and pestle: A mortar is a hollow block of wood or a stone bowl, and the pestle is a heavy rounded tool with a handle. Grain or herbs are put into the hollow or bowl and the pestle is used to grind it.

Mortgage: When the entity lending money to buy property holds the title on the property until it is paid off. If the borrower defaults on the loan, the lender takes the land away.

Mother of vinegar: A bacteria drawn from the air that makes vinegar.

Mower: A horse-drawn mower is pulled through a grain field and cuts the grain down. It leaves the grain in windrows, long, narrow rows of grass 8-10 ft apart. They are made to be ridden and have many levers for adjustability. The driving wheels are usually about 30 in. in diameter. They have two kinds of knives, a toothed knife for cutting grain and a regular knife for cutting grass.

Mucking/mucking out: Removing wet and soiled bedding and cleaning a stable.

Mulch: A cover over the soil after plants have come up which prevents weeds from growing and insulates the ground. It can be plastic, organic material, or newspaper.

Mule: The child of a male donkey and a female horse.

Mustang: A wild horse from the American west.

Mutton withers: A horse with wide, flat withers, such as on a quarter horse.

Nail header: A wood tool that is all one piece with a handle and a square on the end of the handle. In the square is a hole through which unfinished nails are put. The nail header holds the nail while a head is hit.

Nail rod: A long metal rod which is about the width of the desired nail, which is used during forging to cut into pieces to shape into nails.

Nanny: A female goat.

Natural farming: A technique of growing plants without plowing cultivation or fertilizer.

Naturalist: A person who studies the working of nature

and its workings as a whole, as well as creatures and organic things that live in it.

Navicular bone: A small bone inside a horse's hoof that fits horizontally between the short pastern and coffin bone.

Navicular disease: When the navicular bone degenerates causing pain and lameness.

Near side: The left-hand side of a horse.

Neck reining: Turning a horse by using the opposite rein against the neck.

Neck strap: In horse terms, a leather strap buckled around the horse's neck to help new riders, or a martingale.

Negative: Something with a negative electric charge, or electrons which are negative.

Nematode: A worm without segments that is pointed at both ends. Some are parasites.

Net head: In calculating power available from a stream, the total gross head minus the head loss.

New York plow: Designed for deep tilling and used for sugar cultivation. Instead of the width being adjusted by the clevis, it is adjusted at the end of the beam where it connects to the handle-frame.

Nibs: The handgrips on a snath.

Off side: The right side of a horse.

On the bit: When the horse is correctly holding his head near vertical and accepting rein commands.

Open-pollinated: The opposite of hybrid. The seeds are pollinated by a whole crop of seeds that have been protected from cross pollination.

Organic: According to the National Organic Standards Board, agriculture that promotes biodiversity, natural cycles, and sustainability. Pollution from air, soil, and water is minimized.

Outhouse: A small house with a pit under it that is used as a toilet, instead of plumbing.

Ovary: A flower's female reproductive system, located at the base of the pistil. The ovary contains ovules that require fertilization by sperm from pollen.

Oven rake: A tool that looks like a hoe but with a shorter handle, used to rake ashes out of the oven.

Over bent: Also called behind the bit. When the horse tucks in its head to avoid the bit.

Over face: Trying to make a young horse jump a fence when it is beyond his capability.

Overreaching: In horse terms, when the toe of the hind foot catches and injures the back of the pastern of the front foot, which can happen when galloping or jumping.

Ovule: The little eggs inside the flower's ovary. The ovules contain an egg to be fertilized by one sperm from a pollen tube.

Oxen: A team of bovine draft animals, usually steers, which are used to pull heavy loads.

Pacer: A horse who moves its legs laterally instead of diagonally.

Pack horse: A horse who carries goods in packs on either side of its back.

Paddock: A small enclosure for putting animals out to graze.

Paddy: An irrigated or flooded field where rice is grown.

Parasite: An animal or plant that lives off a host animal or plant without benefiting or killing the host.

Parch: To dry or roast by exposing to heat, but especially for making things very dry.

Partial bones: Bones on top of the skull.

Parrot mouth: In horses, an overbite where the top jaw extends forward over the bottom.

Part-bred: A horse that is part thoroughbred and part something else.

Pastern: In animals, the sloping bone in the lower leg connecting the hoof to the fetlock.

Pasteurization: Heating a liquid to a specific temperature for a period of time to kill harmful microorganisms.

Pasture: A fenced field free of harmful objects and plants that is used as a grazing area for animals. The grass is often cultivated like another crop.

Peel: A wooden shovel used to shovel food in and out of a fireplace bread oven.

Perineum: On a female, the region between the anus and the back of the vulva. During childbirth this is the part that stretches the most.

Percolation: When a liquid passes through a porous substance. For example, when water passes through soil at a certain rate, that speed is called its percolation rate.

Permaculture: A patented word created by Bill Mollison which combines permanent and agriculture. It is a method of agriculture and living that looks at the whole landscape and lifestyle to design the most efficient and caring methods for all the species living there.

PETE: Polyethylene terephthalate, which can be identified by its recycling symbol. It will have a 1 in the center with the letters PET or PETE under it.

pH: Stands for the potential of hydrogen and measures on a scale from 0 to 14. The acidity or alkalinity of a solution 7 is neutral, while above 7 is alkaline and below 7 is acidic.

Phosphorus: A non-metallic element that occurs in phosphates and is used in safety matches, pyrotechnics, incendiary shells, etc.

Photosensitive: Being light sensitive.

Photo voltaic: Anything that produces voltage when exposed to radiant energy, especially light. When several solar arrays are connected together, it is a photovoltaic array.

Phyla: In Latin classification, a category within a kingdom, such as the *gymnosperm* phyla in the plant kingdom.

Pier: A column of masonry that supports other structural parts of a building.

Pigeon-toed: A conformation fault in horses where the feet turn inward.

Pipping: When a baby bird starts to peck a hole from the inside of the egg.

Pitch: A substance that is related to tar and is made from pinewood charcoal and resin. It is used to waterproof wood. Also, the amount of slope of a roof.

Pitchfork: A metal-pronged tool with a wooden handle used to toss hay, manure, grain, etc.

Plane: A wooden block made of beech that holds a blade for the plane body. The blade is held in with little shims, or wedges, and is used to smooth wood.

Plaster: A white powder, usually a form of calcium phosphate, that when mixed with water forms a paste that later hardens into a solid. The action of applying the paste is called plastering.

Plat logs: Top wall logs of a cabin which support the lower end of the rafters and ceiling joists.

Plow: Also spelled plough. It is used to turn the earth over in preparation for planting. The blade, or bottom, turns over the soil. The frame is the overall structure and the gauge wheel determines the depth of the furrow. The coulter cuts the furrow slice from the land in front of the share and the clevis is where the drought, or harness, is attached.

Plumb bob: A string with a weight at the end that is used to make sure items are vertically straight.

Pointing up: Fixing problems with dry wall after it is installed.

Points: External features of a horse making up its conformation. When identifying color combinations, it refers to the lower leg's mane and tail, e.g., a bay with black points has black legs.

Poll: Highest point on the top of an animal's head.

Pollen: A fine powder produced by seed-bearing plants, which contain the male parts. It flies through the air or is carried by insects and fertilizes the female parts of another plant.

Pollination: When pollen from the stamen goes into the stigma of a plant, causing reproduction.

Pommel: The center front of an English saddle.

Pony: Any small horse with a height of 14.2 hands or less.

Port: A raised section in the center of the mouthpiece on some curb bits. A low port is a mild bit.

Positive: Something with a positive electric charge, or protons which are positive.

Posting trot: Also called a riding trot. When the rider rises in the saddle in rhythm with the horse's trot.

Potato digger: Similar to a plow, it has two wheels which are followed by a blade that turns up the earth and the potatoes with it. It pushes the plant to one side, so they do not get tangled.

Poult: A baby turkey.

Prairie-breaking plow: A plow that makes a furrow 4 in. deep. It is very heavy and long, and uses a wheel coulter. The clevis is adjusted both side to side, for width of the furrow, and vertically, for depth.

Prepotency: A horse's ability to consistently pass on characteristic traits to offspring.

Pressure canner: A pot with a pressure gauge that brings the contents to a pressure hot enough to kill bacteria.

Prime: When painting, to prime is to cover the surface with a white, brown, or grey flat paint before covering it with color. Priming a hand pump is to add water to the pump to create suction in order to bring water to the surface.

Pritchel hole: A hole in an anvil for making specific items.

Prolapsed: When an organ or part of an organ has fallen down or slipped out of place.

Proof: The amount of ethanol in alcohol. All alcohol has some water, and 100 proof alcohol has 50% water and 50% ethanol, which is drinkable. 198 proof alcohol has very little water and can be fatal if ingested.

Propagation: In a growing plant, methods of reproduction without using seeds, e.g., root cutting.

Protein: A group of complex tiny molecules which contain the basic components of all living cells and are essential in the diet for the growth and repair of tissue.

Pruning: To trim a tree or shrub in order to stimulate growth and train its shape.

Pruning shears: A curved cutter with short blades and a small handle that is used with one hand to prune branches of tree and shrubs. Pruning shears are not scissors, grass trimmers, power tools, or hedge clippers.

Purebred: A horse, or other animal, who had both parents from the same breed.

Purlin: On a timber-frame house, a long beam which sits on top of the bents and connects them together. Usually, a house will have four on each side of the peak of the roof. On a log cabin, the purlins are horizontal logs in a roof which are supported at each end and hold up the rafters.

Quarter round: A 3-6 in. pole that has been cut into quarters and is used for chinking, window and door trim, and molding.

Quarters: The part of an animal's body from the rear of the flank to the top of the tail, down to the top of the gaskin. It is also called the hindquarters.

Quenching bucket: A large tub full of water kept near a forge to cool metal.

Quicksand: A pit filled with loose wet sand that is found in nature. It can trap heavy objects that sink below the surface.

Quidding: When a horse drops half-chewed food from its mouth from age or dental problems. It is fixed by floating teeth.

Quilting: Stitching in a quilt that goes thru all the layers in order to hold the filler in place, often with a decorative design.

Quilting frame: A rectangular frame that holds the quilt tight while it is stitched.

Racehorse: A horse bred for racing, usually thoroughbreds, quarter horses, Arabians, or standardbred.

Radial: Shrinkage when drying wood that causes a board to become skinnier.

Rafter: A sloping beam running from the peak of a roof to the bottom, which helps support the boards and shingles, or other roofing material. It is usually spaced 16-24 in. apart.

Rake: A large wooden rake with a half circle of wood to support the raking part. It is used to rake hay. These can only be made by hand.

Rain pot: A painful skin inflammation on horses that causes raised hair, hair loss, and crustiness.

Rangy: A horse with a larger size and scope of movement.

Ratchet: A mechanical device with a toothed wheel that only allows movement in one direction.

RC: A number rating the reserve of an engine battery. A higher RC number equals a bigger battery reserve in case of engine failure.

Reining: A type of western riding where spins and slides are done in patterns.

Resuscitation: To restore someone to consciousness, to revive. This is normally referring to CPR.

Retting: A process of retting the stalks of flax, hemp, and nettle before it is broken down into fibers so it can be made into cloth and paper.

Reverse osmosis: Finest filtration known, in which water is forced through a membrane. It can filter out salts, sugars, proteins, particles, dyes, etc.

Revolutions Per Minute (RPM): The number of times an engine revolves in one minute.

Ridgepole: A long pole put at the peak of the house that will support the rafters, usually on log cabins.

Ridgling/rig: A male horse that has not dropped one testicle, which can cause stallion-like behavior.

Riding horse: A horse bred especially to be comfortable for riding.

Ringbone: Any bony changes in the pastern or coffin joints that may cause temporary lameness.

Ringworm: A contagious fungal disease that causes small circular patches where hair falls out.

Ripple: A plank with wood or wire teeth through which flax is pulled in order to remove the seeds.

Rising trot: See posting trot.

Roach back: The opposite of hollow back, when the curvaton of the spine goes outward.

Roached mane: Also called hogged mane. A mane that has been shaved close for its whole length.

Road plow: A plow that cuts a furrow 7-9 in. deep. A very durable plow with no wheel for making roads.

Roll roofing: A roofing material saturated with asphalt that comes in rolls.

Roughing in: Installing sewer lines or water pipes under the concrete of the foundation. The line and pipes are called rough ins.

Roaring: A noise made by horses when breathing when they have laryngeal hemiplegia.

Rolag: An even roll of unspun wool that is prepared for spinning.

Roller: A tool pulled by horses or by hand that crushes sod on top of the ground after using a harrow. It forces small stones level with the surface, makes the ground smooth for using a scythe and rake, and presses the soil around seeds. A roller is especially useful for compacting manure gases into light soil and in clay soils to prevent winter killing.

Rolling: Smashing grain between rollers going at different speeds.

Roman nose: When the nose curves outward instead of being flat or concave.

Root ball: The root system of a tree mixed with a ball of dirt clinging to the roots, making a large heavy ball.

Root bound: When a plant's roots have grown so tightly and tangled that they completely fill the containers they are in.

Rosin: A fine-powered byproduct left from distilling pine resin. It is sometimes added to soap to help create lather.

Rototill: To till the ground with a machine that can be pushed by hand. It has several sharp blades turned by a motor that cut and turn the earth rapidly. Although quick, it produces light soil. It also kills worms.

Roundworm: The common name of *Ascarids*, an internal parasite.

Ruptured disc: See herniated disc.

Saddle horn: A very prominent pommel on a Western saddle, also called a horn.

Saddle horse: A riding horse.

Saddle marks: White hairs in the saddle area on a horse.

Sap: A mixture of sugars, salts, and minerals circulating through a plant, somewhat like the blood of a person.

Sap yoke: A piece of wood hollowed out to fit the collector's neck with a hole on each end for a rope or chain to attach a bucket.

Saw: A tool used to cut wood with a serrated edge, usually for big cuts. It usually has a long, sharp blade with teeth made of metal and a wooden handle.

Scion: A fruit tree shoot with buds that is used in grafting on another tree.

Scope: A horse has scope when it has potential and capability of movement. This is considered a special horse.

Scoring ax: An ax with a long handle used to score, or cut a line, into a tree.

Scotch harrow: A harrow made of two rectangular pieces that are chained together and pulled from the ends.

Scotch sub-soil plow: A plow used right after a turning plow in the same furrow. It is used to break up and pulverize the soil further.

Scours: Diarrhea in baby animals.

Scoville unit: A unit used to measure how hot a food is. It was invented for chili peppers and devised by Wilbur Scoville in 1912.

Scratches: In horse terms, a scabby, oozing inflammation on the back of the pasterns just above the heel.

Scythe: A large blade used to cut hay and grain. The blade is attached at a right angle to the snath, or the handle.

Seed drill: A wheeled machine that is drawn behind a team of horses. It has a bin, or hopper, which pulls seeds down into the tubes and feeds the seeds into drills. The drills drop the seeds into the earth and can be set to any depth. The soil naturally drops over the seeds as the drill pulls out.

Seedy toe: Separation of the hoof wall from the laminae. It can be accompanied by laminitis.

Self-pollinator: A plant whose individual flower contains all the parts to successfully pollinate itself.

Self-seeder: A plant that grows from seed which it drops itself, and is spread naturally without any help from a person.

Selvage: The edge of a fabric that is woven so that it will not unravel or fray.

Septic tank: A tank in the ground to which human waste is piped into where it can decompose safely using anaerobic treatment and leech into the soil.

Setting: When a fowl, such as a chicken or a duck, is incubating her eggs by sitting on them and keeping them warm with down from her body.

Sewage: Any material taken away by sewer drains.

Shake: A shingle that has been split from a piece of log, usually 2-4 ft long.

Shank bone: The hind cannon of an animal.

Shares harrow: An effective harrow that digs 2-3 in. deeper than a regular harrow. It has sharp, flat blades shaped like a sled runner.

Shaving horse: Similar to a vise, it is used to clamp wood in place while a drawshave is used on it. It is a four-legged bench with a heavy plank attached at one end. Going from halfway to the seat, there is a bench with a stick that clamps the wood in place. It also has a bottom bar for the worker to rest his or her feet on. The worker sits on the seat end and pushes the bar with the feet to clamp the wood tightly into place. The harder the drawshave is pulled, the harder the worker must push with his or her feet.

Sheath: A protective outer covering around a stallion's penis.

Sheave: A large handful of wheat stalks tied together.

Shingle frow: A thick blade with a handle 18 in. long that is set at right angles from the blade. It is used to make shakes, or handmade shingles.

Shivers: In draft horses, this is an abnormally high leg gait where the horse flexes one or both hind legs and tremors can be seen. It is thought to be caused by EPSM.

Shock: A stack of sheaves of wheat, made to shed water.

Screwband: A metal band used to fasten the sealed canning lid to the jar.

Shovel: A wooden shaft that has a handle shaped like a D and an iron shoe on the shoveling end. It is used for any digging except post holes or shoveling snow.

Shoulder-in: In horse terms, a movement where the horse is evenly bent along the length of the spin away from the direction it is moving.

Shuttle: A handheld tool used in weaving which thread, or another material, is wrapped around to be woven through the warp, creating the weft.

Shy: In horse terms, when the horse jumps suddenly to

one side when startled.

Sickle hocks: In horse terms, when the hocks are bent, giving the hind legs a sickle shape and positioning the legs too far under the body.

Side bone: When the lateral cartilage on either side of a horse's coffin bone gets rigid within the hoof.

Side-hill plow: Also called a swivel plow. It throws the furrow slice downhill. It is pivoted so that it can move from side to side when at the end of a furrow, so the user can plow straight lines instead of in a circular pattern.

Side reigns: Reins used in training to help position the horse's head. They are attached to the bit and to the girth or a training surcingle.

Side-stick collar: A collar made for goats which prevents a female from sucking her own udder.

Silk: The tassel on sweet corn located at the top of an ear.

Sill: The wood under the house that rests directly on the foundation.

Single cultivator: A cultivator that cultivates two rows at a time.

Sippy bottle: A bottle with a special spout that only releases its liquid when it is sucked on.

Sire: A horse's male parent.

Skein: A length of spun fibers, such as flax or wool, that is looped into a loose coil.

Skep: A man-made beehive shaped like a dome and often made of a coil of twisted grasses.

Slab-sided: In horse terms, having narrow ribs.

Slaked/slacked: Lime that has been treated with water to cause it to heat and crumble through a chemical reaction.

Slub: An irregularity in raw wool such as thin spots or thick spots, which are pinched out prior to spinning.

Slurry: The plant pulp that is layered onto a deckle in the making of paper.

Smoker: A tool used in keeping bees which allows a controlled flow of smoke to be put in with bees in order to calm them.

Smoothing plane: A plane 8-10 in. long used to finish a rough surface.

Snaffle bit: A type of bit that acts at the corners or bars of a horse's mouth and uses only one rein.

Snath: The handle of a scythe with two nibs, or handgrips. It is used for harvesting grain. A cradle, or rack, is attached to it. The best snath is a steam-bent, black cherry snath.

Sock darner: A small, rounded tool that is put into a sock to support it while it is being darned.

Softwood: Some may be harder than some hardwoods. The difference is the way they produce seeds. Softwoods let seeds fall to the ground without any covering, such as pinecones.

Solar: Anything relating to the sun or utilizing the energy of the sun.

Solvent: A liquid that can dissolve other substances, often used for removing paint.

Sorghum press: A large mill that is powered by a horse or mule walking around it. It has three rollers that are turned by reduction gears attached to a pole, which is attached to a horse. The juice goes through several strainers and into a holding tank.

Sound: Free from lameness and/or injury.

Spacer board: Also called a sticker. A piece of dried wood put between layers of newly cut wood that is being dried outside.

Spark plug: An electrical device that fits into the cylinder head of an engine and ignites the gas with an electric spark.

Spavin: In animals, a degenerative arthritis in the lower joints of the hock which can be seen as bony swelling. It is also called Bog Spavin.

Spillway: A runoff from a dam which allows overflow to be directed to a designated place, rather than flooding.

Spindle: A stick or pin used to twist yarn or thread when spinning.

Spinning wheel: There are several kinds of wheels. Small wheels with foot pedals are for wool. Big wheels are for fine fibers such as flax, silk, and cotton. Small wheels come in two styles, Saxony, the most common, and Norwegian.

Spline: Peeled off strips of wood prepared for making baskets, which are woven together. It can also refer to a wood strip that fits into any groove or slot between parts, such as on a cabin.

Splints: In animals, an injury to one or both metacarpal or splint bones running up the back of the cannon bone.

Splitting ax: An ax for splitting logs, with a wedge-shaped head and a long handle.

Splitting maul: A combination between an axe and a maul. It has a wedge on one side and a hammer on the other. The wedge is used as an axe and hammer to dislodge things.

Spokeshave: A tool with handles and blades that are used to shave wood. It is used as the final shaving tool when making a helve, or handle, and is also used in making wooden boats.

Spraddle legs: When a baby bird's legs turn outward abnormally because of slippery footing.

Spurs: A small metal device is worn on the rider's boot to enforce leg aids during riding.

Stone boat: A large sled with a front that is curved up so it is about 3 ft from the ground. It is used to haul stones from a field.

Square harrow: A square shaped harrow that is pulled from one corner.

Stallion: An uncastrated male horse.

Starch: A substance found in seeds, fruit, tubers, roots, wheat, and rice, which is a complex carbohydrate. It is used as food and also as a stiffener in paper and fabric.

Starter: Animal feed especially made for chicks, ducklings, and other baby foul.

Stave: In basket making, a long piece of material used to weave the walls of the basket. It is also the handle of a flail.

Steer: Castrated male bovine animal.

Sticker: See spacer board.

Still: An apparatus used in the process of the distillation of a liquid, such as the purification of water or in the making of ethanol.

Stock horse: A horse used in ranch work, such as driving and cutting cows.

Strangles: A highly contagious disease also known as distemper.

Straw: After a grain has been threshed off, the remaining stalk is dried and used for bedding for animals, thatching, weaving, or braiding.

Stringhalt: In animals, the over-flexion of the hind legs in which the leg is jerked up to the belly.

Stripper: A long blade on the end of a straight handle used to strip the leaves off sweet sorghum plants. The tip is curved like a sickle and the rest is straight. The curved part is used to cut stalks and heads.

Strongyles: Also called blood worms, is an internal parasite.

Stud: A male animal used almost exclusively for breeding.

Subfloor: The layer of flooring under hardwood or carpet. It is made of floor joists, bridging, plywood, and/or concrete.

Subsoil: The deeper layer of soil that is lighter colored. This is where water is stored.

Sucker: A small sprout that grows out of the roots of a tree and up out of the ground. It looks like a whole new baby tree. It may also come out of the trunk of the tree.

Sulky cultivator: A cultivator with a seat for the driver.

Sulky plow: A single plow that is mounted on a frame with a seat. A brake allows the plow to be pulled out of the ground without having to do it by hand, and the beam relieves pressure to the horse's neck.

Super: A section of a beehive used to store excess honey. It is put on top of a brood chamber.

Surcingle: In horse terms, webbed stays which goes under the barrel to which side reins can be attached, blankets can be secured, etc.

Suspensory ligament: In animals, ligaments which support the fetlock and spread around the fetlock joint.

Swaddling: To wrap an infant tightly so he or she feels as if they are in a similar place to the womb. Infants find this comforting.

Swingle: A tool that looks like a large knife about 2 ft long. It is used for winnowing. It can also be attached to a stave as part of flail.

Swivel plow: Also called a turn-twist plow. Two plows that are attached to one beam so they can be switched between plowing either right or left. A forward plow turns a depth of 3 in. and the rear plow reaches a depth of 5-7 in.

Table: The front lower section of an anvil.

Tack: Short for tackle, or riding equipment such as saddle, bridle, etc.

Tag/tagging: Clipping the wool away from a ewe's vagina in order to make breeding easier.

Tallow: Hard fat taken from the bodies of cattle, sheep, or horses which is used for candles, leather dressing, soaps and lubricants.

Tangential: Shrinkage when drying wood that causes the wood to shrink along its width.

Tapeworm: An internal parasite.

Tarpaper: Heavy paper full of tar which is used on a roof for waterproofing.

Teaser: A stallion used to test a mare's readiness for breeding, but who does not actually breed with her.

Tetanus: Also called lockjaw. It is a serious bacterial infection that enters the body through a puncture wound.

Thinning: To remove excess seedlings to make more space for other plants to grow larger and healthier.

Thresh: To beat with a flail or other tool to remove the chaff from the grain.

Thrifty: In horse terms, a horse that maintains health on a small ration, also called a good-doer.

Threat: The inside of the bottom of the hook on the chain of a chainsaw.

Thrush: In horse terms, a fungal or bacterial infection in the frog that discharges a bad-smelling liquid.

Ticking: Any strong fabric used for a mattress or pillow coverings.

Tied in below the knee: In horse terms, a conformational fault in which the measurement below the knee is much less than the measurement above the fetlock.

Tie log: A beam of one or more logs that connect and provide lateral support for two opposite walls.

Tilling: Another word for cultivating, but usually used for the initial plowing of a field.

Teepee: A house shaped like a cone, which is made of several wooden poles and a half circle of fabric or leather. It was designed by the Plains Indians.

Tire chain: A special grid of chains made to fit around a tire to improve an automobile's traction on an icy or snowy road.

Tire iron: A metal tool used to pry a tire from the rim of a vehicle.

Title: A legal deed to a property or document that shows the legal ownership of a property.

Titration: A chemical process used to find out how concentrated a substance is.

Tofu frame: A wooden frame measuring 7 in. by 7 in. that has wire mesh or screen in the bottom. The screen is covered in cheesecloth or unbleached muslin and a board 6.5 in. by 6.5 in. is pressed down on the tofu when it is in the frame to squeeze out the whey.

Tom: A male turkey.

Tong: A metal tool for holding onto hot metal. A farrier's tong has two round discs on the end.

Top line: In animals, the line from the back of the withers to the end of the croup.

Top heavy: An animal with a heavy body in relation to the substance of the legs.

Topsoil: The top, darker layer of soil, which is crumblier and where the most nutrients are.

Total gross head: The distance that a stream is moving or dropping. This is used in calculating the power available from the stream.

Trailer: A transportation vehicle that is towed behind another vehicle. It is often used for animals and equipment.

Transcendentalism: A philosophy of the 1800s begun by Margaret Fuller, Ralph Waldo Emerson, Henry David Thoreau, Bronson Alcott, and Emily Dickinson. It advocated simplicity, truth, intuition, and other ideas.

Transesterification: A chemical reaction used in the making of biodiesel in which ethanol and lye are mixed to make sodium methoxide.

Transition: In horse terms, changing from one pace to another. An upward transition would be changing to a faster pace and a downward transition would be changing to a slower pace.

Tread: The bumps on a tire that improve traction on the road.

Tree-pruning hook: A long pole with a hook on the end mounted at right angles from the pole. It is used for cutting branches.

Trimming out: Finishing the plumbing in a house by installing the fixtures.

Trivet: A small piece of metal used to elevate pots and pans off the top of a wood cook stove so they do not get so hot.

Trot: In horse terms, a moderately fast gait where the horse moves from one diagonal pair of legs to the other with a period of not touching the ground in between.

Trunnel: A wooden peg that is used instead of metal nails. They are hammered in with a mallet.

Truss: An assembly of wood or metal formed into a triangle framework usually to support a roof.

Tuber: The fleshy underground stem or root of a plant for reproduction and food storage, such as a potato.

Turning plow: A simple plow with a curved blade, a rotating disc in the middle, and a wheel in the front. The disc cuts a furrow and the bottom turns it over.

Turn out: Turning out horses in a field or a length of time during the day, or a standard of dress for a horse and rider. Also, when making a road, it is a shallow notch in the outside slope so water can flow out.

Tuyere pipe: A metal pipe running through a forge directly to the fire through which air can be blasted with a bellows to make the fire hotter.

Twill: A heavy cloth with parallel lines or ribs, often woven in rather than died, and used for making beds or ticking.

Type: A horse that fulfills a certain purpose, such as a cob, hack, or hunter, but of no particular breed.

Udder: An organ resembling a bag that has mammary glands and produces milk in female mammals such as cows, sheep, and goats.

Undercut: When cutting down a tree, a cut made on a tree at least 8 in. in diameter, on the same side as the direction you want the tree to fall.

Underlay: In a house, a layer of plywood or hardboard sheets on top the subfloor. The plywood lies directly under the hardwood of a wooden floor.

Undershot: A horse deformity in which the lower jaw sticks out farther than the upper jaw.

Unschool: A school of homeschooling in which the home-schooled children are allowed to educate themselves in a more natural way. It is meant to be the opposite of institutionalized education.

Uterus: An organ in the female mammal in which a fertilized egg implants and develops. Also called the womb.

Vent: The anus of an animal, especially of fowl such as ducks and chickens.

Vermicompost: Compost to which worms are added in order to break up the compost, decay it faster, and add worm castings to increase nutrients.

Vermiculite: A mineral added to a variety of materials such as brake linings, as a filler in textured paint, in concrete and in plaster, and as fire proofing. It has also been used in stormwater biofilters and has several gardening uses.

Vise: A clamping device with two jaws that close with a screw.

Volunteer: A plant that grew spontaneously from a self-seeder.

Vulva: External genital organs of a female.

Warp: The stationary, taut threads held vertically by a loom.

Washtub: A wooden or metal tub used to wash clothes in.

Water bath canner: A pot which is big enough to can fruit, but does not get hot enough for other foods to kill the bacteria.

Water sprout: Similar to a sucker, it is a very green shoot which comes out of a tree branch after too much pruning or an injury.

Watt: The standard unit of electrical power. 746 watts equals 1 horsepower.

Weanling: An animal or child who has been recently weaned from its mother's milk.

Weathervane: An arrow or flat silhouette (e.g., a rooster) which rotates on a pole. On the pole are visible indicators of the four cardinal directions. When installing, use a compass to place the vane facing the right direction. The pointing end tells which way the wind is coming from.

Weft: The thread that has been wound on a bobbin and is woven through the warp on a loom.

Wheel: When making pottery, an electric- or foot-powered rotating circular table on which pots are formed.

Whittle: To shape wood with a whittling knife or pocketknife, usually for fine carving.

Winch: A tool that is sometimes motorized, which has a coiled cord and a hook. It is attached to items too heavy for a human to pull and assists in hoisting or pulling heavy objects.

Windbreak: A barrier that slows or stops the wind, often a row of trees or shrubbery.

Windrow: A long row of wheat piled up before making sheaves.

Winnow: To separate the chaff from the grain.

Winnowing tray: A wooden box with handholds on the sides, no end, and no top. It is similar to a large scope.

Womb: Also called a uterus.

Woodlot: A patch of forest on a person's property that is used especially for firewood.

Wort: When brewing alcohol, the unfermented malt or the malt in the process of fermenting.

Wrap-over: A type of roof ridge that, when thatching, folds a thick layer of straw over the edge of the roof-peak and is fastened on both sides.

Wrench: A tool that is used to twist a bolt or a nut.

Yealm: When thatching a roof, a bundle of long straw that has been made into a tight layer of straw, and is then cleaned up so it is level at both ends. Also called yealming.

Yoke: A piece of wood shaped to a person's or animals' shoulders to help in carrying or pulling great weight.

Yurt: A traditional Mongolian portable house with a round shape that provides excellent shelter in extreme weather.

Appendix

The Latin Classification System

Latin names are the scientific nomenclature used for identifying species. They are much more accurate and specific than popular names. For instance, cabbage is a popular name, while *Brassica oleracea* is the Latin name.

Kingdom: All living things are classified into five kingdoms.

Kingdom Plantae – Plants
Kingdom Fungi – Fungus
Kingdom Animalia – Animals
Kingdom Monera – Microscopic single-celled creatures (algae)
Kingdom Protista – Complex cells (seaweed)

Phyla: A further breakdown of classifications.

Mushroom group – *Phylum basidiomycota*
Yeast group – *Phylum ascomycota*
Plantae species are classified into two groups: *Gymnosperm* (conifer, moss, and fern-type plants) and *Angiosperms* (Plants that animals, including humans, eat)

Classes

Angiosperms have two classes: *Monocotyledoneae* (Monocots) and *Dicotyledonae* (Dicots).

Monocots have seeds with one leaf. Plants in this class have narrow leaves and the flower has parts in multiples of three. Dicots have seeds with two leaves. The plant has broad leaves and the flower has parts in multiples of four or five with large colorful petals.

Genera

Within each Monocot and Dicot family there are genera. The genus of a plant identifies exactly which species it is.

Monocot families that should be known:

Arecaceae: Palm family – coconuts and palms. They are the equivalent of wheat in a tropical area.
Gramineae: Grass family – wheat, bamboo, corn, and rice
Liliaceae: Lily family – onions, lilies, and tulips
Musaceae: Banana family

Dicot families that should be known:

Apiaceae: Carrot family – carrots and parsley
Asteraceae: Sunflower family – dandelion, sunflower
Brassicaceae: Cabbage family – cabbage, kale, cauliflower, and turnips
Cucurbitaceae: Melon family – cucumber, melons, squash, etc.
Fabaceae: Pea family – peas and peanuts
Lamiaceae: Mint family – lavender and mints
Leguminosae: Legume family – alfalfa, bean, peanut, pea, and soybeans
Poaceae: Grass family – wheat and barley
Rosaceae: Rose family – rose and apple
Solanaceae: Nightshade family – pepper, potato, and

tomato

Measurements, Equivalencies, Substitutes, etc.

Common Abbreviations of Measurements

cal = calories
c = cup
deg = degrees
EHP = electric horsepower
ft = foot
g = gram
hr = hour
Hz = hertz
in. = inch
Kg = kilogram
L = liter
lb = pound
m = meter
mi = mile
ml = milliliter
mph = miles per hour
oz = ounce
pg. = page
PSI = pounds per square inch
pt = pint
qt = quart
tbsp/T = Tablespoon
tsp = Teaspoon

Home Equivalents of Can Sizes

8 oz = 1 cup
Picnic = 10.5 – 12 oz = 1 ¼ cups
12 oz = vacuum = 12 oz = 1 ½ cups

#1 = 11 oz = 1 ⅓ cups
#1 tall = 16oz = 2 cups
#1 square = 16 oz = 2 cups
#2 = 1 lb. 4oz = 1pt 2 fl oz = 2 ½ cups
#2 ½ = 1 lb. 13 oz = 3 ½ cups
#2 ½ square = 31 oz = scant 4 cups
#3 = 4 cups
#3 squat = 2 ¾ cups
#5 = 7⅓ cups
#10 = 13 cups
#300 = 14-16 oz = 1 ¾ cups
#303 = 16-17 oz = 2 cups
Baby food jar = 3 ½ - 8 oz

Canned Liquid Equivalents

1 can condensed milk = 15 oz, 1 ⅓ cups
1 can evaporated milk = 6 oz, 2 ⅔ cups
1 can frozen juice = 6 oz, ¾ cup

Flour Substitutes

1 cup self-rising flour = 1 c all-purpose flour, 1 ¼ tsp baking powder, pinch of salt
1 cup white flour = 1 ⅜ c barley flour
1 cup white flour = ⅞ c corn meal
1 cup white flour = 1 c corn flour
1 cup white flour = ⅜ c potato flour
1 cup white flour = ⅞ c rice flour
1 cup white flour = 1 c rye meal
1 cup white flour = 1 ½ c ground rolled oats or 1 c. oat flour
1 cup whole wheat flour = 1 c white flour
1 cup whole wheat flour = ⅞ c amaranth
1 cup whole wheat flour = ⅞ c chickpea/garbanzo

1 cup whole wheat flour = ¾ c corn flour
1 cup whole wheat flour = 1 c corn meal
1 cup whole wheat flour = ¾ c oat flour
1 cup whole wheat flour = ⅝ c potato flour
1 cup whole wheat flour = ¾ c potato starch
1 cup whole wheat flour = ⅞ c rice flour
1 cup whole wheat flour = ¾ c soy flour

* When using dark flour, use twice as much baking powder.

BAKING POWDER EQUIVALENTS

1 tsp double-acting baking powder (typical store-bought variety) is equivalent to:

2 tsp homemade (single-acting) baking powder
½ tsp baking soda and 1 c sour milk or buttermilk
½ tsp baking soda, 1 tsp vinegar, and 1 c milk
½ tsp baking soda, 1 tsp lemon juice, and 1 c milk

Baking Powder Ratio

Cake with eggs: 1 tsp baking powder per 1 c flour
Biscuits, muffins, and waffles: 2 tsp baking powder per 1 c flour
Buckwheat and whole grain with no eggs: ¾ tsp baking powder per 1 c flour.

COMMON PRODUCT INGREDIENTS SOURCES

Gum Arabic/Arabic gum powder: *Acacia vera*
Acetic acid: 3.5% solution of vinegar
Alum: In recipes, it is a spice not frequently used except in pickling. As a chemical, it is aluminum powder,

sulfate, carbonate, etc.

Ammonium carbonate: Baker's ammonia or smelling salts

Amyl acetate: Banana oil

Arrowroot: An herb used as a powder substitute for cornstarch, tapioca starch, rice starch, or flour

Ascorbic acid: Vitamin C

Bicarbonate of soda: Baking soda

Calcium carbonate: Chalk or agricultural lime

Calcium hydroxide: Slaked or slacked lime

Calcium oxide: Unslaked quicklime

Calcium sulfate: Plaster of Paris

Citric acid: Derived from acidic fruits

Furfuraldehyde: Bran oil

Glucose: Corn syrup

Glycerin: A by-product of the saponification of vegetable oil or animal fats

Graphite: Pencil lead

Hydrogen peroxide: Peroxide

Iodine: Tincture of iodine (4%)

Isopropyl alcohol: Rubbing alcohol at 70-90% concentration

Lye: Made from ashes

Magnesium hydroxide: Milk of magnesia

Magnesium silicate: Talc

Magnesium sulfate: Epson salt

Methyl salicylate: Wintergreen oil, sweet birch oil, and teaberry oil

Potassium bitartrate: Cream of tartar, pearl ash, and salt of wormwood

Potassium carbonate: Potash

Potassium chloride: Potash muriate

Silica/silicon dioxide: Sand

Sodium chloride: Table salt

Sodium hypochlorite: Bleach

Sucrose: Cane sugar

Talc: Talcum powder, an alternative to arrowroot powder

Tincture of iodine: 47% alcohol, 4% iodine

"Whiting": Chalk mixed with linseed oil to form a putty. Add water and other additives to make whitewash

Other Useful Information

De-stinking a skunked Animal

1 qt 3% hydrogen peroxide
¼ cup baking soda
1 tsp liquid soap

Mix ingredients together, rub deeply into the animal's fur/skin, and rinse thoroughly. It is recommended to complete this process outdoors when possible.

Useful Books

Totally Apples Cookbook by H Siegel and K. Gillingham
The 99 Cent Only Stores Cookbook
Prairie Home Cooking by Judith M. Fertig
Essential Book of Fermentation by Jeff Cox
101 Things to do with Eggs
The Farmer's Wife Canning and Preserving Cookbook by Lela Nargi
The Farmer's Cookbook by Marie Lawerence
Beverly Lewis Amish Heritage Cookbook by Beverly Lewis
The Chai Seed Cookbook
The Amish Cook's Family Favorite Recipes by Lovina Eicher with K Williams
The Mountain Man Cookbook
Almonds Every Which Way by Brooke McLay

The Tea Encyclopedia by Keith Souter
Classic Candy by Abigail R. Gehring
A Farmer's Daughter by Dawn Stoltfus
The Healthy Coconut Flour Cookbook by Erica Kerwien
Healing Foods by Susan Curtis
Nature's Medicine by Joel L. Serdlow
Edible Mushrooms by B. Forsberg and S. Lindberg
Prepper's Food Storage by Julie Languille
Herbs: Smithsonian by Lesley Bremness
Wild Wisdom of Weeds by Katrina Blair
The Howell Book of Dogs by Palika
Complete Book of Home Remedies for Your Dog by Deborah Mitchell
Organic Mushroom Farming and Mycoremediation by Tradder Cotter
Edward R. Hamilton books
Old-Time Country Wisdom and Lore by Jerry Mack Johnson
Back to Basics by Abigail R. Gehring
Modern Survival by Barry Davies
Someone's Watching You
Native American Medicinal Plants by Daniel E. Moerman
The Compost-Powered Water Heater by Gaelem Brown
Ann Getty: Interior Style by Diane Dorran Sacks
Fences, Gates, and Bridges by George A. Martin
Complete Guide to Stonescaping by David Reed
The Joy of Keeping Farm Animals by Laura Childs
Animal Camp by Kathy Steven
Chickens in your Backyard by Rick and Gail Luttmann
Backyard Medicine by J. Burton-Seal and M. Seal
The Coconut Oil Miracle, 4th Edition by Bruce Fife
Dental Herbalism by L.M. Alexander and L.A. Straub-Bruce
The Herb Book by John Lust

Anatomica by Robin Arnold
Foods the Harm, Foods that Heal by Sandra Brazel
Fairy Gardening by J. Bawden-Davis and B. Turner
The Venison Cookbook by Kate Fiduccia
Olive Oil by Ed S. Milton
Complete Guide to Sausage Making by Monte Burch
Dutch Oven Baking by Bruce Tracy
Joy of Keeping a Root Cellar by Jennifer Megyesi
Cider Beans, Wild Greens, and Dandelion Jelly by Joan E. Aller
Food Drying with and Attitude by Mary T. Bell
Jam and Marmalade Bible by Jan Hedh

ABOUT THE AUTHOR

Larry Justice was born on July 23, 1975 in Williamson, West Virginia. He graduated from London High School in 1993. After graduation Larry enlisted in the U.S. Army. Once out of the Army, he tackled many different jobs where he applied his hard work and ethics, and always seemed to excel because of it.

Larry was a very cultured man, as he enjoyed and appreciated so many aspects of life and people. Some of his favorite hobbies were riding motorcycles, working on vehicles, playing pool, bowling, board games, and reading. In addition to these hobbies, Larry was the guy you wanted on your team when playing trivia or needed answers about music.

Larry never met a stranger and always had a genuine care and concern for everyone who was a part of his life or even crossed his path. He loved to help people and would go out of his way to do so. He always had an inviting smile on his face, no matter what was going on when he walked into a room.

His love for and pursuit of God, daily, was not only relentless but inspiring. This was his fuel to love and appreciate others so well! He was so thankful for all that God had done in his life and knew that he was a man of honor, integrity, and principle, because of his relationship with Christ.

Larry passed away on November 20th, 2021 prior to the publishing of this book. He spent three years writing this book during a very difficult time in his life. Prior to going home to be with the Lord, he worked with his fiancée, Keri Wilkins, and his sister, Helena Hahtatley, to pull the pages together in preparation of publishing. Keri and Helena committed to finishing his hard work.